Palgrave Philosophy Today

Series Editor: **Vittorio Bufacchi,** University College Cork, Ireland

The *Palgrave Philosophy Today* series provides concise introductions to all the major areas of philosophy currently being taught in philosophy departments around the world. Each book gives a state-of-the-art informed assessment of a key area of philosophical study. In addition, each title in the series offers a distinct interpretation from an outstanding scholar who is closely involved with current work in the field. Books in the series provide students and teachers with not only a succinct introduction to the topic, with the essential information necessary to understand it and the literature being discussed, but also a demanding and engaging entry into the subject.

Titles include:

Pascal Engel
PHILOSOPHY OF PSYCHOLOGY

Shaun Gallagher
PHENOMENOLOGY

Simon Kirchin
METAETHICS

D0160909

Duncan Pritchard
KNOWLEDGE

Mathias Risse
GLOBAL POLITICAL PHILOSOPHY

Joel Walmsley
MIND AND MACHINE

Forthcoming Titles:

Helen Beebee
METAPHYSICS

James Robert Brown
PHILOSOPHY OF SCIENCE

Neil Manson
ENVIRONMENTAL PHILOSOPHY

Chad Meister
PHILOSOPHY OF RELIGION

Matthew Nudds
MIND AND THOUGHT

Lilian O'Brien
PHILOSOPHY OF ACTION

Don Ross
PHILOSOPHY OF ECONOMICS

Nancy Tuana
FEMINISM AND PHILOSOPHY

Palgrave Philosophy Today
Series Standing Order ISBN 978–0–230–00232–6 (hardcover)
Series Standing Order ISBN 978–0–230–00233–3 (paperback)
(*outside North America only*)

You can receive future titles in this series as they are published by placing a standing order. Please contact your bookseller or, in case of difficulty, write to us at the address below with your name and address, the title of the series and one of the ISBNs quoted above.

Customer Services Department, Macmillan Distribution Ltd, Houndmills, Basingstoke, Hampshire RG21 6XS, England

Phenomenology

Shaun Gallagher

University of Memphis, USA
University of Hertfordshire, UK

First published 2012 by
PALGRAVE MACMILLAN

Palgrave Macmillan in the UK is an imprint of Macmillan Publishers Limited, registered in England, company number 785998, of Houndmills, Basingstoke, Hampshire RG21 6XS.

Palgrave Macmillan in the US is a division of St Martin's Press LLC, 175 Fifth Avenue, New York, NY 10010.

Palgrave Macmillan is the global academic imprint of the above companies and has companies and representatives throughout the world.

Palgrave® and Macmillan® are registered trademarks in the United States, the United Kingdom, Europe and other countries

ISBN: 978–0–230–27248–4 hardback
ISBN: 978–0–230–27249–1 paperback

A catalogue record for this book is available from the British Library.

A catalog record for this book is available from the Library of Congress.

10 9 8 7 6 5 4 3 2 1
21 20 19 18 17 16 15 14 13 12

To Elaine

Contents

Series Editor's Preface

It is not easy being a student of philosophy these days. All the different areas of philosophy are reaching ever increasing levels of complexity and sophistication, a fact which is reflected in the specialized literature and readership each branch of philosophy enjoys. And yet anyone who studies philosophy is expected to have a solid grasp of the most current issues being debated in most, if not all, the other areas of philosophy. It is an understatement to say that students of philosophy today are faced with a Herculean task.

The books in this new book series by Palgrave are meant to help all philosophers, established and aspiring, to understand, appreciate and engage with the intricacies which characterize all the many faces of philosophy. They are also ideal teaching tools as textbooks for more advanced students. These books may not be meant primarily for those who have yet to read their first book of philosophy, but all students with a basic knowledge of philosophy will benefit greatly from reading these exciting and original works, which will enable anyone to engage with all the defining issues in contemporary philosophy.

There are three main aspects that make the Palgrave Philosophy Today series distinctive and attractive. First, each book is relatively short. Second, the books are commissioned from some of the best-known, established and upcoming international scholars in each area of philosophy. Third, while the primary purpose is to offer an informed assessment of opinion on a key area of philosophical study, each title presents a distinct interpretation from someone who is closely involved with current work in the field.

Shaun Gallagher is arguably the most influential and recognizable global authority on phenomenology. As author of twelve books and innumerable journal articles, Gallagher has for many years shaped the current debate on phenomenology. The present book for the Palgrave Philosophy Today series will unlock a whole new research agenda for students and scholars of phenomenology.

While phenomenology is traditionally associated with certain areas of philosophy, especially aesthetics, existentialism and even psychoanalysis, Gallagher's main focus is to show the extent to which phenomenology can play a productive role as part of a scientific practice. Starting from the fundamental premise that our experience is shaped by the basic phenomenon of intersubjectivity, Gallagher makes a compelling argument for the thesis that reductionistic tendencies of science should be rejected, and that recent developments in practical and scientific uses of phenomenology can play a determining role in this project.

This book will be of interest to those interested in the classical accounts of phenomenology. It will also inform and stimulate readers on several contemporary debates about the nature of consciousness and the mind, including the key issues of intentionality, cognition, temporality and the selfhood.

Vittorio Bufacchi
General Editor, Palgrave Philosophy Today
Department of Philosophy
University College Cork

Acknowledgments

I owe thanks to a large number of people who supported the huge project of constructing this rather small book. First, thanks to Vittorio Bufacchi at University College Cork, Editor of this Palgrave Macmillan series, who invited me to write this book. And to Stefano Vincini, at the University of Memphis, who helped gather references and commented on a partial first draft.

I have received significant support as the Lillian and Morrie Moss Chair of Excellence in Philosophy at the University of Memphis. I've also benefited from the support of several research grants and fellowships, research visits, meetings and discussions on topics covered in a number of chapters. These include the Marie Curie Initial Training Network Grant, Towards an Embodied Science of Intersubjectivity (TESIS), at the University of Hertfordshire; the CNRS as visiting researcher in 2010 at the École Normale Supérieure de Lyon, and the Centre de Recherche en Epistémelogie Appliquée, École Polytechnique, Paris; the Australian Research Council project on Embodied Virtues and Expertise, headed by Richard Menary and David Simpson at the Universities of Macquarie and Wollongong, respectively; and the Arts and Humanities Research Council project on the Nature of Phenomenal Qualities led by Paul Coates and Sam Coleman at the University of Hertfordshire.

In addition to the scholarly review of the classical positions of phenomenology that I present here, this work reflects and references a lot of my own research on various contemporary themes and debates. In this regard, I've greatly benefited from collaborations and conversations with a chorus of co-authors whose voices have undoubtedly found expression in some of these chapters. These include Hanne De Jaegher, Ezequiel Di Paolo, Tom Froese, Dan Hutto, Rebecca Jacobson, Katsunori Miyahara, Jean-Michel

Roy, Jesper Brøsted Sørensen, and Dan Zahavi. In specific the following papers, where more developed discussions can be found, have formed the basis for dispersed bits and pieces of some of the chapters in this book. Chapter 2: Gallagher (2012a); Gallagher and Brøsted Sørensen (2006). Chapter 3: Froese and Gallagher (2010). Chapter 4: Gallagher and Miyahara (2012). Chapter 5: Gallagher (1986). Chapter 6: Gallagher (2011b); Gallagher and Zahavi (2012). Chapter 7: Gallagher (2012c); Gallagher and Zahavi (2005). Chapter 8: Gallagher (2012b,d, 2007a, 2000). Chapter 9: De Jaegher, Di Paolo and Gallagher (2010); Gallagher (2012e and in press); Gallagher and Jacobson (2012).

As Aristotle notes, there are some friends to whom debts can never be fully repaid. This includes spouses, of which I have only one. I already owe too much to my wife, Elaine, for her patience and support. She never asks for repayment, but she always has my love.

Introduction: The Situation of Phenomenology

Before you started to read this line of text you were doing something else. Perhaps you just came back from surfing and are sitting on a beach chair; perhaps you have just found a spot in the shade and you have two hours to sit and read and sip your wine before the concert starts in Luxembourg Gardens; perhaps you have just made a cup of tea and are settling into your armchair in front of your warm hearth. Or maybe you're in a jet airliner reading this on the latest electronic text-display gadget. In any and all cases you find yourself already situated, in the middle of something, or having just done something – pulled up a chair, taken a seat – and you are now at a point where you are reading these lines.

Phenomenology begins right here, with one of the oldest problems in philosophy, which is also one of the most contemporary problems in science. It begins with the fact that we, as agents who must act, and as thinkers who try to get a grasp on what we are doing, are always *already situated* in the world. It's this problem that leads Aristotle to acquiesce in accepting the inevitable, namely, in this life we can only live in the second-best way – the imperfect *practical* life, since the very best form of life, the life of self-sufficient contemplation is never fully attainable. We are constantly being interrupted by the demands of our physical nature and the distractions of the world. If by enormous effort we turn our attention away from food and sex and survival and attempt to study our rational capacities – our quest for reasons, our natural inclination to know everything (ala science and gossip) – we are confronted with the very first fact, which is that *there is no very first fact*, and that every fact is preceded by other facts, that every fact, every reason, every thought, every instance of consciousness is already situated in some contingent circumstance.

1

In the history of philosophy it is usually thought that phenomenology informed the later development of existentialism (in thinkers like Heidegger, Sartre, Camus, etc.). This is certainly true. But it is also true that the original motivation for phenomenology was itself an existential one – the already being-in-a-situation, the 'thrownness', the 'facticity' of our existence. This thought – this situation – is one that phenomenology begins with, and the one it eventually returns to. In between it is like all great philosophies, attempting to clear a space, to find a place from which it can survey this very situation of being situated. In this regard phenomenology both succeeds and fails in interesting ways. It continues to do so, since it is not merely a piece of history or a tradition, but is something that continues to be practiced.

In this book I'll take a pragmatic approach to phenomenology. The focus will be on phenomenology as a philosophical and interdisciplinary practice. Accordingly, my primary intention is not to rehearse the history of phenomenology as a philosophical movement (although I will not ignore this completely). Rather I'll focus on its methods and what Edmund Husserl (1859–1938), the founding father of phenomenology, called 'the things themselves' – the ways in which the world comes to be experienced within the various situations that make up our *lifeworld*. The lifeworld (*Lebenswelt*) is one of phenomenology's basic concepts. It's connected to the fact that we are already situated in the world. It is the collection of situations in which we find ourselves involved – it is the world as we live it, not just the world as it opens up in front of us as perceiving subjects, but the world which is at the same time something *already there* operating as the meaningful background for all of our actions and interactions. The lifeworld is the world we take for granted, rather than the world as we study it through science, or represent it through art. The lifeworld, in this sense, is not the world that we take as object, as something distinct from ourselves, but is rather a specification of our existence.

In a world where there is no very first fact, there are several factors that nonetheless seem basic and that constitute our human way of being. Let's call these 'primary facts' and note one of these primary facts about the lifeworld (and therefore about out existence) that will clear away at least one serious misconception about phenomenology. The lifeworld is, from the start of our existence, already populated with others. Before we have a chance to think about this – before we have a chance to theorize, philosophize or 'phenomenologize', before we have a chance to stake out a position of any sort – our capabilities for so doing have already been shaped by other humans who have been with us even before our birth, who have been talking to us even before we could respond, and who have been interacting with us even before we could act on our own. This primary fact, and the *natural attitude* that we take toward it – that is, our taking it for granted – specifies the beginning point for phenomenology.

If we keep this in mind, and if we acknowledge that our experience is already shaped by this basic phenomenon of intersubjectivity, which makes it impossible to obtain anything like a presuppositionless starting point for our philosophical considerations, then we will avoid certain misconceptions about phenomenology. One such misconception is that the practice of phenomenology leads to a kind of solipsism in which we find ourselves entirely wrapped up in a reflective and lonely consciousness. This is simply not the case. Solipsism would only be a problem if one thought of consciousness (our experience of the world) as an object in the world rather than as an opening to (or disclosure of) the world. Phenomenology, however, shows that we are not locked up in some object, or reducible to some objective entity – a brain, or an organism regarded as a purely physical thing, or a set of strictly functional relations. Rather, we are, as Heidegger puts it, *in-the-world* as agents engaged in pragmatically and socially defined projects.

Phenomenology, as something that is practiced, as both a method and a philosophy, has a point of departure and goes in a certain direction. To say that it is a philosophical practice, however, is not to say that it is a way of life, in the way one might think that being a Buddhist, or a yogi, or a movie star is a way of life. As a philosophical practice, it is an approach taken by philosophers in their philosophical considerations, not an attitude taken up in their everyday life. That phenomenology makes a start and goes in a certain direction, taking a certain perspective on its subject matter, means that phenomenology on its own is not in a position to give a full and exhaustive account of experience. It is not, for example, able to provide causal explanations of subpersonal (e.g., neuronal) processes that may underpin some aspects of experience. In this regard, however, phenomenology can play a productive role as part of a scientific and interdisciplinary practice. As a method, it has been used not just by philosophers, but also by researchers in a variety of disciplines that pursue both naturalistic and qualitative investigations. Recent uses of phenomenology in non- or extra-philosophical contexts, however, are controversial, but also, as I will try to show, productive, not only for science, but for a continuing reinvigoration of phenomenology.

Some of these controversies go back to the beginnings of phenomenology, to the situation in which Husserl found motivation to develop a method that was set against naturalistic and psychologistic explanations. As we'll see, however, challenging the relativism involved in scientism does not mean that phenomenology is opposed to the practice of the natural and social sciences. Rather, phenomenology is opposed to the reductionistic tendencies of science, and precisely the claims that are sometimes made by scientists who, ignoring certain lessons learned in the long history of philosophy, suggest that one science can provide the full and complete explanation of everything. We sometimes find such claims being made when a particular science first emerges or when it has had an impressive round of successes. In the history of such things, historicism is followed by economism, which is followed by psychologism, and so forth. Most recently neurologism is frequently put forward as the way to explain it all. The recent neurologizing of disciplines – neuroaesthetics, neuroeconomics, neurophilosophy, and even neurophenomenology – can go either way; in some cases it looks like neuroscience will colonize the target discipline (aesthetics, economics, philosophy, or phenomenology, etc.) and its subject matter; in other cases the discipline at stake has the potential to modulate any strong claim about what neuroscience can explain on its own. These are broader issues that I won't try to resolve here, however.

Chapter outline

In each chapter I will, first, outline some insights in the classical phenomenological accounts that continue to be defining for phenomenology and relevant to contemporary issues. Second, I will show how recent developments in practical and scientific uses of phenomenology are helping to undermine the reductionistic tendencies of science and at the same time helping to redefine phenomenology. Most chapters, therefore, start out with a review of classical phenomenology as we find it explicated in the 20th-century writings of Husserl, Heidegger, Sartre, Merleau-Ponty, and others. The chapters then transition to more contemporary, 21st-century applications of phenomenology, especially in contexts that involve empirical investigations of cognition.[1]

What is phenomenology? In *Chapter 1* I try to answer this question by reviewing several definitions. The answer is complicated by the fact that there is more than one version of phenomenology, and I provide some historical context for understanding this complexity. *Chapter 2* looks back at the classical discussions of psychologism, and the concept of phenomenology as a transcendental enterprise. It also looks forward to prospects for naturalizing phenomenology. In *Chapter 3* I present the basic toolbox of phenomenological methods – the epoché, phenomenological reduction and eidetic variation, and I suggest a 21st-century, high-tech retooling of the latter.

Chapter 4 starts to dig into the basic concepts of phenomenological philosophy. Here I show how the concept of intentionality was, and continues to be central for understanding phenomenology and several contemporary debates about the nature of consciousness and the mind. In *Chapter 5* I suggest that one of the more obscure concepts found in classical phenomenology, the notion of hyletic data, has direct and important relevance for contemporary discussions of embodied and enactive conceptions of cognition. *Chapter 6* presents Husserl's classic analysis of the temporal structure of experience, and introduces distinctions between elemental, integrative, and narrative time scales that are relevant to analyses found in later chapters. I also offer an enactive-phenomenological interpretation of temporality.

In the final set of chapters I try to show how phenomenology can help us sort out issues that pertain to more existential aspects of our personal and interpersonal experiences. In *Chapter 7* I review phenomenological theories about self and self-consciousness. I then look specifically at how the concept of first-person perspective can survive a number of pathological and experimental situations even as other aspects of selfhood are disrupted. *Chapter 8* explores concepts of intention formation and action on the narrative scale, relating these concepts to the phenomenolial concept of lifeworld. The final chapter, *Chapter 9*, delivers on certain promissory notes made about intersubjectivity in previous chapters. Considerations about intersubjectivity are related to questions about method, the nature of consciousness, action and self. The phenomenology of intersubjectivity, however, stands on its own as an important topic related to contemporary debates about social cognition.

1

What Is Phenomenology?

1.1 Phenomenologies

What is phenomenology? There have been books written on this question, including books by some of the major figures in this philosophical tradition. Let's start by taking a look at some of the recent definitions.

> Phenomenology is the study of human experience and of the ways things present themselves to us in and through such experience (Sokolowski 2000, 2).

> Phenomenology is the study of structures of consciousness as experienced from the first-person point of view. (Smith 2008)

These definitions closely reflect the traditional starting point for phenomenology. Husserl, considered the founder of the phenomenological movement, would certainly have accepted these characterizations. He focused on consciousness, and thought of phenomenology as a kind of descriptive enterprise that would specify the structures that characterize consciousness and the world as we experience it. The *first-person point of view* means that the phenomenologist, the investigator of consciousness, studies his or her own experience from the point of view of living through that experience. This sounds a bit like introspection, but as we'll see, phenomenology should not be equated with introspectionist psychology.

> Phenomenology is usually characterized as a way of seeing rather than a set of doctrines. In a typical formulation Edmund Husserl...presents phenomenology as approaching 'whatever

> appears to be as such', including everything meant or thought, in the manner of its appearing, in the how of its manifestation. (Moran 2002, 1)

Again, this follows closely with Husserl's original conception of phenomenology. It is a way of *seeing* rather than a set of doctrines or theories. In fact, part of the way one starts to do phenomenology is to push aside any doctrines or theories – including scientific and metaphysical theories. This pushing aside is part of the method of phenomenology. The phrase 'way of seeing' could be written 'method of seeing' – it is certainly a methodologically-guided way of seeing. Accordingly, some authors suggest that phenomenology is best defined as a method rather than a philosophical theory. The 'whatever appears to be as such' and the 'manner of appearing' or 'its manifestation' – these are all ways of talking about the *phenomena*, which is a Greek word for *appearances*. For Husserl, phenomenology (literally, the 'science of appearances') was a method that attempted to give a description of the way things appear in our conscious experience. *The way things appear in conscious experience* may be very different from the way things actually are *in reality*. But the phenomenologist, on this definition, is not concerned about how things actually are in reality; the phenomenologist is rather concerned about how we experience things.

Why should the way we experience things be of more interest than the way things actually are in reality? Here is a basic insight that phenomenology gives us. Our only access to the way things are in reality (and even to the very idea that there *are* things in reality; even to the very idea that there is something we call 'reality') is *via* consciousness. Phenomenology takes this as a significant fact: the person who opens her eyes and sees the world, sees it and has knowledge of it consciously. This applies to the person in the street as well as to the scientist in the lab. Even if the scientist is using sophisticated equipment to comprehend and measure physical processes, her knowledge of those processes comes by way of her consciousness of them. Even mathematicians reason and solve their problems consciously. Similar to Empiricists like Locke and Hume, who claim that all knowledge comes from sensory experience, Husserl would say that all knowledge comes through consciousness. That's why the phenomenologist thinks that consciousness (the way we experience things) is of more interest than the way things actually are in reality. Phenomenologists give a certain epistemological primacy to consciousness.

Think of it this way. Consciousness is like our window onto the world. Of course we are usually interested in the things we perceive through that window; maybe we are fascinated with the stuff that we find around us. But how do we know that we are getting a good view through our window? For example, what if the window is dirty, or colored, or distorted. What if the way the window is designed, or the window frame, keeps us from seeing everything we want to see. The phenomenologist suggests that before we study the things that we see when we look outside the window, we should first be concerned about the condition of the window – whether it's dirty, colored, distorted, or structured in such a way that it gives us only poor access to the objects on the other side of it. Returning from the metaphor, the phenomenologist thinks that the first step in understanding the basis for knowledge is to study the conditions imposed by consciousness – and specifically the structural features of consciousness, the way it works, and perhaps the systematic distortions that might bias it.

One problem should be evident. Since to study consciousness we have to do so *consciously*, how can we do so without already being caught up in the possible biases or distortions that may characterize consciousness itself. Following in a tradition started by Kant, Husserl proposes a *transcendental* analysis. That is, he proposes to study consciousness not by empirical methods (e.g., the methods of psychology), but by methodologically putting himself into a certain transcendental attitude. I'll come back to the concept of the transcendental in Chapter 2.

One problem with the definitions considered so far is that phenomenology is something more than what we have just described, and more than these definitions can capture, although, to some extent, this is phenomenology as Husserl conceived it at the beginning of the 20th century. Soon, however, other philosophers took up phenomenology and started to do different things with it.

The best example of this was Husserl's student, Martin Heidegger (1889–1976). Here is how Heidegger defines phenomenology.

> Phenomenology means...letting that which shows itself be seen from itself in the very way in which it shows itself from itself. This is the formal meaning of that branch of research which calls itself 'phenomenology'. (Heidegger 1962, 58/34).

Heidegger gets to this definition by reviewing the etymology of the word 'phenomenology'. *Phenomenon*, as already indicated, means something like appearance, or *that which shows itself.* *Logos* means something like 'allowing something to be exhibited'. Phenomenology is the discipline that allows that which shows itself to exhibit itself. Now you may think this doesn't get us very far at all. But it turns out that for Heidegger, that which shows itself are not the things that appear to us consciously; rather it is in some way *Being* itself. That is, Heidegger thinks that phenomenology is concerned with the question of the meaning of Being. Phenomenology is ontology. This is surprising because one usually thinks of ontology as a kind of metaphysics, and on Husserl's concept of phenomenology metaphysical theories are pushed aside. Phenomenology is not a form of metaphysics.

Accordingly, very early in the history of phenomenology, one can find serious differences in how phenomenology is defined. More generally, as different people engage in doing phenomenology, phenomenology itself undergoes some change. So, what phenomenology is, is itself open to question. Indeed, it might be better to talk of *phenomenologies* (in the plural). Rather than trying to find the right definition, then, it might be best to say something about the history of phenomenology. It turns out that the influence that phenomenology has had on a broad range of thinkers and subsequent philosophical developments is part of what we have to understand about phenomenology to truly see what it is.

1.2 Historical background and foreground

It's common to use the term 'movement' when referring to phenomenology as having a philosophical identity. As a movement, it's not entirely unified. Certainly, the term 'school' would be too strong in this respect. Generally speaking, however, phenomenology includes a number of people in its ranks. Husserl, whom we already mentioned as the originator; Heidegger, his most famous colleague. There is then a group of people who are to varying degrees associated with phenomenology, including Max Scheler (1874–1928), Karl Jaspers (1883–1969), and Hans-Georg Gadamer (1900–2002). There are also figures who are more rightly considered part of the lineage of phenomenology, that is, those who continued to develop phenomenology, including Maurice Merleau-Ponty (1908–1961), Jean-Paul Sartre (1905–1980), Simone de Beauvoir (1908–1986), Aron Gurwitsch (1901–1973), Alfred Schutz (1899–1959), among others. One thing you will notice, if you are familiar with any of these names, is that phenomenology has close ties with hermeneutics (Heidegger and Gadamer) and existentialism (Merleau-Ponty, de Beauvoir, Sartre). Moreover, phenomenology starts to flow over the borders of philosophy into psychiatry (Jaspers) and sociology (Schutz). It takes different turns into the thought of Levinas, Derrida, Foucault, and other poststructuralist thinkers and outright critics of phenomenology. The broader, but problematic term 'continental' philosophy is sometimes used to cover all of these thinkers, and others.

Consider a very short list of historical facts that suggest the complexity involved in trying to get a full sense of the history of phenomenology.

- One of the roots of phenomenology was the thought of the philosopher and psychologist Franz Brentano. From 1874 to 1895 he taught a seminar at the University of Vienna which, at various times was attended by Husserl, Meinong, Freud, Kafka (the novelist), Twardowski (the logician), and some of the founders of Gestalt psychology.
- Husserl was educated as a mathematician, studying with L. Kronecker and C. Weierstrass at the University of Berlin. Later, Husserl's phenomenology had some influence on Kurt Gödel, famous for Gödel's theorem (see Føllesdal 1995; Kennedy 2011).
- Husserl wrote his texts in an idiosyncratic shorthand and was said not to be able to think without writing. His manuscripts,

which consist of approximately 58,000 pages of shorthand, were smuggled out of Nazi Germany in the 1930s and are kept in the Husserl Archives in Leuven, Belgium.

- Heidegger read a book by Brentano on the many senses of being in Aristotle's metaphysics, and from that point onward never stopped thinking about one question: the question of the meaning of Being.

- Heidegger, after completing his doctoral studies spent several years at the University of Freiburg and became Husserl's assistant. He took a position at the University of Marburg in 1923, and when in the late 1920s Husserl retired, Heidegger was invited to take his position in Freiburg. In 1933 Heidegger became rector of the university, and joined the Nazi party just days after the university prohibited the retired Professor Husserl, because of his Jewish background, from participating in any university activities.

- Many German phenomenologists who studied with Husserl and Heidegger fled Germany in the 1930s because of the Nazi Regime, emigrated to France and/or the United States, and influenced various aspects of philosophy in those countries.

- Twentieth century philosophy has been characterized in terms of a serious opposition between analytic philosophy and continental (European) philosophy. Phenomenology falls into the latter category. Despite this, Frege and Wittgenstein, important figures in the origins of analytic philosophy, were from the European continent, and Husserl was greatly influenced by Frege. Bertrand Russell, also on the analytic side, carried a copy of Husserl's *Logical Investigations* to prison with him, and read them. Even around mid-century, the analytic philosopher Gilbert Ryle reviewed Heidegger's *Being and Time*, and taught a course on phenomenology at Oxford. Ryle, Quine, Ayer, Strawson and other analytic philosophers attended a conference organized by Merleau-Ponty and other phenomenologists in 1959 at Royaumont (outside of Paris), where there was some (but not much) agreement voiced that maybe analytic philosophy was not so alien to phenomenology.

- Phenomenology as a research program died sometime around 1970 but was reincarnated in the 1990s. It is alive and well today.

The last point is meant as a provocation. It may be regarded as an exaggeration and oversimplification, but let me paint the picture in broad strokes.

1.3 Death and reincarnation

In the 1960s, shortly after the Royaumont conference, two things happened. First, a growing number of American scholars started to discover phenomenology (and existentialism) and became very enthusiastic about these philosophical approaches. More and more philosophers started to publish papers on phenomenology. A professional academic society (SPEP – the Society for Phenomenology and Existential Philosophy) was founded in the United States in 1962. Conferences were organized, courses were being taught etc.

Second, and around the same time (early 1960s), the philosophical scene on the European continent (especially in France) started to shift away from phenomenology and existentialism. In Germany, Heidegger had already rejected existentialism and had entered into his later, less-phenomenological thinking. Sartre moved firmly into his Marxist phase. Merleau-Ponty died in 1961. In Paris, structuralism was already the rage, and shortly thereafter post-structuralism. Foucault, Barthes, Levi-Strauss, and numerous others came into prominence. Derrida, who was influenced by his study of phenomenology started to publish his critical readings (deconstructions) of phenomenology, taking aim at Husserl and Heidegger. At the same time, although Heidegger still seemed to draw some attention in France (he attended a conference at Cerisy-la-Salle in 1955), his own communiqué with French philosophers, *The Letter on Humanism* (1947), actually helped to push French thought away from phenomenology.

Meanwhile, in America, the mainstream interest in the works of Husserl, Heidegger, Merleau-Ponty, and Sartre continued and remained strong until the mid- to late-70s. Although Derrida gave an influential lecture at John Hopkins University in 1966, his works did not appear in English until the 1970s. By the 1980s, however, many philosophers who had been creating scholarly works in the area of phenomenology were fast moving away from this focus and towards post-structuralism. Although American philosophers have often been in the lead with respect to analytic philosophy, it seems that among American philosophers who follow continental theory, they do just that, *follow*; and during these times they were usually about 20 years behind the trend-setters in Paris. In the 1980s, the SPEP meetings still involved a few sessions on phenomenology and existentialism, but most phenomenologists were trading in their *Husserliana* for post-phenomenological texts.

Even before this relative abandonment of phenomenology, however, I would argue that phenomenology was dying a slow death. For example, it's not easy to name a major work in phenomenology that was written after 1960. Of course, there were many books *on* or *about* phenomenology written after 1960, but for the most part these were commentaries – secondary sources that explained and commented on, or that provided detailed textual exegesis of Husserl or Heidegger's works. By 1980 there was a clear question in the air: is anyone doing phenomenological philosophy in an innovative or original sense, or has phenomenology simply become a scholarly exegesis? Many started to think the latter as they moved on to poststructuralist deconstruction – although this itself seemed to consist of simply more critical exegesis, often of phenomenological texts. So, the fashion went from writing explanatory commentaries on Husserl and Heidegger, to either writing deconstructions of Husserl and Heidegger, or defending Husserl and Heidegger from the deconstructionists.

There were, of course, some exceptions, that is, some original works in phenomenology, but not a lot, and most were not of major influence. One exception that did have an important impact was the work of Hubert Dreyfus. Dreyfus, writing in the 1970s and after, used phenomenology to develop a critique of artificial intelligence. He relied mainly on Heidegger and Merleau-Ponty, but this was an important and innovative application of phenomenological principles in an area of research that had not been addressed by phenomenology before. Other possible exceptions who continued to develop phenomenological ideas, but for various reasons did not have a major or widespread impact, are Jan Patočka (1907–1977) in Prague, and Michel Henry (1922–2002) in France. Other thinkers, greatly influenced by phenomenology, like Paul Ricoeur (1913–2005) and Jean-Luc Marion (1946-) are not easily categorized as phenomenologists.

It is safe to say, however, that there was a rebirth of interest in phenomenology in the 1990s, and specifically in works that suggested that phenomenology had something important to contribute to the developing cognitive sciences. Cognitive science, the interdisciplinary study of mind, brain and behavior was motivated by the influence of research in artificial intelligence on psychology starting in the 1950s. By the 1970s it had become an organized research program. Although Dreyfus had used phenomenology to critique AI, the idea that phenomenology could actually make a positive contribution, by pushing cognitive science to consider the importance of consciousness and embodiment struck only in the 1990s. We can understand this connection very clearly if we think about Merleau-Ponty's work 50 years earlier. In the 1940s Merleau-Ponty had been drawing on insights from gestalt psychology, neurology, and developmental psychology, and had integrated them with phenomenology in his first two published works: *The Structure of Behavior* and *Phenomenology of Perception*. Although in the 1980s a number of papers were published that attempted to positively exploit Merleau-Ponty's insights in relation to our understanding of embodied cognition, only in 1991, with the publication of Varela, Thompson and Rosch's *The Embodied Mind*, did a clear statement emerge about the relevance of phenomenology for cognitive science.

I'm suggesting that this connection between phenomenology and the cognitive sciences represents a rebirth of phenomenology; a re-incarnation (with renewed emphasis on embodied cognition). Some phenomenological scholars may regard this claim to be controversial, but today, in the opening years of the 21st century, it is, practically speaking, the primary way phenomenology is being put to use. It is clearly a way to put the insights of phenomenology to work on issues that have defined phenomenology from the very beginning: consciousness, intentionality, perception, cognition, action, intersubjectivity, and so forth. Importantly, however, this reincarnation means not only a rethinking of cognitive science, but also a rethinking of phenomenology (Gallagher and Varela 2003).

1.4 A different phenomenology

If one begins by thinking of cognitive science as it was first formulated in opposition to behaviorism, in terms of computational analysis and information processing, it is difficult to see how phenomenology might participate in the 'Cognitive Revolution'. On this formulation, the scientific study of cognition is a study of how the subpersonal, non-phenomenological mind manipulates discrete symbols according to a set of syntactical procedures, and how this might be cashed out in neurological terms. This, however, is no longer the current view of cognitive science. Faced with a variety of problems implicit in this view, the cognitive revolution took a different turn in the 1980s. This turn corresponded to a new emphasis on neuroscience, and connectionism, which challenged the prevailing computational orthodoxy by introducing an approach based on nonlinear dynamical systems. With this formulation there was a shift away from an emphasis on reductionism, at least in some circles, to an emphasis on the notion of emergence and self-organization. The question was how higher-level personal structures emerged from lower-level subpersonal, self-organizing processes. This turn in the fortunes of cognitive science also motivated a new interest in consciousness and phenomenology.

The current situation in the cognitive sciences is characterized by a growing interest in ecological-embodied-enactive approaches (Chemero 2009; Gallagher 2005; Hutto and Myin, 2013; Thompson 2007; Varela, Thompson and Rosch 1991). Such approaches, motivated and inspired by phenomenological insights, insist that cognition is best characterized as belonging to embodied, situated, action-oriented agents – agents who are in-the-world, as Heidegger and Merleau-Ponty would put it. On this understanding of the cognitive sciences, just as neuroscientists and neuropsychologists work together with researchers in artificial intelligence and robotics, so also phenomenologists and philosophers of mind work together with scientists in order to develop a fuller and more holistic view of cognitive life – a life that is not just the life of the mind, but the life of an embodied, ecologically situated, enactive agent.

This recent redefinition of the cognitive sciences, if it is to include a place for phenomenology, requires that we also conceive of phenomenology in a different way. At the very least we need to see that there is a section of the phenomenological map that can be redrawn along lines that reach across the theoretical divides that separate phenomenology from the sciences. To sketch out this topography we need to look at the topics that have defined phenomenology from the beginning, and then to overlay these traditional lines with the most recent phenomenological constructions that build on, revamp, or extend the original insights.

If we want to understand in detail how it's possible to reconceive phenomenology, and why this is a difficult and controversial task, we first need to understand how phenomenology was initially defined in opposition to naturalism, what that definition ruled out, and what it made possible. We then need to ask whether we can relax this definition, or back out of it, without backing out of phenomenology. This is the topic of the next chapter.

1.5   Further reading

For an introductory bibliography of resources on phenomenology see Gallagher (2011a). Bernet, Kern, and Marbach (1993) summarize major aspects of Husserl's phenomenology, including relevant material on mathematics and logic, and concepts of science and lifeworld. Cerbone (2006) provides an account of the historical development of phenomenology and some critical responses. Lyotard (1991) presents a critical account of phenomenology from a Marxist perspective. Moran (2000) is one of the best of the recent introductions to phenomenology. Patočka (1996) focuses on logic, consciousness, temporality and embodiment in Husserl, plus his own critical contributions to phenomenology. Spiegelberg (1960) provides an exhaustive historical survey.

2 Naturalism, Transcendendentalism and a New Naturalizing

2.1 Mathematics and psychology

In the early-1930s, Raymond Aron, a French philosopher returning from Germany after studying with Husserl met Jean-Paul Sartre, the soon-to-be existentialist, in a café in Paris. After Aron explained what he had learned from Husserl, Sartre became very excited by the fact that, as he put it, with phenomenology one could begin to philosophize by carefully describing one's perception of a wine glass. The following year Sartre went to study in Berlin where he more likely employed beer glasses. Later in his major work, *Being and Nothingness*, he actually does use the example of a wine glass to make a point about bodily movement. In Paris, phenomenology was (and still is) often done in cafés.

The beginnings of phenomenology, in the academic settings of various Prussian-Austrian universities where Husserl worked,[1] were far removed from everyday Parisian cafés. Its roots can be found in debates about the nature of mathematics in the late 19th century, and in a set of problems that can be traced back as far as Plato. Like Plato, Descartes, Leibniz, and a number of other philosophers, Husserl was trained in mathematics. He was also influenced by the emerging science of psychology. He had attended the lectures of Wilhelm Wundt (one of the first experimental psychologists) in Leipzig, and he later studied William James' *Principles of Psychology*. The connection between mathematics and psychology is important for Husserl. It led to his first two writings: *On the Concept of Number* (1887) and *Philosophy of*

Arithmetic (1891). What Husserl tries to show in these writings is that mathematical concepts are in some sense grounded in psychological states, a position known as psychologism. According to this view, logical laws reduce to psychological laws. This is a position that he not only eventually gave up, but also came to aggressively criticize.

The question is whether we should think of logical and mathematical laws as workable only because the human mind is the way it is. Is the mathematical fact that $1 + 1 = 2$, or the logical law of non-contradiction, true only because our minds are structured in such a way that these concepts (the concept of 2, or the concept of non-contradiction) make sense? Psychologism answers in the positive. This implies, for example, that $1 + 1 = 2$ is not true in itself, or that the rules of logic are not true independently of the kind of psyche that we have. Another way to think of this is that if evolution (or God) had designed our minds (or perhaps our brains) differently, then maybe $1 + 1$ would not be equal to 2.

Some philosophers, including Plato, would disagree. The Platonic view is that mathematical and logical concepts and laws have a certain existence independently of human psychology. If humans did not exist, $1 + 1$ would still be equal to 2. If there were no humans, indeed if there were no universe, the law of non-contradiction would still be true. In other words, there is no universe in which the law of non-contradiction is not true. The debates in the philosophy of mathematics are complex ones that involve epistemology and metaphysics. Is the statement '$1 + 1 = 2$' an eternal truth that has its own existence, or a convention that works in one mathematical system, or the product of the human mind? Luckily we don't have to resolve this. What we need to consider is simply this: that Husserl in his early works on mathematics adopted a form of psychologism, but then, before the dawn of the 20th century, he converted to a more Platonic anti-psychologistic view. For Husserl this was almost like a religious conversion, and it shaped his subsequent philosophy. This is where Husserl came into contact with Gottlob Frege who published a review (1894) of Husserl's *Philosophy of Arithmetic* where he criticized the psychologism that he found in that work. There are various debates about whether

Husserl, influenced by the logician Bernard Bolzano, had already moved away from psychologism before Frege's review appeared, but it does seem clear that Frege had an important influence in reinforcing Husserl's conversion to anti-psychologism. In his first major work in philosophy, *Logical Investigations* (1900–1901), Husserl (2001a) provided an argument against psychologism. With this argument Husserl is not far from the position taken by Frege, and one can note that right here there was no hint of what later came to be known as the analytic-continental split in philosophy.

Not unlike Frege, Husserl argues for a general theory of pure logic, understood as a theory of science – that is, as something that would apply to all knowledge. Science, or knowledge in general, considered as a theory, can be understood as a system of interconnected propositions linked by inferential relations. Furthermore, such propositional systems are best studied by examining their linguistic expressions – taken as a set of sentences expressing propositions. A proposition has a certain meaning (which Frege called its 'sense' [German: '*Sinn*']). Propositional meaning exists independently of anyone actually thinking about such meaning, and independently of someone making reference to something, or using a particular linguistic expression. In that case, we don't *invent* mathematical or logical truths, like the Pythagorean theorem; we *discover* them. Propositions are abstract objects that have their existence independently of whether they are ever expressed in a sentence.

When such meanings are expressed in sentences, or, more generally, when the human mind comes in contact with such truths, that is when we grasp the truth of a proposition, Husserl argues, meanings are experienced and are therefore accessible via conscious intuition. They are instantiated in intentional acts, and are therefore open to a reflective (phenomenological) description. This idea that we can experience or intuit such meanings is a beginning point for phenomenology, and in some regard it is a breaking point away from purely logical analysis, which becomes standard in analytic philosophy. To oversimplify things, analytic philosophy stays with the sentences; phenomenology turns its attention to the conscious acts in which we intuit meaning.

2.2 Naturalistic and transcendental accounts

It is important, however, to see that when Husserl starts talking about conscious acts – acts of judgment, but also acts of perception, imagination, recollection, and so forth – he is not taking us back to psychologism. That is, he is not claiming that the meaning, or the truth of the proposition, is *generated* in psychological states or mental acts. Rather, he is talking about our access to meanings that are independent of such acts. Although in his early characterizations of phenomenology Husserl calls it a 'descriptive psychology', he later rightly drops the term 'psychology'. Phenomenology is an attempt to describe our experience of meaning, but not in the way that psychology might try to explain that experience.

On some accounts, the methods of psychology are naturalistic. That is, psychology attempts to give causal explanations for mental processes and psychological states. For example, a neuropsychologist might argue that I am able to remember what my first car looked like because my brain is processing information in a certain way. And my brain is able to process information in a certain way because it has evolved in a certain way and I have had certain kinds of experiences in my life. Psychology, in this sense, is empirical. It looks to empirical facts – how the brain works, what my experiences are, etc. – to explain why certain mental states occur. This is a naturalistic explanation. It's naturalistic because there is no appeal to any kind of mysterious process that can't be explained, at bottom, in terms of physical processes. Nature consists of physical events, and everything we need to explain, whatever we need to explain, is contained in nature.

It is not clear, however, that mathematical truths or the laws of logic are *natural* in this sense. Even if we destroy nature, as we seem to be doing at an ever-increasing rate, and if all rational brains cease to function, the law of non-contradiction would still be true. Again, for Husserl, the issue is not to explain how these laws come into existence, but rather, how we can know such laws. This question leads Husserl to the idea of a transcendental analysis.

The notion of a transcendental analysis was clarified by Kant in the 18th century. A transcendental analysis is an attempt to discover the conditions of possibility for knowledge. Specifically, Kant wanted to discover the categories used by the mind when it engaged in epistemic acts. For example, when I perceive one billiard ball banging into another billiard ball, why do I perceive this as an instance of causality? Kant was unhappy with Hume's answer to this question. Hume suggested that our imagination simply fabricates a relation out of habit (or indolence) after we see such things happen often enough. What we actually see is only one event (one billiard ball rolling) followed by a second event (the second billiard ball rolling). This amounts to succession, but if we see this particular pattern of succession often enough, we start to call it causation. We learn, through empirical experience to see things in a causal way. This is a version of psychologism – causality is really just a product of our overworked imagination. Kant regarded this kind of position as a threat to science. If Hume was right, then science is a kind of fiction that depends on how the imagination works. In order to put science on a 'firm foundation' Kant set out to show that the mind actually follows immutable, unlearned, non-empirical laws (of the same sort as the laws of logic or mathematics), and that such a priori laws constitute reason itself. He did this by means of what he called a transcendental (or 'pure') deduction. Kant, and then Husserl, used the term 'pure' to signify an analysis that is transcendental and that sets aside claims that are merely empirical.

Transcendental, then, means first of all, non-empirical. On the transcendental view, I see certain events in terms of causal relations, not because of certain psychological facts about my life – not because I was born in this time and place or have had x, y, and z experiences, or because I met Freud in Brentano's seminar, or because I'm depressed, or because someone told me to look at the world in this way, or because I learned to see it this way, etc. – but rather because the mind is structured in a certain way, *independently of my experience*. Kant called this the *a priori* structure of the mind – the mind is this way 'prior to' any experience. Causality, it turns out, is one of the categories that define the mind as rational, and it's a universal, transcendental feature of all rational minds. Kant thought that you can't explain this fact by means of a psychological, natural, causal analysis, since the very possibility of appealing to causality in such an explanation is already presupposed. Accordingly, the conditions of possibility of any such explanation, or any such scientific knowledge, can only be discovered through a non-empirical, transcendental analysis.

Notice here that even for Kant there is already a kind of bracketing of the question about whether causality exists independently of the mind. This would be a metaphysical question that is not addressed by a transcendental analysis. What the world in-itself (the *Ding-an-sich*) is like is not knowable, according to Kant. Our way of *knowing* the laws of nature or of mathematics, which are phenomenal laws that apply to empirical reality, depends on the transcendental structure of our mind, but this does not mean that these laws themselves depend on psychological aspects of our experience.

The basic idea is just this. The mind can know things about the world. Psychology explains this fact by invoking causality and empirical facts. The transcendental question is, what makes it possible for the mind to be able to invoke something like causality in the first place? Husserl follows this Kantian transcendental agenda. Unlike Kant, however, he did not think that we needed a transcendental deduction. Rather, he thought that we could actually put ourselves into a transcendental stance or attitude that would allow us to see how the mind (or consciousness), or our experience of the world is structured. This is what Husserl meant by 'intuition' – we can actually 'see' the transcendental structure of consciousness. This kind of intuitive seeing, which brings something to presence in our experience, is a principle in the practice of phenomenology. In this context, 'intuition' doesn't mean having a hunch, or a vague feeling that something is the case. Rather, it means a pure seeing that something is the case in a self-evident way. Intuition does not involve making an inference (i.e., a logical move from A to C, via some other fact, B). It means simply seeing that C is the case. Phenomenology is an attempt to step back and to see how consciousness works.

In a work published in 1911, *Philosophy as a Rigorous Science*, Husserl calls this form of transcendental phenomenology, a rigorous or strict science. In German philosophy of the 19th century, the term 'science' has a very broad meaning. It involves any enterprise that seeks knowledge. That includes natural sciences, human sciences (humanities – the German term is *'Geisteswissenshaften'*, literally the 'sciences of spirit'), and even philosophy. Husserl uses the term 'science' in this wide sense. He attempts to situate himself with respect to (1) Kant (or critical philosophy), (2) Hegel, and (3) more recent, Romantic philosophy, i.e., the historicism of Dilthey and Romantic hermeneutics and its concept of relativistic *Weltanschauungen* [world views]. In addition, he distances himself from any positivism (i.e., the claim that natural science is the only valid form of knowledge) and the natural sciences.

To be clear, Husserl was not opposed to natural scientific explanation. Rather, Husserl was opposed to scient*ism*, the positivistic view that everything is fully explainable by natural science. Specifically he regarded the naturalizing of consciousness, including intentionally, but also the naturalizing of norms, and things like formal logic, mathematics, and ideal essences as wrong-headed. In his arguments against psychologism, in the *Logical Investigations*, for instance, he shows that this extreme naturalism refutes itself by undermining any formal-logical principle or law of nature by reducing it to mere psycho-physical processes. Simply put, on the extreme version of naturalism, if our brain processes evolve over time (which they certainly do), then the laws of nature may be different in the future than they are now. A law of nature would accordingly be relative to the particular neurological or psychological constitution of the historically-situated knowing subject. This is what Husserl wanted to reject.

Although he clearly criticized positivism (scientism, naturalism), he did not reject natural science. Indeed, he was concerned about natural science – i.e., he worried that it did not properly understand its own epistemological foundations. He wanted to make sure that science and our knowledge of the laws of nature were firmly grounded. This was Kant's worry (and Descartes's worry before that). The right foundations cannot be found in psychology, or relativistic historicism. Husserl argues, however, that we should not return to Kant; rather we should take the transcendental project forward. In effect, for him, the new rigorous science, i.e., rigorous philosophy, is phenomenology.

Accordingly, Husserl defined phenomenology in opposition to and as excluding a naturalistic, merely empirical analysis. This addressed, more generally, a long-standing controversy about philosophy's relation to science, which phenomenology itself was meant to answer.

> The question of philosophy's relation to the natural and human-istic sciences, whether the specifically philosophical element of its work, essentially related as it is to nature and the human spirit, demands fundamentally new attitudes, that in turn involve fun-damentally peculiar goals and methods; whether as a result the philosophical takes us, as it were, into a new dimension, or whether it performs its function on the same level as the empirical sciences of nature and of the human spirit – all this is to this day disputed. (1965, 72)

To the extent that phenomenology is transcendental, it does not function on the same level as empirical psychology; it is more fun-damental and it opens up a new transcendental dimension.

Not only did Husserl adopt a traditional concern about estab-lishing a firm epistemological foundation for doing science, he also wanted to define the limits of what science, or naturalism broadly construed, can tell us.

> Naturalism is a phenomenon consequent upon the discovery of nature ... considered as a unity of spatiotemporal being subject to exact laws of nature. With the gradual realization of this idea in constantly new natural sciences that guarantee strict knowledge regarding many matters, naturalism proceeds to expand more and more.... [T]he natural scientist has the tendency to look upon everything as nature, [just as] the humanistic scientist sees every-thing as 'spirit', as a historical creation. By the same token, both are inclined to falsify the sense of what cannot be seen in their way. Thus the naturalist, to consider him in particular, sees only nature, and primarily physical nature. Whatever is, is either itself physical, belonging to the unified totality of physical nature, or it is in fact psychical, but then merely as a variable dependent on the physical, at best a secondary 'parallel accompaniment'. Whatever is belongs to psychophysical nature, which is to say that it is univocally deter-mined by rigid laws. (1965, 79).

On Husserl's view, then, psychology as a legitimate natural science is one thing; phenomenology is something else. Psychology treats consciousness as belonging to natural human or animal organisms. In conducting their studies and experiments, however, psychologists already and unavoidably employ consciousness in the very obvious sense that they tend to be conscious when they conduct their studies. In taking natural, third-person perspectives on cognition and behavior, and in conducting their specific research, psychologists are not concerned with basic philosophical questions that ask about the *a priori* nature of the very consciousness that they must use to do their research.

The idea that consciousness may have certain systematic characteristics that will place *a priori* limitations on what conscious agents (including psychologists) can learn – in a way that is even more basic than any method or technology that psychologists might use to do their research – is not something with which psychologists tend to be concerned. Consider, for example, the temporal structure of consciousness. According to phenomenology, this is something that permeates all experience, all cognitive processes including perception, memory, imagination, judgment, emotion, etc., as well as all action. Although psychological science has long studied reaction times, timing in neuronal processing, the subjective experience of time passing, and phenomena such as time estimation, all such studies employ the notion of objective time and attempt to measure these phenomena, literally, by the clock. Even in studies of working memory, researchers raise questions that can only be answered in terms of objective time – how many units of information, or how much representational content can be held in consciousness for how long? Such questions define the nature of the psychological and neuroscientific investigation of such phenomena. Neither psychology nor neuroscience, however, asks about the temporal nature of experience *as experienced.* The phenomenological question is something like this: what must consciousness be like if the subject is able to experience the passage of time, to remember what just happened, to anticipate what is just about to happen, and to perceive temporal objects such as melodies, sentences, horse races, or indeed, any object that endures or changes. This question marks the subject matter of

Husserl's phenomenological analysis of time-consciousness (see Chapter 6).

In one sense the transcendental investigation seems more basic; in another sense one might think that the neuroscientific investigation is equally basic. One could put the neuroscientific question in this way: how must the brain function if it allows consciousness to have this temporalizing structure? The issue, however, despite Husserl's claim about the fundamental nature of phenomenology, should not be about which type of investigation is more basic. It's rather that these are two different kinds of investigations that are not reducible to one another. Accordingly, phenomenologists maintain a strong distinction between phenomenology as a transcendental study, and psychology or neuroscience as a natural science. Precisely for these reasons, some phenomenologists argue that to naturalize phenomenology would be to do something other than phenomenology, or that even to speak of a naturalized phenomenology is absurd (e.g., Lawlor 2009). Phenomenology is defined as a transcendental discipline, conducted within a transcendental attitude. If one takes the naturalistic attitude, then one is not doing phenomenology. If one ignores Husserl's anti-naturalism and proposes to do phenomenology within the natural attitude, then that just isn't phenomenology.

2.3   The new naturalism

The phenomenologist Eduard Marbach, in his book *Mental Representation and Consciousness* (1993), described the relationship, or more precisely, the lack of relationship between phenomenology and cognitive science. Focusing on investigations of mental imagery, Marbach suggested that the studies carried on in the respective fields of phenomenology and cognitive science, although, on the surface seeming to investigate the same phenomena, are quite divorced from each other. Both enterprises are concerned with cognition, and in some instances, with consciousness, yet they obviously work on different levels and with different conceptions of cognition and consciousness. Explanations of consciousness made by cognitive scientists and philosophers of mind for the most part rely on 'non-conscious physical symbol-manipulating machines or information processors' (Marbach 1993, 4). Thus, for someone like Stephen Kosslyn (1980, 1984) the solution to the problem of mental imagery must be sought in representations that lie below the threshold of consciousness, that is, on the level of information processing and functions that are not accessible to introspection. In contrast, Marbach's training in Husserlian phenomenology leads him to seek solutions on the level of intentionality, and specifically in descriptions of consciousness that are made precise by a methodologically controlled reflective introspection.

For Marbach the main issue is not what the relationship *is* between phenomenology and cognitive science, but what it *ought to be*. Echoing in the background of his text are different versions of the same question: What is (or ought to be) the relationship between 1st-person and 3rd-person explanations? What is (or ought to be) the relationship between personal level (intentional) explanation and explanation on the subpersonal level? Husserl himself had based his phenomenological approach precisely on the distinction between what was available to reflection (experience, intentional consciousness) and what was not (extra-intentional, subpersonal information).

In terms of explaining the processes of imaging, Zenon Pylyshyn sets the general problem in terms of the distinction between personal experience and subpersonal representation:

> It is important to inquire whether the experience of imaging can reveal important properties of the information processing function or of the mental representation of information on which these processes operate (1973, 3).

Pylyshyn then outlines one side of what persists as an adversarial relation between phenomenology and cognitive science.

> But we must not assume in advance that such observation [of experience] will reveal the content of the mental representation. Not only does such observation present serious methodological hazards, it is not prima facie an observation of the functional representation

(i.e., one that figures in the human information-processing function) (1973, 3).

For Pylyshyn, as for Kosslyn and many others, phenomenology can contribute little or nothing of importance to a genuine scientific explanation of consciousness. Thus Dennett (2001), characterizing phenomenology as a first-person science, maintains: 'First-person science of consciousness is a discipline with no methods, no data, no results, no future, no promise. It will remain a fantasy.'

In contrast, Marbach contends that cognitive science will remain blind insofar as it operates without a serious and methodologically controlled description of what it attempts to explain, that is, consciousness, or more generally, mental life. He suggests that if Kosslyn is right in his claim that 'a theory of imagery should be consistent with reliable introspective reports of imagery, and ideally should offer the basis of an account of these experiences' (1978, 223), then cognitive science needs to take its presuppositions from something more sophisticated than commonsense or folk psychology. For Marbach, phenomenology provides a reliable and systematic reflective analysis required for guiding cognitive science. This means that a phenomenological study of consciousness is required as part of cognitive science.

> By this I simply mean to say the following: even though I am inclined to share standard naturalistic views on which, I take it, the mental (including consciousness) will ultimately be *explained* in terms of ordinary physical properties, I do not believe that the *explacanda* themselves are all and only to be found at the naturalistic level of investigation. (Marbach 1993, 9).

On this view, cognitive science needs to relax its borders if, in any particular analysis, it is to target precisely what it is trying to explain. Phenomenology, in this respect, ought to constrain cognitive science. If, for example, we are to understand which brain activities produce or correlate to certain specific states of consciousness, then we first must be provided with '*basic conceptual categories* for talking about the true nature of the mental' (Marbach 1993, 9). Such categories are supplied by phenomenological reflection on conscious experience. Thus, 'in order to convey a truly scientific content to the terms/concepts that cognitive psychology and related philosophy of mind use for determining their objects – i.e. mental phenomena – *a systematic descriptive analysis of consciousness in its own nature must be presupposed...*' (p. 11).

Marbach's advice goes one way on what is clearly a two-way street. If phenomenology should constrain empirical investigations of the mind, it may also be the case that empirical investigations should constrain phenomenology. If it is difficult for cognitive scientists to accept the help of phenomenology, however, it is even more difficult for phenomenologists to accept the idea that empirical science could in any way constrain phenomenology. After all, the clear distinction between a transcendental discipline and the naturalistic empirical sciences seems to be part of the very definition of phenomenology. Yet the idea of 'mutual constraints' and a naturalizing of phenomenology have been proposed by a number of other theorists (Varela, Thompson and Rosch 1991; Varela 1996).

If we think of a strict transcendental phenomenology as a narrow conception of phenomenology, then a broader conception of phenomenology would be one that involves more than the pure description involved in the transcendental project. Viewing phenomenology in this broader way does not, however, 'contradict Husserl's entire conception of phenomenology' (Lawlor 2009, 2).[2] Indeed, Husserl (1977) suggested the possibility of developing a phenomenological psychology. This project would differ from transcendental phenomenology but would still be an investigation of consciousness from the first-person perspective, while remaining within the natural attitude. The task of phenomenological psychology is to study consciousness, not as the transcendental foundation of the sciences and the condition of possibility for all meaning, but as a phenomenon in its own right. The idea that one can do phenomenology, or we might say *use* phenomenology while remaining in the natural attitude signals a way of thinking of phenomenology that is quite different from Husserl's original project. But such an approach is clearly consistent with a broader conception of phenomenology held by Husserl himself. Husserl certainly thought that the results of transcendental phenomenology should not be ignored by science, and the idea that they might inform the natural sciences is not inconsistent with the value of transcendental analysis. He suggested, quite clearly, that 'every analysis or theory of transcendental phenomenology – including... the theory of the transcendental constitution of an objective world – can be developed in the natural realm, by giving up the transcendental attitude' (1960, §57).

First, let's note that beyond Husserl other phenomenologists moved in this direction. Gurwitsch, Sartre and Merleau-Ponty, for example, each pursued what could generally be called phenomenological psychology. Gurwitsch appealed to Gestalt psychology, animal studies, and developmental psychology to support the proper phenomenological characterization of various experiences. For example, if we want to provide a phenomenological description of how we go about solving a problem in the real world, or how, in that context, a certain object can take on the meaning of a tool, we can benefit from something that Gestalt theorists have described very well: a perceptual reorganization involving the *'restructuring of the given situation, the regrouping of the facts of which it is composed'* (Gurwitsch 2009, 246). Sartre, in his phenomenological examination of the imagination relied upon insights from empirical psychology. For example, he refers us to experiments on images associated with presented words, and offers a reinterpretation of these experiments to work out distinctions between symbols and images (e.g., 2004, 107ff). Merleau-Ponty is also well known for his integration of phenomenology, psychology, and neurology. In *Phenomenology of Perception*, for example, he makes extensive use of the experimental literature and case studies. In lecture courses at the Sorbonne in 1950–1952 (under the title *Human Sciences and Phenomenology*) he discusses a 'convergence' of phenomenology and psychology, explicating various misunderstandings on both sides of this relationship (2010, 317). He cites Sartre's analysis of imagination as a good example of how phenomenological (eidetic) analysis can be integrated with psychology, and like Gurwitsch and Sartre, he appeals to psychology as a possible guide for phenomenological insight, suggesting that 'the distinction between phenomenology and psychology must not be presented as a rigid distinction' (2010, 329) – without, of course, denying the distinction.

What we see in each of these cases is, to use Merleau-Ponty's term, a convergence of phenomenology and the natural sciences of psychology and/or neuroscience. This is more than a convergence of results. That is, the convergence is not simply that phenomenology and psychology have reached the same conclusions about specific topics. Indeed, in some cases, there is a critical distance between the view defended by phenomenology and the received view of psychological science. Rather, the convergence pertains to how phenomenology is put to use in the research fields of psychology and neuroscience. It's a convergence on a methodological plane. Moreover, the convergence does not signify a change in the definition of phenomenology. Nor is it a threat to transcendental phenomenology. The transcendental project remains as its own phenomenological project. What we find in Husserl's concept of a phenomenological psychology, however, and in the work of Gurwitsch, Sartre, Merleau-Ponty, and others is a certain pragmatic use made of phenomenological method. Accordingly, some of the 'classical' phenomenologists have already provided a positive response to the question of whether phenomenology can be naturalized.

2.4   Some natural ways of using phenomenology

In contemporary proposals about how precisely phenomenology can be naturalized, we find three general approaches. I'll briefly summarize these here, without providing anything close to the full critical discussion that each one deserves. I'll provide a more detailed account of phenomenological methodology in the next chapter.

2.4.1   Formalizing phenomenology

One approach to naturalizing phenomenology, proposed by Roy et al. (1999), involves translating the results of phenomenological analysis into a formal language that is clearly understood by science, namely, mathematics. We can call this the CREA proposal, since it was proposed by an interdisciplinary group of researchers at the Centre de Recherche en Epistémologie Appliquée (CREA) in Paris – Jean Petitot (a mathematician), Jean-Michel Roy (a philosopher), Bernard Pachoud (a psychiatrist), and the late Francisco Varela (a neurobiologist). They write, 'It is our general contention... that phenomenological descriptions of any kind can only be naturalized, in the sense of being integrated into the general framework of natural sciences, if they can be mathematized. We see mathematization as a key instrument for naturalization...' (Roy et al. 1999, 42).

We can understand this proposal as building on the work of Marbach (1993) who suggested a formal symbolic language for phenomenology. One important question is whether it is possible for mathematics to capture the lived experience described by phenomenology. The description of lived experience, of course, already involves expressing the experience in language. It takes an additional step to formalize those verbal or written descriptions. This is a strategy that can be employed to clarify word meaning and to facilitate scientific communication. As Marbach (1993; 2010) suggests, formalizing the language can improve the possibility of formulating intersubjectively shareable meanings. As in science, terminological problems are addressed through the use of formalized language systems like those found in mathematics. Marbach thus attempts to develop a formalized notation to express phenomenological findings, not just about the content of experience, but about its structure.

Husserl's analysis of episodic memory, for example, suggested that it involves the re-enactment of previous perceptions. He relies on the notion of 're-presentation' (*Vergegenwärtigung*); literally, 'to make something present again'. Whereas perception is an intentional reference to something present, and thus an activity of 'presentation', memory refers to something absent. Even intentional reference to something absent, however, requires a presentational activity where reference to that which is not present is made 'as if' it were given to me in perception (Marbach 1993, 61). The 'as if' is the re-presentational modification. Marbach, following Husserl's own proposals for formal notation,[3] attempts to make the structure of re-presentation clearer.

Let '(PER)x' signify the act of perceiving some object, x. Remembering x involves (PER)x, not as an actual and occurent act of perception, but as a reenactment of a past perception. To signify this in the notation, the parentheses become brackets: [PER] x. Furthermore, an element of belief (signified by **) distinguishes a reenactment in memory from an imaginary enactment. In other words, in contrast to imagination, episodic memory involves a belief that in the past I actually did perceive x. Let 'p' signify that the perception of x is in the past rather than in the future (to differentiate it from expectation). Marbach thus attempts to capture the structure of an act of episodic memory in the following formulation:

(REP p**[PER])x

This states that a re-presentation of x occurs by means of 'a perceiving of x bestowed with the belief of it having actually occurred in the past'.

Things get more complicated (see Marbach 2010), but the virtue of formulating a notation like this should be clear if it can show clearly the complexity of consciousness and the explication of that complexity provided by phenomenological reflection. The hypothesis that at some suitable level of abstraction, the phenomenological and the neurological notations would turn out to be consistent, leads directly to the CREA proposal made by Roy et al. (1999).[4] Mathematics is purportedly a formal and therefore neutral language with which we can set out results that are either first-person (the results of phenomenological reflections) or third-person (the results of natural science). Specifically, the CREA proposal suggests that a sufficiently complex mathematics, specifically the mathematics of dynamical systems, can facilitate the translation of data from phenomenological and naturalistic realms. In Varela's (1996) specific proposal for a neurophenomenology we can see a good example of how phenomenology, experimental brain science and dynamical systems theory can be integrated in a way that pushes cognitive science in a new direction.[5]

2.4.2 Neurophenomenology

The aim of neurophenomenology is to incorporate phenomeno-logical investigations of experience into neuroscientific research on consciousness. Neurophenomenology focuses especially on the temporal dynamics of conscious experience and brain activity (Thompson, Lutz and Cosmelli 2005). Varela formulates the 'working hypothesis' of neurophenomenology in the following way: 'Phenomenological accounts of the structure of experience and their counterparts in cognitive science relate to each other through reciprocal constraints' (1996, 343). By 'reciprocal constraints' he means that phenomenological analyses can help guide and shape the scientific investigation of consciousness, and that scientific findings can in turn help guide and shape phenomenological investigations. An important feature of this approach is that dynamical systems theory can mediate between phenomenology and neuroscience. We can thus distinguish three aspects of this approach:

1. Phenomenological accounts of the invariant categorical and structural features of lived experience;
2. The use of formal dynamical approaches to model these structural invariants; and
3. Neurophysiological measurements of large-scale, integrative processes in the brain.

Let me say a word about dynamical systems theory before going further since it's something that will be frequently mentioned in the following. The behavior of a dynamical system cannot be explained on the basis of the behavior of its separate components or in terms of an analysis that focuses on the synchronic, or static, or purely mechanical interactions of its parts within an isolated moment of time. In non-dynamic or static models, time is merely a medium in which a mechanistic system operates; in a dynamical system time is intrinsic to the operation of the system. The parts of a dynamical system do not interact in a linear fashion; rather, they interact in a non-linear way, reciprocally determining each other's behavior. This involves a process of self-organization in which the parts remain dynamically coordinated to each other over a period of time. In explaining experience, then, neurophenomenology holds that a variety of processes in the brain, body and environment become temporally coupled in dynamic coordination.

In neurophenomenology, the idea of reciprocal constraints means not only that the subject is actively involved in generating and describing specific experiential invariants, and that the neuroscientist is guided by these first-person data in the analysis and interpretation of physiological data, but also that such phenomenologically enriched neuroscientific analyses provoke revisions and refinements of the phenomenological accounts, as well as facilitate the subject's becoming aware of previously inaccessible or phenomenally unavailable aspects of his or her mental life. Examples of this can be found in neurophenomenological studies of epilepsy (Le Van Quyen and Petitmengin 2002) and pain (Price, Barrell and Rainville 2002).

As proposed by Varela (1996), neurophenomenology involves training experimental subjects in phenomenological method. That is, subjects will employ phenomenological reflection and develop descriptions of their own experience, which then may be used to facilitate responses in experimental trials. Since the practice of neurophenomenology in the lab requires training subjects to employ phenomenological methods, we'll discuss this approach in more detail in the next chapter.

2.4.3 Front-loaded phenomenology

A related approach to integrating phenomenology and experimental cognitive science has been called 'front-loaded phenomenology' (Gallagher 2003; Gallagher and Brøsted Sørensen 2006). This approach is closely connected with neurophenomenology in the sense that front-loaded phenomenology can draw on the results of neurophenomenological experiments. Rather than starting with the empirical results (as one would do in the CREA proposal) or with the training of subjects (as one would do in neurophenomenology), the front-loading approach starts with the experimental design. The idea is to incorporate phenomenological insights into the design of experiments, that is, to allow the insights developed in phenomenological analyses to inform the way experiments are set up. The phenomenological insights might be drawn from Husserlian transcendental investigations, or from neurophenomenological experiments, or from the more empirically oriented phenomenological analyses found, for example, in Merleau-Ponty (1962). To front-load phenomenology does not mean to presuppose or automatically accept the phenomenological results obtained by others. Rather it involves testing those results and more generally a dialectical movement between previous insights gained in phenomenology and preliminary trials that will specify or extend these insights for purposes of the particular experiment or empirical investigation.

The idea that one can incorporate the insights of phenomenology into experimental protocols without training subjects in the method is not meant as a rejection of the neurophenomenological approach. Front-loaded phenomenology, however, can address certain limitations involving training in neurophenomenological procedures. Specifically not every experiment can be designed to allow for the training of subjects in phenomenological methods. For example, in some cases one wants the subject to be naïve about what is being tested. In other cases one might be testing subjects who are unable to follow phenomenological method (e.g., young children or subjects with specific pathologies). In such cases, it may still be possible to employ the front-loading technique.

Experimental design is always based on some concept, contrast or distinction. Most often such ideas come from previous experiments. If one traces these ideas back far enough, however, one finds that some of the concepts and distinctions are based on previously operationalized concepts that are themselves drawn from folk psychology, our everyday natural attitude, or varying philosophical traditions. In this regard there may be less control involved in experimental design than the experimenters believe; specific theories lurking in the background may already introduce certain biases that are shaping the kind of conclusions that can be drawn from the experiments. To the extent that the concepts and distinctions incorporated into the experiment are generated in careful phenomenological analyses, closer to experience and less influenced by established theoretical considerations, the scientist gains a certain degree of control that is otherwise missing.

These are some of the ways that one can naturalize phenomenology, in the sense of integrating phenomenological data, methods and insights into natural scientific experiments in cognitive science, including psychology and neuroscience, without engaging in naturalistic reductionism. Practically speaking one of the most straightforward and productive ways of providing opportunity for this kind of integration is for phenomenologists to work together with psychologists and neuroscientists. Just this kind of engagement may be what Dan Zahavi has in mind when he writes:

> To naturalize phenomenology might simply be a question of letting phenomenology engage in a fruitful exchange and collaboration with empirical science. Phenomenology does study phenomena that are part of nature and therefore also open to empirical investigation, and insofar as phenomenology concerns itself with such phenomena it should be informed by the best available scientific knowledge. (Zahavi 2010, 8)

Phenomenology does not directly address the questions of subpersonal mechanisms or causal factors. And yet phenomenology can offer some insight to studies of consciousness and cognition, at the very least by providing personal-level *descriptions* of the *explicanda* for those studies. Furthermore, it is a matter of historical fact that phenomenology (in the work of Gurwitsch and Merleau-Ponty, for example) has always learned from disciplines such as psychopathology, neuropathology, developmental psychology, cognitive psychology, and neuroscience. The influence goes both ways, in a process of mutual enlightenment (Gallagher 1997).

'Mutual enlightenment' is a relatively mild way to put it, however. A more radical proposal would be to pursue what Merleau-Ponty (1963) called the 'truth of naturalism' and the idea that 'it would be necessary to define transcendental philosophy anew in such a way as to integrate with it the very phenomenon of the real'. The 'truth' of naturalism is not the naturalism Husserl cautioned against, but a redefined non-reductionist naturalism that correlates with a redefined phenomenology.

2.5 Further reading

Gallagher and Schmicking (2010) offer a collection of essays that explore the connections between phenomenology and cognitive science, including one by Marbach on formalizing phenomenological notation. Marbach (1993) introduces the idea of formalizing phenomenological notation and reviews the relation between phenomenology and cognitive science. Mohanty (1989) offers an interpretation of Husserl's transcendental phenomenology from a perspective informed by analytic philosophy. Petitot et al. (1999) is a collection of essays that explore the naturalizing of phenomenology. Zahavi (2012) is a collection of essays that explores a variety of topics in phenomenology.

3
Phenomenological Methods and Some Retooling

3.1 The natural attitude

As we saw in the previous chapter, phenomenology starts with a transcendental rather than a naturalistic analysis of consciousness. How do we do a transcendental analysis? Husserl suggests that we need to effect a change in attitude, and specifically by moving from what he calls the natural attitude to the phenomenological attitude.

We are all familiar with the natural attitude, even if we don't know it. Being in the natural attitude means simply taking for granted everything that we do take for granted. For example, for the most part, we assume that we live in a real world – that the world around us is real. We don't even think about that (unless we're in philosophy class, or undergoing some strange experience, such as a hallucination). Ordinarily, we simply assume that the objects around us are real. This is a very practical attitude to be in; perhaps it's even evolutionarily necessary for our survival. If we are walking through the woods and come upon a bear, it would not be a good thing to suddenly become metaphysically skeptical about whether this animal actually exists. So, the natural attitude is quite natural for us to be in. Husserl describes it thus:

> [Each perceiving subject] 'knows', is certain, that the surrounding world that is posited as existing in the manner of immediate intuition is only the intuited piece of a total surrounding world and that things continue on further in endless (Euclidian) space. Likewise,

41

the experiencing subject knows that the currently remembered temporal piece of what exists is only a piece of the endless chain of what exists; a chain that stretches back into the endless past and reaches out into the endless future as well...And that holds of things with respect to all their thing-properties, with respect to their rest and motion, their qualitatively changed and unchanged situations, etc. To be strictly accurate, [in the natural attitude] the subject knows itself as one which sometimes judges correctly, one which sometimes falls into error, as one which occasionally succumbs to doubts and confusions, and also as one which occasionally presses on to clear conviction. But the subject knows also, or is certain, in spite of all this, that the world is and that it, the experiencing subject itself, is in the middle of this world, etc. (Husserl 2006, 3)

In the natural attitude we play and work, conduct business, pay our taxes, visit our friends, love our partners, raise our children, attend our classes and study science, etc. As scientists we take a natural attitude in our labs; as business executives we take a natural attitude in our corporate offices; as family members we take a natural attitude in our homes, etc. There are some very specialized experiences that we might have, or specialized ways of thinking. For example, if, in studying science, we start to think about the molecular or atomic structure of things, this seems a somewhat different attitude to take toward the surrounding world. Or if, as a business person we see everything in terms of economic accounting, that also is an unusual attitude. Even so, these kinds of modifications are made within the more general natural attitude, and presuppose that attitude. The scientist drives to her lab in her car, stopping at red lights, and so forth. She assumes that her test tubes are made of glass, and that they continue to exist even when she goes home at night. Science and business, etc., involve theories or practices that we more or less believe in, but they also assume the most general thesis of the natural attitude – that there is a world that we live in. Being in this natural attitude characterizes our everyday life.

This immersion or situatedness in the natural attitude is precisely the motivation for a philosopher to adopt a different attitude. That is, if we want to get a critical perspective on the way the natural attitude works – and therefore on the way that we live our everyday life – we need to effect some kind of modification of that attitude. For the phenomenologist, this does not mean that we dismiss the natural attitude, or leave it behind. Rather, it means we put it in brackets.

3.2 The epoché

The first method that Husserl gives us is the beginning step in gaining a phenomenological perspective on the natural attitude. As he explains it, he wants us to suspend the natural attitude, to disengage from it. If we think of the natural attitude as a collection of beliefs, judgments, opinions, or theories about how things work – these could be scientific theories or folk (common sense) theories – then the first step into the phenomenological attitude is to bracket these beliefs, judgments, opinions, and theories. This means to suspend one's beliefs and judgments, to put one's opinions and theories out of effect. To suspend judgment does not mean to doubt, but simply to set the judgment aside. This includes the most basic judgment that the world exists and is real. To suspend the natural attitude does not mean that we should start believing that the world does *not* exist, but rather to set aside any belief about the reality or non-reality of the world. Husserl refers to this first step as the *epoché* (a Greek word for suspension of belief – putting things in parentheses or brackets – pronounced 'ep-okay').

Okay, let's try it. Let's assume you are sitting reading this book, or looking at your computer screen right now. Let's assume that on the desk or table in front of you there is not only the book, or the computer, but some other object. Maybe it's your computer mouse; maybe it's your pet mouse; maybe it's an apple (a piece of fruit, not the computer). It doesn't matter what the object is. We want to do an experiment with it. I'll assume it's an apple, but, again, it can be anything that happens to be there. Now, simply suspend your belief in its existence. So, you no longer believe that the apple exists – you suspend your judgment about its metaphysical reality. This does not mean that you start to believe that the apple is *not* there; it means you believe nothing with respect to the existence or inexistence of the apple. Once you do this what do you have left? Actually, despite the fact that you have suspended your belief about the existence of the apple, the apple hasn't gone anywhere; you still see the apple there – right there where it was before you suspended your belief. Can you describe what it looks like? Yes, because it is still something you experience. The *epoché* requires you to suspend everything you believe about it – that it is an apple, that it exists, that it doesn't exist, that it has weight, that it is something good to eat, that it will rot if you leave it there too long, that it has density, that it is something you can bite into ... etc. Even when you suspend all of these opinions, it remains right there in front of you and you can describe how it appears in your experience. Phenomenologists call this the phenomenological residuum. It's what's left over after you perform the *epoché*.

Accordingly, with the *epoché* you are also putting out of effect all theories. E.g., that the apple is made up of molecules, or atoms, or at bottom some billions of particles. Also, that if you lift the apple and then let it go, it drops because of gravity. All of these theories attempt to explain the object from a scientific point of view. But science here is suspended. So is metaphysics. Does the apple exist? Is it composed of atoms? Does it have a molecular structure? Not only do I not know, as a phenomenologist I don't even care. These are not questions that I want to address.

What then is my concern, as a phenomenologist? Why am I practicing this *epoché*? The answer to this goes back to one of Husserl's motives for practicing phenomenology. Remember he has an epistemological concern to make sure knowledge, including scientific knowledge, is on a firm foundation. Since consciousness is our only access to knowing anything, we have to understand how consciousness works. This method of *epoché* is a first step towards that understanding. We suspend our metaphysical and scientific judgments not only about the apple, but about everything on the desk, and everything in the surrounding world, and about the world itself. But that doesn't leave us with nothing – it leaves us with the continuing experience of the world. That is, it leaves us with our consciousness of the world.

You can think of this as a variation of methodic doubt, as found in Descartes' *Meditations*. Descartes begins by doubting everything. He's not sure that he can trust his perceptions or his reason; he could be simply dreaming up the world; or there might be some kind of evil demon that makes him believe that there is a world, when in fact there isn't. He is not sure one way or the other. But then he finds one thing that he cannot doubt. The fact that he is doubting, which is a form of thinking. Even if the evil demon is tricking him into thinking that he is thinking, he is still thinking. Accordingly, the one thing that he cannot doubt is the *Cogito* – the '*I think*'.

Roughly, Husserl follows Descartes just to this point but no further. For Husserl the *cogito* is just this consciousness. It's the one thing that he can't suspend or bracket out. Importantly, however, he doesn't take Descartes' next step. To make the next step, Descartes, at least on one interpretation, uses logical inference to say, *ergo sum* – I think, therefore, I am. That is, he employs logic, and gets involved in argumentation of a metaphysical type. In contrast, Husserl stays with the *cogito* – with the bare fact of consciousness. But it turns out that even within the *epoché*, even when all that we have is consciousness, we also have everything else. Consciousness is necessarily consciousness *of something* (that is, consciousness has the characteristic of intentionality), and the something doesn't disappear just because we put it into brackets. Despite the fact that the *epoché* leads me to suspend all judgments and beliefs about the apple in front of me, the apple is still there in front of me – that is, I am still conscious of the apple. And if I suspended all of my beliefs and judgments, etc. about the whole world, about the universe *in toto*, I would still have all of my experiences that are experiences of the world within which I am situated. This puts us in a position to do phenomenology, since phenomenology begins with the description of the world *as experienced*.

This world as experienced is the very starting point of knowledge. For example, if I'm a scientist who studies bats, you might ask me: What precisely do you study? I say, 'I study bats'. You might then ask, 'What precisely do you mean by bat?' Now as a scientist I might be tempted to give you a scientific definition of a bat – relying on certain zoological categories (Chiroptera Megachiroptera or maybe Microchiroptera) for example. But this is already a product of a certain zoological theory. You might respond, 'Forget the theory, I just want to know what you mean by a bat. How would I recognize one if I saw one?' Of course I might then appeal to folk knowledge and say, "I'm sure you've seen bats before; everyone knows what bats are." That may be true (or not). But you, phenomenologist that you are, continue to oddly insist that I give you a clear idea of what a bat is. At some point it would come down to getting a bat and showing you the very thing that I study. 'Here it is. Notice the wings and how they're shaped. Notice the rodent-like body.'

At this point we would be getting closer to what Husserl has in mind. All science starts with our consciousness of the world. So, what precisely – i.e., *precisely* – do we see, hear, feel, perceive? Whatever that is, and without the intervention of scientific theories, common sense beliefs, opinions, assumptions, presuppositions, etc., that would be the starting point, the foundation of all further knowledge. Only that experience would be first evidence that we could use to say what a bat is, even before we say that bats actually exist, that they have such and such properties, etc. But consider that we would want to do this, not just for bats, not just for any of the objects or things around us, but for the very notion of object itself, for world, indeed, for experience. Consciousness itself – the way that we experience – can become the target of phenomenological analysis too.

More generally, all meaning – the meaning of the world itself – can be traced back to experience – the way things appear to consciousness. Using the *epoché*, we can, without contradiction, cut through, as it were, the empirical connection between the experience and all thingly existence. We thereby achieve a kind of *distinctio phaenomenologica*. But what does that mean? What kind of cutting through is that? Is it not true that experiences are experiences of experiencing humans and, hence, that they have a relationship to a body and an insertion in nature? Can I change anything about that? To be sure, it just so happens to be that way. But we can indeed consider the experiences in and for themselves, without considering them in their empirical relation. We can disengage each natural positing (positing of the existence of nature) in the sense that we undertake scientific considerations, in which we make no use at all

of any positing of nature and where, accordingly, these considerations keep their validity, whether or not nature or an intellectual-
embodied world exists as such. (Husserl 2006, 36)

3.3   The phenomenological reduction

The second step in phenomenological method is usually referred
to as the phenomenological reduction (PR), although this is sometimes used to refer to the entire process, including the *epoché*. The
PR simply means that we turn our attention toward the phenomena as they appear to us. With the *epoché* we are no longer interested in metaphysical or causal questions; now we take what we
experience just as we experience it. Our attention is turned just
to that – to how we are experiencing, and to how things appear in
that experience. On that basis we simply describe what we experience. It turns out that what we experience is somewhat complex.
For example, our experience itself may differ from one instance to
another. In one case I may be seeing things clearly; but in another
I may be experiencing pain (e.g., a headache) and not seeing things
clearly. It's important to describe what I see, and how I see it.

What you see, even if it's a simple thing like the apple on the
desk in front of you, may be somewhat complex. For example, in
your visual experience of the apple you can note that you see a
certain complex color – it's red, but there are various shades of
red that pattern the surface. Perhaps it is not sitting in clear light
and there are shadows falling across its surface. Nonetheless, you
seem to see it as having a more-or-less consistent color, despite
the variations that come from the shadows. Also, there are some
things you can describe about its shape. But notice that you can't
see the entire apple all at once. You always see it in profile. It's
quite amazing that even though you can't see its inside, you see
that the apple has (must have) an inside. And although you can't
see the other side of the apple, you see it as having another side.
In some way you see this without seeing the other side. Of course
you can also manipulate the apple or your own position so that
you see more of it. But there seems to be a rule here that says you
can't see more than one profile at a time, and you never can see

the entire apple at once, although you do see it as a whole. You can also explore the apple by touching it or by tasting it. If you close your eyes you can still describe what you learn from touching the apple and manipulating it. Or you can take a bite and try to describe what you taste. Such explorations, however, only point to other ways in which the apple is perceived incompletely.

In all of this you are concerned only with the apple as you experience it. Again, you are not interested in giving a theoretical account; you're interested only in a pure description. But wait, this doesn't seem to be a pure description in the sense of a 'pure' – that is, transcendental – description. It really seems to be an empirical description since you are relying on your perceptual senses – you are describing what it feels like, what it looks like, etc. How, then, do we make this a transcendental project?

Some phenomenologists talk about a *transcendental reduction* that takes the PR to another level. But let's first note that what we are describing is not the apple as such. Rather, we are describing our lived experiences of the apple. To maintain the *epoché*, we would have to be careful to say not that the apple is red but that I experience the apple as red; so, in the PR, I don't say that the apple *is* red, but that the apple *appears to be* red. This experience of the apple (or whatever) has its own existence, and as such, it exists in a certain way. Within that experience the apple appears from a certain perspective. This is a characteristic of the experience, not of the apple. Each experience presents the apple incompletely, and this is an essential feature of the way we experience things.

Despite the fact that the object of perception is never perceived completely, we can say something different about the experiences themselves. Can we say that one's experiences themselves are given in completeness? At least according to Husserl's 1913 book, *Ideas*, experiences are not given in profiles, but are given in an absolute way (Husserl 1982). There is no other side to the experience *per se* that I cannot get to. It is absolutely complete in its very experience. When we attend to the experience itself – which is an attending to the way that we are experiencing the world – we are starting to grasp certain aspects of experience that can be considered transcendental. There is here a certain apriori aspect that constrains every visual perception that we have, namely, that it involves a perspective which limits the way in which any object appears to us. This is something pervasive in our visual experience of the world. Moreover, we know this by phenomenological intuition, which means we do not have to infer that this is the case, since the experience itself is given absolutely. We should add a qualification, however, as we start to notice that the experience is *not* given so absolutely or completely, since even experience takes time. When part of the experience is present, some previous part of it is no longer there. This too, however is something we can describe. In effect, within the PR there is the possibility of a further transcendental reduction to the pure experiences themselves, and taken just as such.

3.4   Retooling the eidetic reduction

One more important piece of the phenomenological method concerns the idea that within the transcendentally reduced sphere of consciousness we can grasp the essence of the phenomenon. This is termed the eidetic reduction. *Eidos* is the Greek term translated as essence. Husserl explains the technique involved in this procedure as a form of imaginative variation. The idea is that we use our imagination to change various features of the phenomenon. For example, we can imagine the apple we see on the table in front of us being bigger or smaller than it is; being green instead of red; being redder than it is; being more round than it is; being heavier or lighter than it is; being more or less sweet or bitter than it is. We could imaginatively vary the way the apple appears by imagining walking around it or seeing it in a different context. There are all sorts of things that we could change about the apple. Through all of these changes it nonetheless remains an apple. The question, then, is what kind of change could we imagine that would actually change it from being an apple into something other than an apple. Whatever those characteristics are which cannot be changed without changing it from being an apple, then those characteristics belong to the essence of being an apple. The essence of something is equal to the set of invariables that we can discover through this process of imaginative variation.

Eidetic variation, then, is a method for discerning or gaining insight into essences. It's clearly a form of conceptual analysis based on our imaginative abilities. Husserl frequently talks about essences and about intuiting (or seeing) essences (*Wesensschau*) (1977, 72–87). For this reason he is sometimes referred to as a Platonist. Once we understand the procedure of imaginative variation, however, the idea of seeing essences is not so mysterious or Platonic. The phenomenologist does not interpret the essence of something in metaphysical terms, or as an *idea* in some mind-independent realm. Rather, the essence is intended in our experience by employing phenomenological method. The aim, then, is to bring this essence to immediate and intuitive givenness, that is, to allow it to emerge as a conceptual truth within the scope of one's experience. This means, however, there are certain limitations involved in this method. Specifically, not unlike the use of thought experiments in analytic philosophy, eidetic variation depends on the cognitive abilities of the investigator. Indeed, one can ask whether our imagination is trustworthy enough to attest to every metaphysical possibility, or might it occasionally reflect nothing but our own ignorance on the subject matter (Zahavi 2005, 140–142)? This is especially an issue in research areas that involve a high degree of complexity, where we may be dealing with biological constraints and human behavior, and differences that are more nuanced than those between apples and oranges.

There are several ways to address the limitations involved in eidetic variation. One of these is to turn to empirical or factual variations as a supplementary or corrective strategy.

> If we are looking for phenomena that can shake our ingrained assumptions and force us to refine, revise, or even abandon our habitual way of thinking, all we have to do is to turn to psycho-pathology, along with neurology, developmental psychology, and ethnology; all of these disciplines present us with rich sources of challenging material. (Zahavi 2005, 141–142)

A good example of how appeal to empirical cases may offer a corrective to the limitations of our imagination can be found in Husserl's claim that colors and sounds cannot change into each other (1977, 75). Simply because he cannot *imagine* this possibility, however, doesn't mean that it is *actually* impossible. Here we can see the importance of intersubjective verification, since in fact, one can find people who experience synaesthesia, and for whom colors and sounds do change into each other. Empirical research on synesthesia can also indicate the range of possibilities and can demonstrate that the regional (ontological) boundary between colors and sounds can be more malleable than might be ordinarily expected (e.g., Ward 2008). This turn toward factual variation becomes all the more important when we extend our interest to the complexities of human life, embodiment and situatedness. For example, what would we imagine the loss of a limb to be like if no one had ever experienced and reported such a loss? If we relied on our own uninformed imagination, would we have imagined the possibility of phantom limbs and their peculiar experiential properties? Most real-world phenomena, and living bodies in particular, especially those with highly developed brains, are often too complex, unpredictable, non-linear, and so forth, for us to imaginatively vary them in an exhaustive and adequate manner. Accordingly, pathological conditions can be useful factual variations that facilitate the discovery of the essential structures of human existence. Empirical investigations of neonates and young infants as well as non-human animals can be of similar help.

At the same time, despite examples of successful cross-disciplinary studies that employ factual variations, the exploration of the space of empirical variability is hardly systematic. It's also necessarily constrained by factual, technical, and ethical circumstances. In the case of non-human organisms some of these constraints are circumvented via invasive interference with the organism and/or its environment. In the case of experiments with humans, clever protocols may allow us to push the boundaries of our knowledge. Even so, the range of possibilities is limited, and such experiments often run up against concerns about ecological validity. It is never certain that experimental controls introduced for good scientific reasons don't change the phenomenon under observation. This is, once again, the problem of factual contingency, which Husserl tried to avoid by having recourse to pure imagination.

But if the phenomenon of interest is too complex for imaginative variation, and its empirical variability is limited, are there other possible ways to gain eidetic insight? One way to address this takes us in directions that have been explored by research procedures used in simulation and modeling. In fact, certain methodologies employed in evolutionary robotics and in research in the field of artificial life are akin to a form of Husserl's imaginative variation (Froese and Gallagher 2010).

Artificial life (Alife) is an interdisciplinary field of research that investigates the phenomenon of life via artificial means (mainly in terms of computer simulation, robotic hardware, or bio-chemistry) modeling the specificity of life and mind within a mathematical framework of non-linear dynamics and the concepts of self-organization and emergence (cf. Bourgine and Varela 1992; Langton 1989; Boden 1996). There have been related developments in robotics toward a biologically inspired consideration of embodiment and situatedness (e.g., Brooks 1991; Steels 1994), specifically with respect to 'evolutionary robotics' (ER), which most often involves simulations of artificial agents rather than actual hardware implementations (Cliff et al. 1993; Harvey et al. 2005).

ER, for example, is concerned with how adaptive behavior emerges out of the non-linear interactions of a brain, body and world as a systemic whole (Beer 1997). One simple way to achieve this is to embed a control system within a sensory-motor loop and place it within an environment. ER tries to take the human designer out of the loop as much as possible. To be sure, it is still necessary to specify what defines an agent, its environment and the desired behavior, but the particular way in which this behavior is realized depends on an evolutionary process. In this way there is a minimal and controllable impact of design assumptions, and it is easier to investigate the minimal conditions for a behavioral capacity (Harvey et al. 2005). Often the evolutionary process leads to novel and surprising solutions that undermine our preconceptions about the necessary conditions for a certain behavior to emerge, although it is still possible to use dynamical systems theory to understand and formalize the system's behavior in a unified mathematical model that spans brain, body and world (Kelso 1995) as well as various temporal scales (Thelen and Smith 1994).

In regard to theoretical science these procedures allow for creating 'opaque thought experiments' by which it is possible to systematically explore the consequences of a theoretical position (Di Paolo et al. 2000). The idea is that one can use theories about the empirical world to inform the design of ER or Alife models, and that these models in turn constrain the interpretation of the theories (Moreno 2002). This can happen negatively, as when the Alife methodology is used as a subversive tool to undermine theoretical claims for necessity, but also positively, as when it is used to synthesize a model that serves as a proof of concept (Harvey et al. 2005). Although it is not always the aim to explicitly model philosophical assumptions in the process of synthesizing an artificial system, in practice it is difficult – if not impossible – to avoid doing so at least implicitly. The systems we create embody our presuppositions, and this fact has been pointed out, with great effect, by Hubert Dreyfus, who has traced the limited success of traditional artificial intelligence (AI) to its underlying Cartesian philosophy (e.g., Dreyfus and Dreyfus 1988). More recently Michael Wheeler (2005) has suggested that the field's subsequent turn toward embodied-embedded AI coincides with an underlying shift to a more Heideggerian phenomenology. In other words, the focus on designing robotic systems that can robustly adapt to dynamic environments in real-time can be viewed as a scientific investigation into the nature (the essence) of ongoing pragmatic coping. In general, the advantage of probing philosophical positions with ER and other Alife methods, rather than by means of traditional thought experiments or eidetic variation alone, is the increased capacity to deal with complex systems in fully controllable settings.

There are advantages to engaging in such simulation methods as a practice, because it forces one to test one's intuitions in terms of the operation of an implementation. As one finds in the history of ideas in general, an understanding about the limits of one's thinking (or one's model) 'cannot be attained except by a series of successive steps and by a sedimentation of meaning which makes it impossible for the new sense to appear before its time and apart from certain factual conditions' (Merleau-Ponty 1964, 89), similarly, it is a humbling experience to consistently have cherished presuppositions and expectations undermined by an opportunistic evolutionary algorithm. Over time this subversive process starts to affect the way in which one approaches problems, expanding the range of possible explanations to be considered.

Some recent examples of experiments using such methodologies have challenged versions of philosophical internalism. ER has been successful at synthesizing artificial agents that are capable of engaging their environment in a robust, timely and adaptive manner, switching between qualitatively different behaviors depending on situational changes and in ways that do not depend on internal mechanisms (Wheeler 2008). For example, a single dynamical system was optimized to perform two qualitatively different behaviors, chemotaxis and legged locomotion, without providing *a priori* structural modules, explicit learning mechanisms, or an external signal for when to switch between them (Izquierdo and Buhrmann 2008). The agent's ability to switch its behavior appropriately when moved from one situation into another is explained in terms of the interactions between the controller's dynamics, its body and environment, thereby calling into question the internalist assumption that the necessary and sufficient conditions for context-switching behavior must reside in the individual alone. Another ER study demonstrates that even a purely reactive system (i.e. a system whose outputs are at each moment determined only by its current inputs), can engage in non-reactive behavior due to the ongoing history of interaction resulting from its situatedness (Izquierdo-Torres and Di Paolo 2005). It is therefore conceivable that a natural agent's behavior, which appears to depend on some internal state, may actually depend on a *relational* state. This work reinforces the idea that embodied behavior can exhibit properties that cannot be deduced directly from those of the individual's internal processes.

We will discuss another example where simulation methods can supplement phenomenological method in the investigation of intersubjective interaction in the final chapter.

The suggestion, then, is that simulation models considered as opaque thought experiments are indeed a kind of imaginative variation: they lead us to insights about the nature of complex biological phenomena by enabling us to consider 'life as it could be' (Langton 1989). This can occur both in a negative and positive manner: a working simulation model is an undeniable existence proof of an in principle possibility, which can therefore effectively undermine established necessity claims, as well as establish new claims of sufficiency.

The major drawback of this variation by artificial modeling, with regard to the eidetic method performed by a conscious subject, is that the results lack self-evidence. In contrast to the realization of an eidetic intuition, simulations of emergent phenomena are opaque in the sense that they require further analysis before their conditions of possibility are properly understood. Operational models are at best abstract possibilities, and their factual validity always has to be verified by further empirical research. However, the effects of this drawback are mitigated because the computer provides a stable medium for repeated runs, systematic variations, and detailed analysis. These simulation models thus occupy an odd position between eidetic and empirical research, sharing commonalities with both. From this perspective they can form an important methodological link between phenomenology and science.

In order to gain insight into essences we need to ascertain those variations which turn the target phenomenon into something else. Otherwise our conceptions could be contingent on the selected facts or based on prejudice (Zahavi 2005). But what if, for whatever reasons, the appropriate empirical variations are unavailable? In some cases the phenomenologist can turn to an imaginative variation that is not based on empirical fact. As suggested above, however, phenomena that pertain to biological and specifically human behavior and experience are so complex, that we cannot always grasp the imaginative possibilities in a unified intentional act. In this regard simulation techniques can be considered technological extensions of our imaginative capacity, providing a crucial link between phenomenology and the increasingly complex (non-linear, dynamical, self-organizing) phenomena studied in the empirical sciences. Simulations have significantly less difficulty in dealing with the complex dynamics of holistic system/environment interactions, a problem that is particularly pressing with regard to gaining a better understanding of the essential aspects of biological embodiment. A simulation model, as an opaque thought experiment, is essentially a type of imaginative variation whose meaning is not immediately self-given. The use of such models to understand relevant phenomena, like action in a complex world, is, as Tom Froese puts it, a kind of 'out-sourcing' of phenomenology, a type of eidetic method that exceeds the imaginative capacity of a human subject to perform it without the aid of technology (see Froese and Gallagher 2010 for a fuller discussion).

Husserl presents phenomenology as a critical and rigorous science whose task is to disclose and examine the fundamental claims and assumptions presupposed by the positive (objective, dogmatic) sciences: 'Our investigation should be critical and undogmatic, shunning metaphysical and scientific prejudices. It should be guided by what is actually given, rather than by what we expect to find given our theoretical commitments' (Zahavi 2003, 44). In this regard there is a considerable affinity between the critical elements of the artificial and the imaginative methods of variation.

3.5 Some questions about the first person perspective and language

One thing to note about the methodologies of *epoché* and PR presented here is that they are conducted in the first person. In other words, the phenomenologist investigates his/her own experience. 'I' examine my own consciousness. As a result, one objection that is often raised against phenomenology is that it is subjective. Certainly, it would seem that looking at my own experience is a subjective exercise, both in the sense that the object of study is my own subjectivity, and that the first-person approach seems closely tied to my subjective view on things. Accordingly one should rightly ask questions about the objective validity of this method. Why isn't this simply subjective opinion? In contrast to empirical science, for example, where the aim is to gain objective knowledge through the use of controls, there seem to be no controls involved in doing phenomenology.

Phenomenology's response to this is twofold. First, phenomenology does indeed admit to being a first-person study of subjectivity. In this respect the issue concerning subjectivity is not about the subject matter – consciousness, cognition, experience – since even empirical psychology studies this. The issue concerns the approach: first-person vs third-person – the latter associated with natural science. A third-person approach studies consciousness from the outside and indirectly, so to speak. It measures what happens in the brain or in behavior, and then makes inferences about consciousness. Phenomenology points out that there are serious limitations involved in this third-person method. One thing that is not clear is where precisely third-person categories come from. One possibility is that science starts with something like commonsense (i.e., neither precise nor controlled) assumptions about its subject matter. Neither the explanandum (in this case, consciousness) nor the various concepts used to define consciousness, are strictly (using a controlled methodology) or clearly defined. Third-person approaches, in this way, may not be so objective (free of biases) after all.

Second, phenomenology distinguishes between two senses of objectivity.

1. Objectivity in the sense of excluding biases.
2. Objectivity in the sense of studying something as an object (and this usually means, 'from the outside').

In discussions of science these two senses of objectivity are often confused. Phenomenology claims objectivity in the first sense, but not in the second. That is, phenomenology claims that its first-person approach is objective (in the first sense) because (a) with the *epoché* it is careful to rule out any presuppositions or biases that come by way of pre-established beliefs, theories, opinions, etc. And (b) phenomenology also appeals to the importance of intersubjective validity. That is, the phenomenologist even if she works alone, appeals to a conception of objectivity that depends on others; even if phenomenological reflection is something each individual does on their own, the phenomenologist looks to others to make sure that there is some intersubjective consensus about experience. As Zahavi expresses it, 'Only insofar as I experience that Others experience the same objects as myself do I really experience these objects as objective and real' (2003, 116). Furthermore, phenomenology rejects the idea of objectivity in the second sense because the thing we are studying in phenomenology is precisely *not* an object; rather, it involves a subject and the subject's experience of the world. When we turn the subject into an object, or when we try to study this from the outside, we miss the essential characteristics of subjectivity. We can learn about the brain as an objective entity; we study behavior as something objectively observable; but the character of consciousness is such that it is not an object, so any method that makes it into an object distorts it, and is less objective (in the first sense).

A similar objection that is often heard is that phenomenology is a form of introspection, and in the history of psychology introspection has been rejected as a valid method. But this is not as clear as it seems. A number of scientists admit that introspective methods are still an important part of experimental science. The question is whether one wants to use a methodologically controlled form of introspection, or something less. But more to the point, phenomenology distinguishes between its own methods and the methods of introspection. Both are first-person methods – both involve first-person reports, for example. But note that what science calls introspection is not always a matter of reflection. Most of the time when a scientist asks a subject to report what they experience (e.g., 'Tell me when you see the dot of light move'), the subject does not reflectively consult her stream of consciousness to see what's there; they rather look to the world around them (they use ascent routines). Likewise, phenomenology is not simply about subjective experience understood as an internal felt sensation or phenomenal consciousness. As we'll see in the next chapter, phenomenology is about intentionality; that's why we were talking, above, about apples and the world around us. In introspection, without phenomenological methods in place, we tend to think of our first-person reports about our experience of the world as simply a report about the way the world actually is, and our reports about experience itself as subjective (biased) and untrustworthy. Phenomenology addresses both of these issues with careful and controlled methods.

A different kind of objection is raised against phenomenology from a different quarter. Hermeneutics (theory of interpretation) contends that since phenomenology needs to use language – descriptions, of course, rely upon the use of language – such use introduces uncontrolled biases that may be built into language itself. Language itself has structure – grammatical and syntactical structure. So, the question goes, how do we know that the structure introduced by language doesn't distort the supposed structure of consciousness?

This kind of objection was raised against Descartes, for example. When Descartes came to discover the *Cogito*, he expressed it in Latin. *Cogito* means 'I think'. The full Latin expression is 'Ego cogito'. But in Latin you don't need to say 'Ego' (I) because that's built into the ending of the verb. Descartes was then, naturally, led to ask, what is this "I" or Ego that thinks. He called it the 'res cogitans' – the thing that thinks. Some philosophers have pointed out that Descartes should have said that this "I" or Ego was simply a piece of grammar. That is, Descartes is led by the very structure of language to think that there is something called an ego involved in consciousness. But that may just be the result of linguistic structure and the way that we are forced to say things because of our language.

Accordingly, hermeneutics shows that language (not only grammar but also vocabulary, which comes with certain historically determined meanings embedded) subverts any claim to unbiased descriptions so that there are never 'pure' descriptions. Of course, as we saw in the last chapter, this is precisely what Husserl worried about. This is similar to the claim of historicism – that we (and our language) are so bound up in our own historical era, and that the biases of this era are expressed in our language. So, my description of the apple on the desk would be quite different from Shakespeare's description of the very same phenomenon, the yon red globe of apple-John old and withered and likely rotten at the heart.

In this regard, the response of phenomenology is twofold. (1) Phenomenology ultimately makes an appeal to intersubjective validity. One can even do cross-cultural phenomenological studies and negotiate among different languages to abstract the essential commonalities of description. Phenomenology aims for universality (pure transcendental description), but it doesn't claim that it is easily achieved. (2) Phenomenology is not a one-off affair. One doesn't say, okay, I've already done the phenomenology of the apple on the table. Just as in experimental science, one can do many experiments, so in phenomenology, one can go back and do further phenomenological analysis, and then consult the phenomenological descriptions and reports that are provided by others, etc. One can try descriptions in different words. Accordingly, phenomenology does not claim that the phenomenological reduction is an easy, straight-forward, no-problem methodology. Indeed, just such considerations motivated Merleau-Ponty to say:

> The greatest lesson of the reduction is the impossibility of a complete reduction. That is why Husserl is always interrogating himself anew on the possibility of the reduction. If we were absolute spirit, the reduction would not be problematic. But since, on the contrary, we are given over to the world, since even our reflections take place in the very temporal stream they themselves are trying to grasp (i.e., since they *sich einströmen* ['merge into the stream'], as Husserl says), there is no thought which embraces all our thought. The philosopher, as Husserl's last writings still insist, is a perpetual beginner. (1962, xiv)

3.6 Further reading

Crowell (2001a) examines various debates about phenomenological method and transcendental philosophy. Depraz, Varela and Vermersch (2003) outline a methodological approach to exploring human experience that relies on Husserlian phenomenology and describes the concrete activity of reflection on one's own mental life. Gallagher and Zahavi (2012) include a chapter on phenomenological methodology and outline an approach to using phenomenology in the context of the empirical cognitive sciences. Kern (1977) discusses three different ways to understand the phenomenological reduction.

4 Intentionalities

One of the central concepts in phenomenology is that conscious-ness is characterized by intentionality. This concept has a long history, and it continues to play a central role in philosophical considerations right up to the present day. Husserl appropriates this concept from Brentano, who in turn finds it in medieval phil-osophy. The medieval philosophers trace it back to Aristotle, who claims to be explicating a saying from Empedocles: 'Like is known by like' (*homoia homoiois gignôsketei*).

In contrast to Empedocles, who means that the knower is composed of the same materials as the world that is known, Aristotle interprets the knowing relation in terms of his hylo-morphic theory. This theory states that every physical thing is composed of both form and matter. Matter (*hyle*) is the physical stuff; form is a bit more complicated. One term for form is *'mor-phe'* which means shape. But the shape of something determines its function, and that determines its definition or essence. Here Aristotle uses Plato's term *'eidos'* which is translated as essence or form. In regard to the act of knowledge, Aristotle contends that Empedocles' statement should mean that the mind knows the form but not the matter. One reason for this is that the mind itself is not composed of matter; rather it has an immaterial nature. As Aristotle defines it, however, the soul (mind) is the *form* of the body. The soul or mind is itself a form rather than a mater-ial thing. Hence, 'like is known by like' means that in the act of knowledge the form (essence) of the thing is known by the form (the mind). Specifically, the mind abstracts the essence from the object known, and, of course, nothing material enters the mind as such (*De Anima* 424a, 17–20).

Medieval philosophers, like Thomas Aquinas, refer to this relationship between the form of the object and the knowledge act of the mind as intentionality. The object as it is known by (or exists in) the mind is termed the intentional object and in contrast to the existence of the object in the world, its existence in the mind is called its 'inexistence', or intentional existence. This is the idea that Brentano takes as the basis of his theory of intentionality in his 1862 work, *Psychology from the Empirical Standpoint*.

> Every mental phenomenon is characterized by what the Scholastics of the Middle Ages called the intentional (or mental) inexistence of an object, and what we might call, though not wholly unambiguously, reference to a content, direction toward an object (which is not to be understood here as meaning a thing), or immanent objectivity. Every mental phenomenon includes something as object within itself... (Brentano 1995, 88–89)

In Brentano's original theory, the object of knowledge is something psychological; it exists in the mind; it has intentional inexistence (i.e., not real existence, but a kind of internal, ideational existence). The intentional relation is not, according to Brentano, a real relation (i.e., a relation between two physical things, for example, a causal relation), but a 'mixed' relation, which means that one relatum is real (an object in the world) and the other is non-real (something that has mental existence).

4.1 Husserl's theory of intentionality

Husserl is not the only one to go back to Brentano. Contemporary analytic philosophy also draws on Brentano's theory of intentionality. Some versions of the notion of representation as found in philosophy of mind and cognitive sciences involve a Brentanian conception. The representation (in mind or brain) has reference to the perceived object and is what makes the perception be *about* the object. Intentionality is the 'aboutness' or the 'directionality' that is involved in perceiving or knowing anything. Intentionality is also taken to be the 'mark of the mental', where this is definitional for what the mental is.

> Every mental phenomenon includes something as object within itself, although they do not all do so in the same way. In presentation something is presented, in judgement something is affirmed or denied, in love loved, in hate hated, in desire desired and so on. This intentional inexistence is characteristic exclusively of mental phenomena. No physical phenomenon exhibits anything like it. We can, therefore, define mental phenomena by saying that they are those phenomena which contain an object intentionally within themselves. (Ibid.)

Husserl, however, criticizes Brentano's view and specifically the idea that the intentional object has some kind of existence (or inexistence) in the mind, or that the mind contains an intermediate representation between the perceiver and the object perceived. Intentionality for Brentano involves two things:

(1) the aspect of 'aboutness' or 'direction toward an object'; and
(2) the internal existence of the object perceived, judged, believed, loved, hated, etc.

Husserl clearly accepts the first, but questions and rejects the second. The first aspect, as Husserl and other phenomenologists like Sartre put it, is this: *all consciousness is consciousness of something.* The term 'intentionality' derives from the Latin *intendere*, which means to aim in a particular direction, similar to drawing and aiming a bow at a target. Intentionality has to do with the directedness toward an object, or the *of-ness* or aboutness of consciousness. It has to do with the fact that when one perceives or judges or feels or thinks, one's mental state is about or of something. But the disagreement between Husserl and Brentano is about how this is possible.

Brentano would argue that intentionality is possible only by means of some internal object or representation. The intentional object would exist in the mind, as part of a mental or psychological process; it would count as a replication or representation, perhaps caused by the stimulus (the perceived object). In contrast, for Husserl, the intentionality of perception means that the perceived object is itself the intentional object, and that we have a direct perceptual access to that object, without any intermediary.

One of the seeming advantages of Brentano's theory of intentionality is that it can account for the fact that we can be conscious of things that do not physically exist. We can think about a fictional character such as Hamlet; we can deliberate about an abstract concept like justice; we can remember some past (no longer existing) event; we can imagine what Athens would have looked like when Socrates was walking around the Agora. We would say that all of these intentional objects clearly exist in our head, but not out in the world. They would exist as intentional objects, having the same status as intentional objects as in the case of perception, and we would be conscious of them as such.

The problem with this, however, is that the intentional object would be in some sense real – it would be something really existing, as a psychological entity, in the head of the thinker. According to Husserl, however, fictional and purely imaginary things are not real in any sense, and certainly not reducible to a purely psychological reality. They are not real, but also, more positively, they are transcendent to consciousness. Hamlet is not real, but Hamlet does have a certain (non-real) existence that is independent of any individual mind. The intentional object of my consideration, when I think of Hamlet, or justice, or a past event, or ancient Athens, exists in a certain ideal way, but not one that is reducible just to my thinking about it.

One way to think of this is that the *meaning* of Hamlet, justice, a past event, or ancient Athens is constituted not simply by my own thinking; the meaning transcends the mind and exists as such, not as a real object, but as an existing sense (*Sinn*). In such cases the intentional is not hovering before my eyes, out there in physical space; but it does have an (irreal) existence over and above anything that is going on in my mind.

At the same time, however, Husserl realizes that when we perceive a physical object, or when we think or make judgments about some non-physical object, we do so from a certain perspective. The way that I see the palm tree next to my house is not precisely how you see it since you see it from a different angle from where you stand; the way I think of Hamlet is not precisely how you think of Hamlet since you've played the part and I haven't. This kind of consideration leads Husserl to the concept of noema.

Before we discuss the concept of noema, it may help to take a quick look at what Husserl says in the *Logical Investigations*. He discusses intentionality in Investigation 5. In §20 he distinguishes between the quality and the matter of an act of consciousness. This prefigures a later distinction he makes between the noetic act and the noematic content of consciousness. Any intentional mental act has a certain character or quality. For example, an act of perception is different from an act of memory, which is different from an act of judgment. The judgment quality of an intentional act, for example, may be similar if our judgment is 1 + 1 = 2 or if it's 'Elvis is the king of rock and roll'. The matter, or material judged about, however, is different. Likewise we can hold the matter steady and change the quality of the act. For example, we can imagine that the café is crowded, we can hope that the café is crowded, or we can see that the café is crowded. Husserl says that the quality is an aspect of the 'concrete act-experience'. We could say that it is the very attitude or posture intrinsic to the mental act. The object, however, is not intrinsic to the mental act; indeed, it transcends it. The intentional objectivity – e.g. that the café is crowded – is not a real constitutive part of the mental act. Moreover, it makes no difference what sort of being the object has – whether it is real, or ideal, possible or impossible – for example, we may hope that the café is crowded with unicorns – the object is such that its sense or meaning does not depend on our consciousness of it, although in terms of the matter – the subject matter we might say – our consciousness remains 'directed upon' it. If the question is how can something that is non-existent (a crowd of unicorns, for example), i.e., having no existence in itself and having no existence as a constitutive part of my mind, be an object of my consciousness, Husserl's answer is that it is so in the order of intentionality, with respect to its meaning as the subject-matter of my mental act. Its mode of existence just doesn't come into the explanation of its intentional status.

One important implication of this is that the intentional relation is not a causal relation. One might think that the physical presence of something in the environment might cause, via perception, some change in my brain and thereby establish a relation between knower and known. The fact that there can be an intentional relation between the knower and a non-existent crowd of unicorns, however, suggests that the intentional relation cannot be causal, unless one thinks that something that does not exist can be a cause.

What Husserl calls the 'matter' of an act of consciousness is that aspect of an act that defines its direction towards the transcendent object. Or it may be better stated that the matter of the act is the manner in which it is directed. As Husserl notes, even if one fixes act-quality and the intentional direction towards an object, something else can vary. I can make two judgments about the same object but with a certain intentional difference regarding sense. Thus, for example, I may make a judgment about a triangle, regarding it as equilateral, and a judgment about the same triangle regarding it as equiangular. The same object is judged with a different sense or 'in a different fashion' (2001a, 121).

> The matter, therefore, must be that element in an act which first gives it reference to an object, and reference so wholly definite that it not merely fixes the object meant in a general way, but also the precise way in which it is meant. (2001a, 121, italics deleted)

In other words, the matter specifies the grasping of the object *as* a certain something. In this regard, the formula of intentionality, that *all consciousness is consciousness of something* is incomplete; more completely it should state: all consciousness is consciousness of something *as* something. The matter specifies the object as this object in a certain way. It delivers the 'interpretive sense' (*Auffassungssinn*) of the object.

These two distinguishable parts of an intentional act – quality and matter – are abstractions from the full-fledged intentional act and are what makes it intentional.

4.2   Noesis–noema

Intentionality means (1) all consciousness is consciousness of something. Both Brentano and Husserl accept the first aspect of intentionality, i.e., that it is a directionality toward something. Husserl rejects what Brentano considers a second aspect: that there is some kind of internal 'inexisting' intentional object in the mind. In place of that second aspect, Husserl would say that the fact that consciousness is characterized by intentionality means that (2) consciousness has a certain structure which can be expressed as 'consciousness of something as something'. This structure can be analyzed into two (abstract) parts: the consciousness-of (which Husserl calls the noesis or noetic structure), which, as we have just seen, has a variety of possible quality characters, and the 'something', the intentional object which is always taken in a certain manner, as a certain subject-matter. This 'matter-character' is what Husserl comes to call the *noema* or noematic correlate.

The noetic act of consciousness can be an act of perception, memory, imagination, etc. I can be conscious of the same object in different ways: I can perceive an apple tree, or remember one, or imagine one; I can judge the apple tree to be large; I can dislike the tree because it is blocking my view, etc. In each case it is exactly the same apple tree. The difference is only in the character of the act of consciousness directed at it. The noetic act can be complex. My judgment may be fed by my memory of certain facts (I may remember falling out of an apple tree as a kid); by imagining certain things (e.g., imagining what it would look like if the apple tree were not there); by my dislike of apple trees, etc. Likewise, my consciousness of the apple tree has one intentional object – the apple tree. But I am always experiencing the apple tree in a certain way. As perceived, it appears visually from a certain perspective. Like the apple on my desk, I can see the apple tree only from one side at a time, for example, although when I see it from one side I also implicitly see it as having more than one side. If the wind is blowing, or if clouds are interrupting the sunlight, the appearance of the tree is constantly changing. Also, if I move and change my angle of perception, there is a corresponding shift in the appearance of the tree. Throughout all of these noematic changes, the intentional object is the same apple tree. Likewise, if I close my eyes and then remember what the apple tree just looked like; or if I imagined what that apple tree would look like in a different place; or if I judged that the apple tree was getting too big – all of these differences would have corresponding noematic changes. The noema is the meaning or sense (German: *Sinn*) that the apple tree has for me as I perceive or remember or judge, etc. – the apple tree *as experienced*, or as it appears to me.

Consciousness always has this kind of intentional structure where on one side we have the noetic act (or act of consciousness) and on the other side we have the noematic meaning – the way things are experienced. It's clear from the above analysis that the noema is not the intentional object, however. When I open my eyes and look, I see the apple tree, right there where it is, next to the house, just off to the left of where I'm standing. I do not see the noema. The noema is rather how I see the tree – as shimmering in the breeze, as something in my way, as something I can reach out and touch, as a source for food, as something I could draw, etc.

There is an ongoing debate about what Husserl really means by the noema. What sort of status does it have? Recall that Husserl was influenced by Frege. Frege made a distinction between sense (*Sinn*) and reference (*Bedeutung*). Using this distinction we can say that the intentional object is the thing to which we consciously refer in the various acts of consciousness; the noema is the sense or meaning of that thing as we intend it. Frege understood this distinction in linguistic terms. A word has both a sense and a reference. For example, the word 'apple' refers to a real piece of fruit on the table. It also signifies a certain meaning – it points to a definition framed by other words. If we think of intentionality in the example of judging something, then it is easy to think of it as having a structure similar to a proposition. 'The apple is on the table.' This is very much like the notion of a propositional attitude in analytic philosophy. I take an attitude of judging toward a proposition: [I judge that] 'the apple is on the table'. The propositional content (what the proposition means) would then be equivalent to the noema.

This Fregean interpretation of Husserl's concept of noema has been defended by a number of phenomenologists, most notably, Dagfinn Føllesdal (at Stanford) and Hubert Dreyfus (at Berkeley). Given their location, this has sometimes been referred to as the

West Coast interpretation. On this interpretation, the intentionality of consciousness is equivalent to, or is at least closely related to the *intensionality* [with an 's' instead of a 't'] of language. In contrast, the East Coast interpretation comes from one of Husserl's students, Aron Gurwitsch, who, after arriving in the US taught at Brandeis and then the New School in New York. Gurwitsch focuses on perception rather than judgment and suggests that the noema is equivalent to, or at least closely related to the perspectival aspects that we experience in perception – i.e., that I see the apple tree from one side, off to my left, in the sunlight, shimmering in the breeze, etc.

The debate thus concerns the relation between the object-as-intended (the noema) and the object-that-is-intended (the intended or intentional object itself) – respectively, the apple-tree-as-perceived and the apple tree itself. According to the West Coast reading, the noema is a type of representational entity, an ideal sense or meaning that mediates the intentional relation between the noetic act and the object. On this reading, consciousness is directed towards the object by means of the noema and thus only achieves its openness to the world in virtue of this intermediary ideal entity (Smith and McIntyre 1982, 87). According to the competing East Coast interpretation, intentional experiences are intrinsically self-transcending; their being is constituted as being *of* something else, and they do not first achieve a reference to the world by virtue of some intermediate representational entity. As a consequence, it is argued that the noema is to be understood neither as an ideal meaning, nor a concept, nor a proposition; it is not an intermediary between subject and object; rather, it is the object precisely *as experienced*. The noema is the perceived object as perceived, the recollected episode as recollected, the judged state-of-affair as judged, etc. This does not imply, however, that there is no distinction between the object-as-it-is-intended and the object-that-is-intended, but this distinction, according to John Drummond (1990, 108–109, 113), is exactly a structural difference that is reflected within the noema. In so far as an investigation of the noema is an investigation of any kind of object, aspect, dimension, or region, considered in its very manifestation, in its very significance for consciousness, the object and the noema turn out to be the same but considered from different perspectives in an act of reflection.

The noema, as the sense or meaning of the intentional object – the object as it is known – is neither fully immanent nor fully transcendent to the act of consciousness. It is, on the one hand, as Zahavi (2003, 58) suggests, transcendent to consciousness, but only in the sense that it depends on the intentional object, since it is that object-as-intended, and that object is not reducible to an immanent kind of existence. It is, on the other hand, not transcendent to consciousness in the sense that it is nothing more than an abstraction that cannot exist outside of its correlation with the noetic component of intentionality. If one insists that objects have meanings independent of their being known, this does not mean that there are noemata floating around, independent of the intentional relation. Husserl says as much about quality and matter, and it can equally be said of noesis and noema. Noemata are knower-relative.

In this regard, let me suggest something that can at the same time point to an alternative conception of intentionality. Noemata are comparable to affordances. The Gibsonian notion of affordance is best understood in the context of embodied action (see Gibson 1966; 1979). The environment presents an affordance to the agent if it allows a possibility for a certain kind of action. A chair affords sitting; a pencil affords writing; a mountain affords climbing (or perhaps dis-affords climbing if it consists of un-climbable cliffs). Affordances, however, are not purely objective properties of things. They are properties that depend on the agent who has a kind of body with bendable joints that will enable sitting, or who knows how to write, or who is in good physical shape for mountain climbing. In the same way that the affordance depends on the embodied capacities of the agent, I suggest that the noema depends on certain knowledge capacities (which may also be practical knowledge capacities or skill capacities) of the conscious subject. To the extent that I experience something as meaning something, what the meaning (sense, noema) is (and perhaps, at the limit, even that there is meaning at all) depends not solely on the object, but on my own cognitive resources.

4.3 Enactive intentionality

The idea that noemata are comparable to affordances points to some further considerations about intentionality taken up in more recent developments in the area of embodied cognition. In both phenomenology and the analytic philosophy of mind, the discussion of intentionality goes beyond a narrow discussion of mental state or act-intentionality. Husserl introduced the concept of operative (*fungierende*) intentionality in contrast to act-intentionality, which he explains in terms of noetic and noematic aspects. The concept of operative intentionality attempts to capture the fact that the experiencing agent is intentionally engaged with the world through actions and projects that are not reducible to conscious noetic states, but involve what Husserl calls 'bodily intentionality' (1977, §39). Merleau-Ponty (1962) takes up the analysis of intentionality just at this point. Actions are intentional – have intentionality and meaning – not only in the sense that they are willed, but also in the sense that they are directed at some goal or project. Moreover, this intentionality of action is something that can be perceptually understood by others.

Likewise, in analytic philosophy of mind, we find discussions of agent intentionality that go beyond the question of mental state intentionality. Neo-behaviorist and neo-pragmatist conceptions of intentionality, for example, share a common feature: an externalist view that intentionality is something that we can discern in behavior and is not necessarily hidden away inside the head (see Haugeland 1990). The neo-behaviorist view is exemplified by Dennett's concept of intentional stance, which he explains in terms of observing an agent engaged in rational behavior, and on that basis ascribing intentionality, i.e., treating the agent as someone 'who harbors beliefs and desires and other mental states that exhibit intentionality or 'aboutness', and whose actions can be explained (or predicted) on the basis of the content of these states' (1991, 76).[1] In this account we can immediately see two things: first, that this conception of an intentional agent (or system) starts with considerations about the agent's behavior, but also refers us back to questions about mental state intentionality (in terms of beliefs and desires). Second, that this conception relates intentionality to social cognition, our ability to attribute mental states to others.

Let's note first that, in contrast to claims made by the neo-behaviorist model, in our actual practice of intentional ascription, we do not always treat another agent's meaningful action as a rational behavior, or as an instrumental action directed at a particular desired goal. If, for example, we see someone gesturing or nodding their head as they listen to a lecture, we do not fail to attribute a certain intentionality to them in this respect, even though we do not always understand the intentionality expressed in gesturing or head-nodding as motivated by specific beliefs (e.g., about the meaning of the gesturing or head-nodding) or desires (e.g., to impress the lecturer) (Gallagher and Miyahara 2012; Miyahara 2011). Another example involves the intentionality associated with sexuality. As Merleau-Ponty puts it:

> Erotic perception is not a *cogitatio* aiming at a *cogitatum*; through one body it aims at another body, and it is carried out in the world, not in a consciousness. A spectacle has sexual signification for me, not when I represent, even confusedly, its possible relation to the sexual organs or to states of pleasure, but when it exists for my body, for this power which is always ready to form the given stimuli into an erotic situation and to behave therein in a sexual way. (Merleau-Ponty 1962, 139)

Erotic intentionality is not a matter of instrumental rationality, and not reducible to a set of mental states, propositional attitudes like beliefs or desires, or even to a set of observable behaviors, or to some attributional/inferential link between the two. It's a form of intentionality that seemingly goes beyond the terms of belief-desire or folk-psychology.

Objections to the neo-behaviorist view can also be raised insofar as it portrays social cognition and our everyday interactions with others in terms of theoretical inference or 'mindreading'. Here we set this critical issue aside and return to it in Chapter 9 where we take up the issue of intersubjectivity.

In contrast to neo-behaviorists, some neo-pragmatists, like Brandom (1994; 2000), appeal to an account of intentionality that depends on social/normative concepts. Brandom explains the concept of intentionality in terms of what he calls the practice of *deontic scorekeeping*, i.e., our mutual implicit practice of keeping track of each other's and our own actions in terms of *normative status* (1994, ch. 3). On this view we understand the intentionality of the other implicitly in terms of certain commitments or entitlements specified by social norms, although we do not always *acknowledge* such normative statuses *explicitly*. Accordingly, we ascribe intentionality to an entity who is capable of having a particular set of commitments and entitlements, namely, *inferentially articulated* or *discursive* commitments and entitlements instituted by social linguistic norms – that is, the implicit norms that determine the social appropriateness of our linguistic practices including inferential reasonings. In this regard Brandom thinks it's 'norms all the way down' and that '... only communities, not individuals, can be interpreted as having original intentionality. [... T]he practices that institute the sort of normative status characteristic of intentional states must be *social* practices' (1994, 61). That is, we track, and occasionally acknowledge, other people's intentionality in virtue of what they are doing and saying, what they are expected to do or say, what roles they play, what kind of place and time it is and what such factors mean to us in the shared social situation, rather than by somehow looking for mental states hidden behind their behaviors.[2] We ascribe intentionality to actions to the extent that we have a practical grasp on their socially instituted significance.

On this basis, we have no problem in ascribing intentionality to gestures and head nods. According to neo-pragmatism, gestures are just another kind of phenomenon that people keep track of by virtue of their socially instituted significance and normative status. In understanding another's head-nodding, for example, we attribute to that person a discursive commitment to the claim that the lecturer made, which he or she may or may not explicitly acknowledge, instead of positing a belief or internal mental state about the content of the claim.

Thus, the neo-pragmatist account of intentionality avoids some of the problems found in the neo-behaviorist account. According to neo-pragmatism, something is an intentional agent only if it acts according to norms that are socially based. Certain insulting gestures, for example, are culturally relative, and we should not understand someone from a different culture who accidentally made an insulting gesture to be acting as an insulting intentional agent. More generally, if a creature (e.g., a non-human animal) *completely* lacks understanding of social norms, and is not expected to act in accordance with such norms, it seems that the ascribing of intentionality itself would be inappropriate. Just here, however, neo-pragmatists do run into a problem, namely, in their attempt to account for our commonsense ability to recognize intentionality in the behavior of a variety of non- or pre-social entities. One simple example is that we tend to attribute intentionality to geometrical figures moving in certain patterns on a computer screen (Heider and Simmel 1944), as well as to non-human animals, and human infants whom we do not regard as following specific social norms. We do ascribe intentionality to such entities even thought they lack understanding of social norms. Neo-pragmatists, then, seemingly fail to explain our everyday practices of ascribing intentionality to such creatures.

One suggestion for resolving this problem points to a more basic issue. Cash (2008) suggests that on a neo-pragmatist account, we can ascribe intentionality to animals and infants *'based on the similarity of their movement* to the kind of actions, which if performed by a person would entitle us to ascribe such intentional states as reasons'* (2008, 101; emphasis added). That is, neo-pragmatists can ascribe intentionality to a non-social entity, but only by recognizing some kind of similarity between that entity's behavior and the behavior of a socialized human. If we ask what is involved in this claim about similarity, there seem to be two possible answers. The first would be a form of pattern recognition plus inference from analogy. That is, we might take the movement of certain non-social entities as having intentionality by detecting a common dynamic pattern between their movements and the behaviors displayed by people. This solution fails, however, based on the simple fact that at least in some instances where we ascribe intentionality to animals or moving geometrical figures on a computer screen, there is no objective behavioral similarity to humans (Miyahara 2011). A second, alternative explanation is that we take ourselves as the model on which to base the comparison. At some level of abstraction I might recognize the behavior as something that I would do if I imagined myself in that entity's specific situation. This involves a host of other problems concerning the model of social cognition at stake here. Again, for purposes here we need to set these issues aside for later discussion in Chapter 9, on intersubjectivity. For now I'll just suggest that there are ways to resolve such problems by appealing to phenomenological accounts of social cognition that do not involve similarity.

More to the point, with respect to questions about intentionality, the phenomenological conception of operative intentionality is not only consistent with a certain version of neo-pragmatism, but suggests a quite different conception of the mind and consciousness than the one found in either standard internalist conceptions or the traditional accounts of act-intentionality inspired by Brentano. This conception of intentionality is also consistent with enactive phenomenology – that is, a version of phenomenology that emphasizes action-oriented perception (e.g., Heidegger, Merleau-Ponty, Dreyfus, and enactive theorists like Noë 2004; Varela, Thompson and Rosch 1991).

On the enactive view, we engage with others in ways that depend on embodied sensorimotor processes. We do not first perceive non-intentional movements, and then make inferences to what they mean. We perceive the actions and emotional expressions of others as a form of intentionality – i.e., as meaningful and directed. Enactive perception of others means that we see their emotional expressions and contextualized actions as meaningful in terms of how we might respond to or interact with them. Others present us with social affordances. Accordingly, our understanding of others is pragmatic and it references their actions in context: it is not indexed to Cartesian mental states that purportedly explain their actions.

Another way to say this is that we ordinarily perceive another's intentionality in the form of 'operative intentionality' rather than mental 'act intentionality'. As we indicated above, the concept of operative intentionality attempts to capture the idea that the experiencing agent is intentionally engaged with the world through actions and projects that are not reducible to simple mental states, but involve an intentionality that is motoric and bodily.

Actions have intentionality because they are directed at some goal or project, and this is something that we can see in the actions of others. Operative intentionality is quite different from mental state (or act-) intentionality, which is garnered in reflective inference or judgment (Merleau-Ponty 1962, xviii). The latter seems to be what we appreciate when we try to explain or predict another's behaviors from a detached, observatory standpoint, or reflect upon anothers' behaviors rather than when we enactively engage with their intentional behavior. In contrast, we usually experience both others and ourselves in terms of operative intentionality, an intentionality 'which brings about the natural and prepredicative unity of the world and of our lives, which appears more clearly... in our visual field than in objective knowledge' (Merleau-Ponty 1962, xviii). With respect to social cognition, we normally perceive another's intentionality in terms of its appropriateness, its pragmatic and/or emotional value for our particular way of being, constituted by the particular goals or projects we have at the time, our implicit grasp on cultural norms, our social status, etc., rather than as reflecting inner mental states, or as constituting explanatory reasons for her further thoughts and actions.

Consider the following example suggested by Miyahara (2011). Suppose you are driving a car along a busy street and see a person restlessly looking left and right at the edge of the street where there are no crosswalks. You slow down a little in case he runs onto the street, or at least you ready yourself to press the brake pedal. If the passenger in the car with you asks why you slowed down, you might answer that the person looked like he *wanted* to cross the road. In this reflective explanation it seems as if the person had been experienced in terms of his mental states, i.e., his *desire* to cross the road, which constitutes a reason for a further action of crossing the road. This, however, is a way of putting it that is motivated only in reflection. In fact, in the original action, placing your foot on the brake pedal just is part of what it means to experience the intentionality of the person at the edge of the road. As Merleau-Ponty put it:

> Our bodily experience of movement is not a particular case of knowledge; it provides us with a way of access to the world and

the object, with a 'praktognosia', which has to be recognized as original and perhaps as primary. My body has its world, without having to make use of 'symbolic' or 'objectifying function' (1962, 140–141)

Making such bodily responses to the world or to an object, or in social contexts, to others, is a way of encountering such entities, which not only cannot be reduced to actions guided by the mediation of reasonings, but is also more primitive than the kind of recognition of the world that guides action only indirectly.

Enactive phenomenologists claim that this intersubjective and pragmatic understanding is the basic kind of understanding we have of others' and our own intentionality, and that this intentionality is primary and non-derived. On this notion of intentionality 'the unity of the world, before being posited by knowledge in an explicit act of identification, is lived as already made or already there' (Merleau-Ponty 1962, xvii). Intentionality is determined by what the agent is doing and what the agent is ready to do – i.e., in the agent's sensorimotor skills to cope with the situation at hand – and that holds for both stepping off a curb and stepping on the brake, and for any action or interaction that might follow.

On this view, one doesn't need to go to the level of mental states (propositional attitudes, beliefs, desires, inside the head) to encounter intentionality – operative intentionality is in the movement, in the action, in the environmentally attuned responses. This operative intentionality is the real (non-derived, primary) intentionality.[3] Anything like attributed intentionality in terms of mental states is derived from this, and in most cases of everyday interaction, is unnecessary, redundant, and not necessarily real.

As suggested, this account is also consistent with the neo-pragmatist view. Brandom points in this direction.

> A founding idea of pragmatism is that the most fundamental kind of intentionality (in the sense of directedness towards objects) is the *practical* involvement with objects exhibited by a sentient creature dealing skillfully with its world. (2008, 178, emphasis in the original)

Brandom pictures this intentionality as more basic than language-based '*semantic* intentionality', and as involving feedback-governed processes that extend into the world, and which exhibit 'a complexity [that] cannot in principle be specified without reference to the changes in the world that are both produced by the system's responses and responded to…. [Such practices] are "thick", in the sense of essentially involving objects, events, and worldly states of affairs. Bits of the world are *incorporated* in such practices' (178).

This notion of intentionality also provides a better account of both erotic intentionality and our attribution of intentionality to non-humans. In erotic perception, which is not a *cogitatio* but a sexual significance for me 'when it exists for my body', we

> discover both that sexual life is one more form of original intentionality, and also brings to view the vital origins of perception, motility and [symbolic] representation by basing all these 'processes' on an intentional arc…. (Merleau-Ponty 1962, 157)

Erotic intentionality, like every instance of operative intentionality is not an 'I think that…' but an 'I can. …' – it is whatever I recognize as something to which I could respond or with which I could interact erotically.

Consider again the attribution of intentionality to the Heider and Simmel geometrical figures on a computer screen. I do not have to take them as *similar* to human, socially/normative actions to understand the intentionality which, in fact, is in their very movement. Indeed, since this movement is not random and was programed into them by human experimenters, their movement doesn't simply resemble, but it *is* a display of human action. I perceive the movement as something with which I could interact to some end. One could easily picture a larger scale virtual reality where I, as a human subject, am in the scene with the geometrical figures, and where I could intervene, play the game in a meaningful way, so to speak, for example, to prevent one figure from 'chasing' another. This possibility for intervention on my part is what I see in their movement as meaningful, and what constitutes the basis for my attribution of intentionality. If the movements were entirely random, this possibility would not be present. At the same time, this notion of intentionality can explain why I don't take such figures as true intentional agents: this feeling is due to the fact that they are presented in an environment (the computer screen) where the possibility for my involvement is largely restricted. At best, my involvement would have to be a simulation on my part. On the one hand, I see the possibility for intervening, but, on the other hand, I know that I actually cannot intervene. It is this ambiguity that is reflected in my ambivalent appraisal of the figure's intentionality.

This enactive, neo-pragmatic, phenomenological concept of operative intentionality is precisely the relevant concept needed to support a non-traditional conception of consciousness. As we'll show in Chapter 9, consciousness is intersubjective from the very start, and this means that there is no mystery about where this non-derived intentionality comes from. It comes from the others with whom we interact, or more precisely, it is generated in our interaction. To the extent that we are all born into a community, our environment is full of intentional practices from the very beginning of our life. We develop and shape our intentionality by being initiated into social and normative practices in virtue of actual interactions with other people, primarily with our caregivers, and in virtue of our innate or early-learned sensitivity to them or to opportunities for such interactions. This means that non-derived intentionality is not something that is first generated in my own isolated mind, or in brain processes that are not already directed to and by others. In this regard, the mind is constituted by our enactive engagements with an environment that is both physical and social. Accordingly, intentionality means that we are, as Heidegger put it, 'in-the-world'.

4.4 Further reading

Brentano (1995; original 1874) presents a seminal theory of intentionality as the mark of the mental. Husserl (2001a, Investigation V) presents his own view. Mohanty (1971) outlines the concept of intentionality as found in Brentano and Husserl. Føllesdal (1969) and Smith and McIntyre (1982) outline the 'West coast' interpretation of Husserl's concept of noema; Drummond (1990) and Sokolowski (1987) defend the 'East coast' interpretation which is also found in Gurwitsch (1964). The correct view, in part, can be found in Husserl (1982). Dreyfus (1991) includes several discussions of intentionality as Heidegger develops the concept.

5

Embodiment and the Hyletic Dimension

5.1 Hyle: a sensational concept

Since the time Plato wrote the *Theatetus* the concept of sensation has been an issue in the history of philosophy. Modern theorists characterized sensations as either mental events (Descartes, Condillac) or physical modifications (Hobbes, Spinoza, Locke) or as neutral elements that are both mind and matter (Mach, Russell). Maine de Biran noted quite correctly that the term 'sensation' signified too many things:

> If one, in fact, uses the same term *sensation* to express now a simple affective modification, now a product composed of an impression, a movement, an operation, etc., is it not to be feared that the identity of expression will often serve to confuse things quite different and to confirm illusions to which we are already sufficiently inclined? (1929, 54)

Gestalt psychologists challenged this traditional notion of sensation. Koffka, for example, states that sensations 'are certainly artificial products, but not arbitrary ones' (cited in Merleau-Ponty 1962, 10n4). That sensations are not arbitrary would suggest that there is some natural event, some ground of experience at the basis of perception from which the concept of sensation is abstracted. Merleau-Ponty, however, makes a stronger claim: sensations are artifacts, abstract 'products of analysis' that correspond 'to nothing in our experience' (1962, 3).

Worries about the traditional concept of sensation motivated Husserl to shift his terminology from the vocabulary of 'sensation' (*Empfindung*) to the vocabulary of *hyle* (hyletic data), which is the Greek term for 'material'. Husserl associates the latter term with the Kantian concept of matter or sense content. The Kantian distinction, to put it simply, is between material and formal aspects of cognition. For Husserl 'hyle' signifies the formless content that has the potential to receive form. He gives a number of examples: 'color-data, touch-data and tone-data, and the like...sensuous pleasure, pain, and tickle sensations, and so forth, and no doubt also sensuous moments belonging to the sphere of "drives"' (1982, 192/203; also see 1977, 166). Although the list does not tell us precisely what hyletic data are, it does indicate two general types of hyletic data: data that are the result of externally oriented sensing, and data that are associated with bodily processes and experiences, e.g., touch, pressure, warmth, cold, and pain sensations. Hyletic data are not something that we are directly conscious of, but they are aspects of consciousness in some way. They are thus not physiological happenings. According to Husserl, by themselves hyletic data are meaningless, experiential elements of consciousness that are not directly perceived in our everyday experience. But one can become aware of them through an act of reflection.

Husserl provides eight principles to guide our understanding of hyletic data.[1]

(1) Hyletic data are contents in the schema: apprehension – content of apprehension (*Auffassung – Auffassungsinhalt*). For simplicity I'll refer to this as the *noetic schema*. The idea is that hyle becomes informed or interpreted by certain noetic apprehensions having various intentional characters. Husserl explains:

> We find such concrete data of experience as components in more comprehensive concrete experiences which as wholes are intentional, and this in a way that these sensuous moments are overlaid by an 'animating,' sense-bestowing stratum. ... Sensuous data present themselves as material for intentional formings or sense-bestowings at different levels. (1982, 192f/203f)

A conscious act, such as perception, is based on a pre-reflective performance of the apprehension-content schema. But neither the hyletic data, nor the animating apprehensions themselves are perceptual objects; they are rather the operative and necessary conditions that constitute properties of the perception of an object.

(2) Although hyle is the *sine qua non* of appearances it does not need to be animated or endowed with meaning by an apprehension (e.g., 1982, 192/204). Thus it seems that there are some hyletic data – a surplus – that are not in the noetic schema. There are more hyletic data than enter into our cognitive processes. This seems consistent with contemporary neuropsychology which holds that more stimuli than are required for conscious purposes are registered on the physiological level. Only those relevant to an intentional project may be incorporated at the level of consciousness. (see Marcel 1983).

(3) Hyletic data are non-intentional, but enter into the intentional structure of consciousness. Husserl calls them real (*reell*) components, constituents, or moments of consciousness that are in some manner 'present' in consciousness.

> For all lived experiences divide into these two fundamental classes: the one class of lived experiences consists of acts which are 'consciousness of'. These are lived experiences which have 'reference to something'. The other lived experiences do not. The sensed color does not have a reference to anything. (1982, 192/203)

> Hyletic data have no intrinsic meaning. Noetic apprehensions bestow meaning on these data. Hyle is 'irrational stuff without any sense, though, of course, accessible to rationalization'. (1982, 197/208)

(4) Hyletic data are pre-reflective lived experiences that can be grasped only abstractly in reflection. Husserl calls this a 'hyletic reflection' and claims that it involves an abstraction of hyle from its role in the noetic schema. That is, hyletic data are abstractions. In this respect, he warns, reflection can 'generate new phenomena' and transform its object.

(5) Hyletic data compose a constantly changing flux of sensed material. Although the object as it is experienced can in some cases remain unchanging and identical through time, the hyletic sub-structure is constantly changing. For example, a noematic color that remains unchanged throughout a changing perceptual consciousness 'is adumbrated in a continuous multiplicity of color sensations'. (1982, 226/237).

(6) Hyletic data are always members of a sense-field or sense-Gestalt.

> Precisely considered, the visual data belonging to the object and universally to any perceptual object, have a hyletic unity of lived experience, the unity of a closed sensuous field-form (*Feldgestalt*). (1977, 154)

Any attempt to reflectively abstract particular data tends to disrupt the unity of the hyletic Gestalt.

(7) Hyletic data are said to be already there and always available. They are pre-given for the conscious apprehension that animates them. The apprehension is the 'animation' of the pre-existing datum of sensation. 'In the moment in which the apprehension begins, a part of the datum of sensation has already expired and is only briefly retained in awareness' (1991, 110/147). This is nicely explained by William McKenna (1982) who describes his experience of suddenly becoming aware of the fact that he had been smelling the aroma of cooking for sometime, in a way that did not at first register as such. For him this olfactory sensation was there, affecting his system, before he was aware of it or was able to interpret it.

(8) Hyletic data are somehow related to the human body. In regard to this final point, Husserl provides a developing and sometimes ambiguous series of thoughts on the relationship between hyletic data and the human body. Husserl, working as a phenomenologist, had set aside any theory concerning a physical performance of the body in perception. In effect, the body had been bracketed in the *epoché*. Thus, he could write:

Hyletic data are data of color, data of tone, data of smell, data of pain, etc., considered purely subjectively, therefore here without thinking of the bodily organs or of anything psychophysical. (Husserl 1977, 166–167)

Husserl specifically cautions against confusing hyletic data with perceived objective properties. Moreover it is precisely in the perception of one's own body that this distinction can be made clear. E.g., in the case of a toothache, 'the perceived object is not the pain as it is experienced [lived through], but the pain in a transcendent reference as connected with the tooth' (2001a, 770–771/866). It is clear, then, that hyletic data do not belong to the body as it appears to consciousness (the body-as-object), but are real contents of consciousness necessary for the constitution of the body as, e.g., painful.

5.2   The critique of Husserl's theory

Herbert Spiegelberg (1960, 148) reports in his historical account of the phenomenological movement that 'Husserl never seems to have felt satisfied about the status of the hyletic data.' Other phenomenologists have expressed their dissatisfaction with Husserl's theory, including Gurwitsch, Merleau-Ponty, and Sartre. The objections raised by Gurwitsch and Merleau-Ponty against the traditional theory of sensation apply equally to Husserl's notion of hyle. Hyletic data are abstractions, objectified by reflection, and not truly found in experience. Both Gurwitsch (1966, 175–286) and Merleau-Ponty deny the existence of a noetic schema:

There is no hyle, no sensation which is not in communication with other sensations or the sensations of other people, and for this very reason there is no *morphe*, no apprehension or apperception, the office of which is to give significance to a matter that has none. (Merleau-Ponty 1962, 405)

According to Merleau-Ponty, perception is primary and the *hyle-morphe* distinction is the result of abstraction.

When I consider my perception itself, before any objectifying reflection, at no moment am I aware of being shut up within my own sensations (1962, 405). Pre-reflective experience is a unity that is already perceiving, a field that is already perceived. (1962, 241)

Husserl anticipated these objections. He warned of the dangers of a reflection that transforms and objectifies, and he is in agreement with Gurwitsch and Merleau-Ponty that hyletic data are always members of a sense-field and have an intentional unity precisely in perception. There are, however, two objections raised here that go absolutely against and beyond Husserl's theory. First, Gurwitsch and Merleau-Ponty reject the apprehension-content (noetic) schema. Second, and following from this, Merleau-Ponty states, in agreement with Gurwitsch, that the 'simplest sense-given available to us is a sense-field that is 'already charged with a meaning' and is not dependent on apprehensions (*Auffassungen*) to bestow meaning on it (1962, 4). This is precisely what it means to be in a field – that there is a specific semantic 'belonging', a particular significance that the field defines. This means that sense experience is intentional from the start: 'to sense is to intend qualities' (1962, 4). Such qualities are not sensations, 'they are the sensed (*sensibles*), and quality is not an element of consciousness, but a property of the object' (1962, 4).

Thus, in Husserl's terms, Merleau-Ponty would say that consciousness is entirely noetic and intentional. There are no hyletic data to be found in consciousness. Despite his own warning about reflection, Husserl had confused hyletic data with sense qualities that belong to the objective world and are only intentionally in consciousness rather than really contained as components of mental processes. Husserl could say that he would 'no longer confuse [hyletic data] with appearing moments of physical things – coloredness, roughness, etc' (1982, 192/203), only because he had reflectively abstracted hyletic data from the perceptual process that is intentionally implicated in-the-world (Merleau-Ponty 1962, 226). Thus, what Husserl had referred to as hyle is genuinely transcendent with respect to consciousness.

Jean-Paul Sartre levels similar criticisms at Husserl's theory. According to him, Husserl had attempted to bridge the Cartesian dualism of consciousness as *res cogitans* (thinking thing) and the

world as *res extensa* (extended thing) by introducing into pure
noetic consciousness the elements of hyletic data. For Sartre, if
hyle is anything, it is transcendent to consciousness and therefore complicates rather than resolves the dualism (1956, lix).
According to Sartre, if hyle were to have the *officium* or duty of
importing reality into consciousness, it would need to possess the
character of resistance. But, such resistance is lacking because
consciousness transcends hyle without even being conscious of it.
The result is that hyle fails to explain anything and itself becomes
problematic.

> In giving to the *hyle* both the characteristics of a thing and the
> characteristics of consciousness, Husserl believed that he facili-
> tated the passage from the one to the other, but he succeeded only
> in creating a hybrid being which consciousness rejects and which
> cannot be a part of the world. (1956, lix)

Sartre concludes that the concept of hyletic data is a pure fiction that 'does not correspond to anything which I experience in
myself or with regard to the Other' (1956, 314).

Similar conclusions have been reiterated by Quentin Smith
(1977), who shows that, if one takes Husserl at his word and follows
his instructions concerning the reflective grasp of hyletic data, one
is still unable to discover such data in consciousness. According
to Husserl, one can reflectively intuit hyletic data by abstract-
ing these contents from the sense-bestowing noetic schema of
apprehension-content. Thus it follows, according to Smith, that
the distinguishing mark of hyletic data is the absence of all interpretation and meaning. Yet, if we follow Husserl's instructions
systematically and attempt to abstract these data from any interpretation that would translate the data into appearances of qualities we discover the impossibility of hyle.

> In fact, I am confronted with the destruction of my very project of
> intuition itself. I learn that the intuition of the hyle is an impossi-
> bility. For the sensation that I am trying to intuit cannot be intu-
> ited as being anything, for if it were intuited as a certain 'what',
> this 'what' would constitute an interpretation of the sensation.
> (1977, 363)

Take, for example, the hyletic whiteness supposedly involved in the perception of a white paper.

> Since what is immediately given to my reflection is the color *of the paper*, I must try to exclude the apprehension of the white *as a property of the paper*. I must try to see a 'raw white'. And to a degree it seems I can do this. I can hold the white before my mind and consider it as a 'whiteness'. (1977, 365, emphasis in the original)

Has the phenomenologist reached the intuition of a hyletic datum? The answer seems to be 'no'. All I am doing is intuiting the white color of the paper that was given to my perception, but reflectively considering it in abstraction from its perceptual givenness. I have removed its objective meaning, and replaced it with a new meaning, the meaning of 'a hyletic sensation', a meaning that is posited by my reflective consciousness. All I've done is imported the white color of the paper into a supposed component of my consciousness. If in fact one searches Husserl's texts to find a description of pure hyletic data, only descriptions of quality-appearances can be found. In other words, hyletic data turn out to be, as Merleau-Ponty, Gurwitsch, Sartre and others had suggested, sense-qualities that belong to the objective world and that appear intentionally in the noematic correlates of noetic acts.

Should we accept the conclusion that, since we are unable to reflectively intuit hyletic data, or since we seem to end up with objective sense-qualities anytime we try to do so, hyletic data simply don't exist? This argument resembles an *argumentum ad ignorantiam*, i.e., since I have not been able to phenomenologically intuit hyletic data, they do not exist. One could argue in the same way that, since I have not been able to phenomenologically intuit my state of sleep, I do not sleep. It still seems possible that hyletic data exist but are simply not available to phenomenological intuition. In that case, however, the question becomes: what kind of evidence can there be for the existence of hyletic data?

5.3 Hyle and quale

Let me note that the kind of conclusion arrived at in this debate about hyletic data resembles the conclusion that a number of people have put forward in contemporary debates about the notion of qualia, that is, the qualitative or phenomenal feel of consciousness, or what Thomas Nagel (1974) calls the 'what it is like' to experience something. Michael Tye (2000, 48), for example, states about qualia that there are 'no such things as the qualities of experiences ... they are qualities of external surfaces (and volumes and films) if they are qualities of anything'. Husserl's concept of hyletic data seems related in some way to the question of qualia. Looking at the color red feels different from looking at the color green. Tasting chocolate feels different from tasting cauliflower. There are different qualitative features that seem to belong to experience itself in these different cases. Are hyletic data the same as qualia? They both seem to signify a sensation of, for example, redness or chocolate tastiness. Or is hyle supposed to be something that underpins qualia – something that enables us to experience the chocolaty taste. If the concepts of hyletic data and qualia are not equivalent, there is at least some close parallel between them. Both hyle and quale are said to be a matter of pre-reflective or first-order (phenomenal) experience, and are reflectively/introspectively accessible. Both involve sensory experiences – color, sound, taste. Both are declared non-existent in the same way: a matter of abstraction or mistaking objective/intentional qualities for internal or phenomenal. Indeed, once one gets rid of the noetic schema (as Gurwitsch and Merleau-Ponty want to do) there is not much difference between hyletic data and qualia.

Consider, for example, some of the common understandings of qualia that are rejected by Dennett in his famous essay 'Quining Qualia' (1988). First, qualia are sometimes considered to be raw sensory experiences generated by external stimuli.[2] But should we think that what we experience is anything other than the redness that belongs to the apple itself, or the tastiness of a particular drink? Another common understanding is that we *apprehend* qualia, but that qualia remain neutrally the same as our apprehension changes over time. This is related to the idea that they are intrinsic – *independent of one's dispositions to react to the world* – rather than relational. A further conception is that qualia can be isolated (abstracted) from the rest of experience in some way.

Dennett, in a way reminiscent of Smith's argument against hyle, argues against the idea that we can isolate qualia from everything else.

> One dimly imagines taking such cases and stripping them down gradually to the essentials, leaving their common residuum, the way things look, sound, feel, taste, smell to various individuals at various times, independently of how those individuals are stimulated or non-perceptually affected, and independently of how they are subsequently disposed to behave or believe. The mistake is not in supposing that we can in practice ever or always perform this act of purification with certainty, but the more fundamental mistake of supposing that there is such a residual property to take seriously, however uncertain our actual attempts at isolation of instances might be. (1988, 45)

Thus, on contemporary functionalist accounts of consciousness, qualia, and along with them, hyletic data, should be rejected. The properties of the thing experienced, e.g., the redness of the apple, should not be confused with a property of consciousness or with the physiological processes that generate consciousness. As Dennett puts it: 'The properties of the "thing experienced" are not to be confused with the properties of the event that realizes the experiencing' (1988, 72).

Let me complicate this contemporary debate with reference to both enactive and extended conceptions of cognition. Although both of these approaches suggest that the mind is not simply 'in the head', and that cognitive processes are distributed over brain, body and environment, they disagree on a variety of issues. Extended mind theorists defend a functionalist account of cognition and downplay the role of the body (e.g., Clark 2008), and they argue that cognition and action can involve mental representations (e.g., Clark 1997; Clark and Grush 1999; Rowlands 2006; Wheeler 2005). In contrast, enactive theorists argue for radical embodiment (e.g., Thompson and Varela 2001) and defend an anti-representationlist view (e.g., Gallagher 2008a; Hutto and Myin, 2013; Thompson 2007). More relevant to our considerations in this chapter, there are also disagreements in regard to phenomenal consciousness.

Enactivists challenge the traditional and internalist views of qualia. Thus, Noë (2004, 227) contends that in general 'what determines phenomenology [i.e., phenomenal quality] is not neural activity set up by stimulation as such, but the way the neural activity is embedded in sensorimotor dynamic'. Despite the fact that an extended mind theorist like Clark (2008) can voice approval of Noë's emphasis on embodied skills as opposed to qualia, however, Clark (2009, 963) backs away from endorsing a strong externalism about consciousness, and excludes phenomenality from his claims about extended mind. He rejects the idea that consciousness, 'our qualitative mental life (the elusive "what-it-is-likeness" that seems to characterize a subject's experience' could be distributed over brain-body-environment, and specifically rejects suggestions made by Cosmelli and Thompson (2010), Noë (2004), and others, for an enactive account. He concludes, 'as things stand, there are no good reasons (of a dynamical, enactive stripe) to endorse the vision of an extended conscious mind' (Clark 2009, 964). In this regard he cites and sides with Jesse Prinz (2009) who also rejects accounts that attempt to show how phenomenal consciousness might be essentially embodied.

> The claim that consciousness extends into the body is only marginally more plausible than the claim that consciousness leaks out into the world. We have never found any cells outside the brain that are candidates as correlates for experience. Such cells would have to co-vary with conscious states in content and time course. Every component of the body that we can experience is represented in the brain, and when the corresponding brain areas are damaged experience is lost. Conversely, bodily experience can continue after the body is damaged, as in the case of phantom limb pain. There is, in short, little reason to think the correlates of experience extend beyond the cranium. (Prinz 2009, 425)

This corner of the debate is focused on questions about how we can understand the causal and constitutive mechanisms that explain how the what-it-is-like, qualitative aspect of consciousness is generated. That is, the issue at stake concerns the vehicles (neural *vs.* non-neural processes) of phenomenal consciousness or qualia. On the internalist view, neural processes constitute qualia; non-neural processes, at best, are causal contributors. In another corner, however, there are questions about the very existence of internal phenomenal qualities, and in this regard it might be thought that enactivists should side with the anti-qualia arguments of someone like Dennett.

While some functionalists, like Clark, may lean towards an internalist conception of phenomenal consciousness, and others like Dennett may lean towards a neo-behaviorist interpretation (i.e., there just are no qualia), I'll argue that the enactive phenomenologist does not have to follow either of these options. To make this case I want to show that something important has been overlooked or ignored in both the debate about hyle and the debate about qualia. To be clear, as I've suggested, I do not claim that the concept of hyletic data is identical to the concept of qualia, but that there are parallels between the two concepts, and parallel arguments made against the two concepts. What I want to suggest now is that in both Husserl's theory and the criticisms leveled against the concepts of hyletic data and qualia, the role played by the body with respect to 'what it is like' to experience something has been overlooked or ignored. By putting the role of the body into focus, we can move toward a more enactive-phenomenological (vs. functionalist-behaviorist or functionalist-internalist) position in respect to these debates.

5.4   Embodiment and hyletic experience

For Husserl, the body is suspended within the *epoché* and remains transcendentally an obscure problem. For functionalist philosophers of mind, the body is nothing more than a physiological, mechanistic processor. Only in turning away from certain aspect of bodily existence do both the purely transcendental and the purely functionalist attitudes lead to the conclusion that there is nothing of hyle or quale in experience.

On the one hand, the criticisms of Husserl's theory presented above are cogent in so far as they insist that hyletic data are abstractions and as such not to be found in experience. It also seems right to say that there is no hyle that is not in communication with other sensations. There is no isolated datum. Primarily, before any reflection, there is always a field or Gestalt, and the field is always, in a broad sense, a synaesthetic one. On the other hand, the critics wrongly equate hyletic experience with objective or appearing sense-qualities, qualities that belong to the objective field and that appear only intentionally in consciousness. On this reading, *what it is like* becomes what *it* is like. The critics are motivated to identify hyletic data with transcendent sense-qualities because they cannot find hyletic data *in consciousness*. If it is right that hyletic data or qualia are not components of subjective consciousness pure and simple, does that mean that such phenomena must be placed in the objective or intentional order?

On this view, we would have to ignore a multitude of somaesthetic experiences – experiences of the lived body (the body-as-subject) – that have bearing on perception and other cognitive processes, and that seem to operate as a kind of hyletic experience and certainly come close to qualia. Clear examples are phenomena such as pain or itch or tickling, etc. which Husserl himself listed in his examples. Yet it is precisely these hyletic experiences associated with lived bodily processes that Husserl and his critics overlook. They deal strictly with what could be called 'exogenously originating hyletic experience' associated with 'external' perception. By ignoring the examples of *somaesthetic* hyletic experience, Husserl defends, and his critics criticize a theory of hyle that is one-sided and inadequate to begin with.

Consider the number and variety of somaesthetic hyletic experiences in the following incomplete inventory: Pain, with various qualifications, burning, prickling, itching, 'crawling' of the skin, giddiness or light-headedness, faintness, throbbing, tightness, nausea, 'lump in throat', fullness, distension, tension, heartburn, tingling, the feeling of being smothered, palpatation, 'cardiospasm sensation', flutter, hollowness or emptiness, pressure, heaviness, soothing, sinking, hunger, cramp, swelling, 'turning' of the stomach, erotic sensations such as orgasmic ejaculation and genital sensations, bowel sensations, 'quiver', sweating, limbs 'asleep', chills, pull, 'pins and needles', numbness, weakness, dirtiness, sensations of blocked openings, dizziness, 'thickness' or slowness in movement, 'flushing' (as in a blush), innumerable sensations associated with pregnancy, and sensations of warmth, coldness, etc.

Can these examples, overlooked or ignored by Husserl and his critics, be relegated to the transcendent objective order? Consider the experience of pain in the case of headache accompanying eyestrain. This is an hyletic experience even before the headache is identified or felt as pain. In eyestrain one starts to experience difficulties in reading or changes in the environment before one experiences the pain *as* pain. There is something it is like to experience the text one is reading as growing more difficult, or to experience the light in the room as being suddenly inadequate. But clearly this does not mean that the objective qualities of the text or the lighting have changed. The 'what it is like' is not reducible to the qualitative properties of the text or the lighting. Moreover, this qualitative hyletic experience does not disappear when it is consciously interpreted as headache; rather, this is precisely the time that it appears as what it is, a bodily pain. If I then reflect on this pain, in the way that I try to reflect on the whiteness of the paper, and isolate the qualitative hyle of painfulness, do I thereby intuit only an abstract property of my objective body? Is the pain that I experience the pain of the objective body in the same way as the redness that I experience is the redness of the apple? Does this mean that the pained or painful experience – the original hyletic experience – does not exist?

Here there is an important distinction between taking these phenomena as objective characteristics of the body-as-object – characteristics that I perceive as happening in or to my body, *versus* taking them as aspects of the body-*as-subject* – bodily experiences that have an effect on the way that I experience the world. Let's stay with this last thought. If I am in pain, this affects the way that I experience the world. Again, the example of eyestrain is pertinent.

> [W]hen the eyes become tired in reading, the reader does not perceive his fatigue first, but that the light is too weak or that the book is really boring or incomprensible... Patients do not primarily establish which bodily functions are disturbed, but they complain about the fact that 'nothing works right anymore', 'the work

does not succeed', that the environment is 'irritating', 'fatiguing'. (Buytendijk 1974, 62; see Sartre 1956, 332–333)

Likewise, I might have a pain in my leg, and accordingly, because of the pain, perceive the mountain path as steeper than it is, or too challenging. My perception, in the latter case is 'painful' – infected by a pain that plays a prenoetic role in perception – not pain as the object of perception, not as a property of my leg, or of the path, but as a subjective factor that shapes my perception. Typically, there is not a simple, isolated somaesthetic datum – there is rather a cocktail, a mélange of aspects that make up hyletic experience. My trek up the mountain results in a perception that is informed by a combination of my pain, my hunger, my feelings of dirtiness, fatigue, slowness and kinaesthetic difficulty, the weight of my backpack, etc. (Bhalla and Proffitt 1999; Proffitt et al. 1995; 2001). The mountain path looks quite different and less challenging after a good night's sleep, not because of certain objective qualities that belong to the path, but because of my bodily (hyletic) state. These hyletic aspects are qualifications on my perception – qualitative feelings that constrain my being in-the-world in some specific way. There's a difference in *what it is like* to be on the mountain path in the morning after a good night's rest, and *what it is like* to be on the very same mountain path at the end of a long day of hiking. At the same time, these experiences are experienced not purely and simply, but are modulated by intentionality. My physical state may be felt as an overwhelming fatigue that is a barrier to any further climbing; or it may contribute to a feeling of satisfaction as I sip a glass of wine in front of the fire at the end of the day. My phenomenal experience, if not part of a noetic schema, is nonetheless not independent of my intentions and my surroundings.

5.5   Deepening the enactive interpretation

This mutual modulation between intentionality and hyletic/somaesthetic experience means that how I perceive things is qualified by what I can do, which is itself qualified not only by the physical state of my body, but by *what it is like* to be in the particular state that I'm in. What Husserl calls the 'I can', and what Gibson calls my affordances, are defined not simply by sensory-motor contingencies (Noë 2004), but also by prenoetic hyletic-somaesthetic factors. It is not simply the fact that the size and shape of the thing, and the fact that I can reach it with this hand, constitute the 'grabbiness' of the thing – if my pain prevents or slows my reach, then the thing is not so grabby. This applies also to the more traditional examples of qualia – e.g., an experienced color is not simply an abstraction of the objective color, purely felt in consciousness – the phenomenal felt quality of redness. I may see the redness of the red apple as even more red, and specifically an inviting and pleasurable red, if I am hungry. Moreover, the effects of the color environment are felt in the posture, muscle tonicity, and action possibilities of the whole body, as shown in cases of dysfunction of cerebellum or frontal cortex, when these effects are not integrated into an intentional situation or adjusted to certain tasks.

> The gesture of raising the arm, which can be taken as an indicator of motor disturbance, is differently modified in its sweep and its direction according as the visual field is red, yellow, blue or green. Red and yellow are particularly productive of smooth movements, blue and green of jerky ones; red applied to the right eye, for example, favours a corresponding stretching of the arm outwards; green, the bending of the arm back towards the body. The privileged position of the arm – the one in which the arm is felt to be balanced and at rest – which is farther away from the body in the patient than in the normal subject, is modified by the presentation of colours: green brings it back nearer the body. (Merleau-Ponty 1962, 209, citing a study by Goldstein and Rosenthal 1930)

What it's like to experience the color red or green is not just an abstract state of phenomenal consciousness – it is affected by, and it affects our postural readiness to act, which may be experienced as a feeling of discomfort or awkwardness, or alternatively, a feeling of extreme readiness pertaining to engaging in a particular action.

Whatever we call such phenomena – qualia, hyletic experiences, somaesthetic factors – they delimit our perception and action possibilities, as well as our cognitive possibilities. A recent study dramatically demonstrates the importance of this fact (Dansiger et al. 2011). The study shows that the rational application of legal reasons does not sufficiently explain the decisions of judges. Whether the judge is hungry or satiated may play an important role.

> The percentage of favorable rulings drops gradually from ⟩ 65% to nearly zero within each decision session [e.g., between breakfast and lunch] and returns abruptly to ≈65% after a [food] break. Our findings suggest that judicial rulings can be swayed by extraneous variables that should have no bearing on legal decisions. (Dansiger et al. 2011, 1)

Such qualitative hyletic factors appear 'extraneous' only if we try to think of cognition as something that is disembodied. The clear lesson is that the defense should bring a sandwich to the courtroom and give it to the judge before sentencing.

To think about qualia or hyletic data purely in terms of phenomenal consciousness is surely an abstraction. To think of such things in terms of brain-body-environment, in the context of an embodied agent, enactively engaged in the world – suggests that we should not dismiss them as nothing at all, but ask what role they play in our perceptual and cognitive life. An enactive phenomenology would take these issues in just this direction; the *what it's like* to experience X informs not just the know-how of cognitive abilities (memory, imagination, recognition) but also the know-how (or the 'I can' or the affordances) of various action engagements with the world.

At the same time, these considerations suggest a richer enactive account, where we don't reduce phenomenal experience to what Alva Noë (2004) describes purely in terms of sensory-motor contingencies or embodied skills (there is clearly more to the body than just this), or retreat to a qualia-in-the-brain position (ala Clark 2009) – but rather, reframe the concept of qualia (phenomenal consciousness, what it is like) in terms of embodied, prenoetic processes.[3] In this respect we can easily give up the odd vocabularies of qualia and hyletic data. But there is still *something it is like*. Not what *it* is like, but what *I* am like as I experience X – where

'I' means the embodied agent rather than pure consciousness. What it is like *for me*, the embodied agent engaged in the world, to experience X – this is surely something that calls for further phenomenological investigation.

5.6 Further reading

Husserl (1989) presents his most sustained analysis of embodied perception and the concept of the 'I can'. Merleau-Ponty (1962) offers a critique of overly intellectualist and empiricist accounts of the mind. Varela, Thompson and Rosch (1991) builds on Merleau-Ponty's analysis of embodied cognition, and introduces the influential concept of enactive perception. Gallagher (2005) provides a detailed and phenomenologically inspired account of embodied cognition. Other works that emphasize the embodied nature of consciousness in phenomenology include Leder (1990), Wider (1997), and Zaner (1971).

6 Time and Time Again

6.1 Experiencing time

We experience the world in a relatively orderly way. Things are laid out in space in such a way that some are to my right, some are directly in front of me, and some are to my left. Some things are in the foreground and some are in the background. This spatial organization allows us to discriminate, from moment to moment, what is currently reachable from what is not currently reachable; it allows us to keep track of things, to come back to them again even if our attention drifts away towards something else in the environment. This organization is relative to my bodily position. There is much to say about the role of one's body in organizing the spatiality of the first-person perspective and the egocentric frame of reference (see especially Merleau-Ponty 1962, 98ff). In itself, however, the environment is not entirely set or stable; things can move or be moved. Water is more fluid than the glass that contains it, or the table in front of me that supports the glass. Imagine if the glass and the table were fluid like the water. Our lives would not only be messier than they already are, we would have a difficult time sorting out one thing from another. The lines of the book I'm trying to read would start to run into the glass of water and start to sink into the table. Things would be constantly blending with each other in such a way that we would all need to spend our lives as chemists at the molecular level trying to keep things sorted out. Philosophical distinctions are hard enough to maintain in a world without this kind of ontological fluidity.

Now think of this kind of fluidity in the temporal dimension where, indeed, one might be tempted to think that things are in fact very fluid. After all, philosophers tend to talk about the flow of time and the stream of consciousness (Bergson 1999; Husserl 1991; James 1890). Yet there is some important order involved in this temporal flow. We are able to distinguish past from present, and present from past. We are able to say that one event came before another, and that this other event came after that one. What if this were not the case? One can easily imagine one event blending into another or happening simultaneously. Actually, such things happen all the time. Sometimes, even in our awareness or memory of them, happenings seem to blend together into one experience, perhaps with different degrees of coherency. I may be listening to music and waiting for the kettle to boil as I read this book, and at the same time I may be aware of the children playing in the next room. The previously mentioned spatial arrangements help me to differentiate some of these things. But what would happen if the past-present-future distinctions collapsed? What if I could not distinguish in temporal order between the present whistle of the tea kettle, the children playing yesterday, and the music I will listen to tomorrow. Or, to take the phenomenologist's favorite example, what if the notes of the melody I am listening to were all run together, and I couldn't keep the previous note distinct from the current note. Imagine a new high-tech machine designed to facilitate your listening pleasure, making it much more efficient and allowing you to listen to a hundred songs in the time it usually takes you to listen to one. Call it the iPod 2050. Its advanced technology accomplishes this efficiency by taking all of the notes of a song's melody and playing them all at once, so you hear the entirety of the song in an instant.

Luckily the world doesn't work this way. You might think that the world itself does some of the work of keeping things temporally sorted. But that can't be the complete story. We, as conscious agents, also have to do some of the work. This can be made clear by considering a rare condition that disrupts the temporal structure of visual experience. This is the case of motion blindness (motion agnosia). Neuronal processes in the medial temporal cortex are specialized for the visual detection of motion. Damage to this part of the cortex, for example, following stroke, results in a situation where visual perception of form and color may be preserved, but perception of motion is disrupted. A person suffering from motion agnosia experiences the world as seemingly without motion, frozen in place, for several seconds at a time. For her, things in the world stay in place during that time period, but then suddenly seem to jump around and are rearranged in new positions. Getting ready to cross a busy street a person with this condition sees a plethora of cars frozen in place and then suddenly sees them all rearranged tens of yards different from their previous positions. She may know they are moving, perhaps by auditory clues, but simply can't see their movement. Visually, for such a person, the temporal structure of the world seems very different (see Schenk and Zihl 1997; Zihl et al. 1983). This kind of condition suggests that even if the world itself is structured in an orderly temporal fashion, the way that we experience that order depends on how our experience is structured.

Let's go back to the melody I'm listening to. It's stretched out as a series of notes and each note takes a short bit of time to sound itself out. How exactly is it possible for me to hear a melody? It might seem that I have to be able to hear more than one note at a time. For example, if I could hear only the note that is currently sounding, then I would have only a perception of one note. So it must be that I hear more than the note that is currently being played, if indeed I *hear* a melody. I must also hear the notes that were previously played since, if I want to say that I actually hear a melody, then I have to hear a series of notes lined up one after the other. I have to be able to hear the movement of the melody, so to speak. Part of the difficulty involved in describing how this works is that not only is the melody flowing by in time – it's a temporal object with it's own temporal structure – but also *my experience* is flowing – constantly changing – so that we would say that the moment of consciousness (A) in which you just read that phrase 'moment of consciousness' is itself past – and the moment of consciousness (C) that will be current when you reach the end of this longish sentence is yet to come, although it will come very shortly. And the past moment of consciousness (A) is now even further past than it was when you were experiencing the moment (C), which is now itself no longer future, but just past. This movement or change or streaming of consciousness never ceases, unless consciousness itself ceases.

6.2 Husserl's analysis

Husserl, in a set of lectures in 1905, and then for many years afterwards, worked out a theory of the temporal structure of consciousness. His account was influenced by a number of thinkers, including Brentano, William James, and psychologists Carl Stumpf and William Stern.[1] Rather than rehearse the complicated development of Husserl's account, I'll summarize his basic ideas.

Each moment of my experience seems to be present for only a moment, and then to slip away into the past, even if the object that I am conscious of remains present and unchanging. Things become more complex if the object of which I am conscious is itself a temporal object, something that undergoes constant and obvious change, such as a melody. In that case we have two successions to explain – the successive flow of consciousness and the succession of the temporal object. In some way the flowing retreat of consciousness is able to maintain an orderly sense of the melody as it expires in time. According to Husserl (1991), the consciousness of such temporal objects is integrally related to the temporal structure of consciousness itself.

Consciousness always includes a narrowly directed intentional grasp of the now of whatever is being experienced in the moment, for example, the current note in a melody, the current word in an uttered speech-act, or the current phase of any enduring object. But this *primary impression* never happens in isolation; by itself it is an abstraction which cannot deliver an ongoing sense of an enduring object. On Husserl's account, consciousness includes two other structural aspects: the *retentional* aspect, which provides us with a consciousness of the just-elapsed phase of the enduring object, thereby providing past-directed temporal context; and the *protentional* aspect, which in a more-or-less indefinite way anticipates something which is about to be experienced, thereby providing a future-oriented temporal context for the primary impression.

To take Husserl's favorite example, if we are listening to music, the retentional aspect of consciousness keeps the intentional sense of the previous notes or measures available even after they are no longer audible. Furthermore, as I listen I have some anticipatory sense of where the melody is going, or at the very least, that the melody is heading toward some indeterminate conclusion. The protentional aspect of the act of consciousness also allows for the experience of surprise or disappointment. If the melody is cut off prematurely, I experience a sense of incompleteness, precisely because consciousness involves an anticipation of what the imminent course of experience will provide, even if this remains relatively indeterminate.

According to this account, retention is not a particular thing in consciousness that we hear; rather through the retentional aspect we experience the just-past musical tones *as just-past*. Furthermore, there is no simultaneity between the retentional aspect of consciousness (which is a current feature of consciousness) and that which is retained (which is just past). The just-past tones don't remain present in consciousness, like some reverberation; rather they are experienced as something that has just happened, and so precisely as just-past. Consciousness retains the sense of what has just been experienced, not by retaining the event itself, but by its tacit or pre-reflective awareness of the just-past phase of consciousness.

If we view a horse race, our perception is not restricted to a durationless snapshot now of the horses' movements – if it were, we would sense no movement at all. Perceptually, it is not as if the horses suddenly appear out of nowhere in each new moment. On the one hand, we want to say that we actually perceive the horses racing rather than that we perceive their present position and then add to that the recollection of where they were a moment ago. We do not engage in an act of comparative remembering in order to establish the temporal context of their current position. On the other hand, it is not the case that all the previous parts of the race remain perceptually present in the same way as the horses' current positions. If that were the case, they would perceptually fill

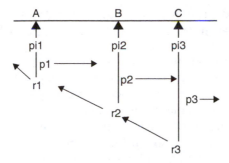

Figure 6.1   Husserl's model of time-consciousness (from Gallagher 1998)

the entire space they had just traversed. The past movements do not remain visually present in some vague ghostly manner. Retention does not keep a set of fading images in consciousness. Rather, at any moment what we perceive is embedded in a temporal horizon. What I see is part of or a continuation of, or a contrasting change from what went before, and what went before is still intentionally retained so that the current moment is seen as part of the whole movement. Consciousness retains the just past with the *meaning* or *significance* of having just happened.

The diagram (Figure 6.1) summarizes Husserl's model. The horizontal line ABC represents a temporal object such as a melody of several notes. The vertical lines represent abstract momentary phases of an enduring act of consciousness.

Each phase is structured by three functions:

- *primal impression* (pi), which allows for the consciousness of an object (a musical note, for example) that is simultaneous with the current phase of consciousness;
- *retention* (r), which retains previous phases of consciousness and their intentional content;
- *protention* (p), which anticipates experience which is just about to happen.

Although the specific experiential contents of this structure from moment to moment progressively change, at any given moment this threefold retention-primal-impression-protention (RIP) structure is present (synchronically) as a unified whole.

> In this way, it becomes evident that concrete perception as original consciousness (original givenness) of a temporally extended object is structured internally as itself a streaming system of momentary perceptions (so-called primal impressions). But each such momentary perception is the nuclear phase of a continuity, a continuity of momentary gradated retentions on the one side, and a horizon of what is coming on the other side: a horizon of 'protention,' which is disclosed to be characterized as a constantly gradated coming (Husserl 1977, 202)

Husserl specifies that retention involves a double intentionality. Retention keeps the intentional sense of the particular experienced object available even after it has already slipped into the past. He calls this *transverse* intentionality (*Querintentionalität*). Furthermore, since retention is the retention of a past phase of experience itself (one past phase embedded in another, and so on), then built into this retentional function is the unitary sense that *I* am the one who has just had this experience. The experience is not part of a free-floating anonymity; it is continuous with my occurrent experience; it remains, for me, part of my stream of consciousness. Husserl refers to this as *longitudinal* intentionality (*Längsintentionalität*). It's also clear that transverse intentionality depends on longitudinal intentionality – that is, my experience of the passing object depends on my pre-reflective retaining of my passing experience.

The protentional aspect provides consciousness with an intentional sense that something more will happen. The content of protention is never completely determinate, however. Indeed, to the extent that the future itself is indeterminate, the content of protention may approach the most general sense of 'something (without specification) has to happen next'. In addition, what Husserl says of the double intentionality of the retentional aspect, can also be said about this protentional aspect of consciousness. I am not only consciously anticipating the next part of the melody, or whatever, but I am anticipating *my experience* of what is about to happen. My anticipatory sense of the next note of the melody, or of where this sentence is heading, or that I will continue to think, is also, implicitly, an anticipatory sense that these will be experiences *for me*, or that *I* will be the one listening, speaking, or thinking. My experience of the passing or enduring object is at the same time a non-observational, pre-reflective awareness of my own flowing experience.

6.3 The ubiquity of temporality

Husserl's analysis focused on consciousness and the kind of synthesizing structure required for the coherent experience of temporal objects. Although is not clear that, as Marvin Farber once claimed, 'these considerations hold for life in general' (1928, 129), it can be said that this type of analysis, as Merleau-Ponty recognized, can also be applied to embodied action and has more recently been applied to dynamic models of enactive perception.

We can begin to see how this works in very basic early actions. Video studies of the movements of infants younger than three-months show that there is more organization in these movements than the casual glance reveals. Close to one-third of all arm movements resulting in contact with any part of the head lead to contact with the mouth, either directly (14%) or following contact with other parts of the face (18%) (Butterworth and Hopkins 1988; Lew and Butterworth 1995). Moreover, a significant percentage of the arm movements that result in contact with the mouth are associated with an open or opening mouth posture, compared with those landing on other parts of the face. In these movements the mouth *anticipates* arrival of the hand.

The anticipation involved in early hand-mouth coordination suggests that from early post-natal life onwards, human (and most likely animal) movement involves an apparent timing that reflects an intrinsic or inherent temporality (Gallagher 2011b). The distinction between timing and temporality is important. Timing is something that we can see and measure, and it can be accidental or merely coincidental. The fact of a more consistent timing, the fact that the mouth almost always anticipates the hand, for example, suggests deeper temporal processes involved in bodily systems capable of such timing. Accordingly, it is not just a matter of the system carrying or processing temporal information; rather, the important thing is that the system is capable of self-organizing its processing and its behavior in a temporal fashion. For the system to have this anticipatory aspect in its movement, it needs to have a practical orientation towards what is just about to happen. In addition, for purposes of motor control, throughout its movement the system also needs to keep track of the just previous movement that has brought it to its current state, and this is especially true if the movement is intentional, and if a conscious sense of movement is generated.

This *intrinsic* temporality, found in bodily movement and action, manifests itself at both the subpersonal and the personal levels of analysis, and it is expressed in Henry Head's definition of the body schema. Head noted that the body schema dynamically organizes sensory-motor feedback in such a way that the final sensation of position is 'charged with a relation to something that has happened before' (Head 1920, 606). He uses the metaphor of a taximeter, which computes and registers movement as it goes. Merleau-Ponty borrows this metaphor from Head and suggests that movement is organized according to the 'time of the body, taximeter time of the corporeal schema' (1968, 173). This includes an incorporation of past moments into the present:

> At each successive instant of a movement, the preceding instant is not lost sight of. It is, as it were, dovetailed into the present…. [Movement draws] together, on the basis of one's present position, the succession of previous positions, which envelop each other. (Merleau-Ponty 1962, 140)

This kind of effect of the past on the present is a rule that applies more generally on the level of neural systems: a given neural event is normally encoded in the context of preceding events (Karmarkar and Buonomano 2007), and, as we'll see below, not necessarily on a linear model.

These retentional aspects of movement are integrated into a process that includes the ubiquitous anticipatory or prospective aspects already noted in the hand-mouth coordination in infants.

Empirical research has shown that anticipatory or prospective processes are pervasive in low-level sensorimotor actions. Visual tracking, for example, involves moment-to-moment anticipations concerning the trajectory of the target. Our gaze anticipates the rotation of our body when we turn a corner (Berthoz 2000, 126). Similar to the mouth's anticipation of the hand, when I reach down to the floor to grab something, my body anticipates a change in its center of gravity and angles backward so I don't go off balance (Babinski 1899). Reaching to grasp an object involves feed-forward components that allow last minute adjustments if the object is moved. On various models of motor control, for example, a copy of the efferent motor command sent to a comparator mechanism creates 'anticipation for the consequences of the action' (Georgieff and Jeannerod 1998) prior to sensory feedback, allowing for fast corrections of movement. Forward control models involve an anticipatory character so that, for instance, the grasp of my reaching hand tacitly anticipates the shape of the object (e.g., a cup) to be grasped, and does so differently according to what I intend to do (e.g., to drink from the cup or to throw it) (see Jeannerod 2001; MacKay 1966; Wolpert, Ghahramani and Jordan 1995). My grasp forms in a teleological fashion. As these examples show, anticipation is 'an essential characteristic' of motor functioning, and this underpins our capacity to reorganize our actions in line with events that are yet to happen (Berthoz 2000, 25). Similar anticipations characterize the sensory aspects of perception (see Wilson and Knoblich 2005 for review). Since these prospective processes are present even in infants, the 'conclusion that [anticipatory processes] are immanent in virtually everything we think or do seems inescapable' (Haith 1993, 237).

What is inescapable, ubiquitous, and pervasive for human experience and action is not just the anticipatory aspect, but the full intrinsic temporality of the processes involved. A good model for this, as Berthoz (2000) suggests, is the Husserlian analysis of the RIP (retention-impression-protention) structure of experience. A number of theorists have proposed to capture the sub-personal processes that would instantiate this Husserlian model and underpin motor performance using dynamical systems theory (Thompson 2007; van Gelder 1996; Varela 1999). On this view, action and our consciousness of action arise through the concurrent participation of distributed regions of the brain and their sensorimotor embodiment (Varela et al. 2001). The integration of the different neuronal contributories involves a process that is understood as an integration of three different scales of duration (Pöppel 1988; 1994; Varela 1999), the first two of which are said to be directly relevant to protentional-retentional processes.

1. The elementary scale (the 1/10 scale, varying between 10–100 milliseconds)
2. The integration scale (the 1 scale, varying from 0.5 to 3 seconds)
3. The narrative scale involving memory (the 10 scale)

Neurophysiologially the elementary time scale corresponds to the intrinsic cellular rhythms of neuronal discharges within the range of 10 milliseconds (the rhythms of bursting interneurons) to 100 milliseconds (the duration of an excitatory-postsynaptic-potential/inhibitory-postsynaptic-potential sequence in a cortical pyramidal neuron). Neuronal processes on this scale are integrated into the second scale, which, at the neurophysiological level, involves the integration of cell assemblies, distributed subsets of neurons with strong reciprocal connections (see Varela 1995; Varela et al. 2001). Phenomenologically the second scale corresponds to the experienced living present, the level of a fully constituted, normal cognitive operation; motorically, it corresponds to a simple action, e.g., reaching, grasping.

The important point in this analysis is the integration of the close-to-momentary processing events of the elementary scale into the extended present of the integration scale. Neuronal-level basic events having a duration on the 1/10 scale synchronize (via phase-locking) and form aggregates that manifest themselves as incompressible but complete acts on the 1 scale. The completion time is not dependent on a fixed integration period measurable by objective time, but rather is dynamically dependent on a number of dispersed assemblies. Moreover, the integration does not necessarily preserve an objective linear sequence in the events. For example, a 50 ms interval followed by a 100 ms interval is not encoded as the combination of the two. Instead, the earlier stimulus interacts with the processing of the 100 ms interval, resulting in the encoding of a distinct temporal object. Thus, temporal information is encoded in the context of the entire pattern, not as conjunctions of the component intervals. (Karmarkar and Buonomano 2007, 432)

The temporal order that manifests itself at the integration level is the product of a retentional function that orders information according to an enactive, pragmatic pattern (a pattern that is useful to the organism and keyed to ongoing or possible action) rather than according to some internal or external clock. One example may be the intentional binding that occurs when subjects are asked to judge the timing of their voluntary movements and the effects of those movements. Subjects judge the time between their voluntary movement and its effect to be shorter than between an involuntary (passive) movement and its effect (see Engbert et al. 2007; Haggard et al. 2002; Wenke and Haggard 2009). In addition, the temporal window of the integration scale is necessarily flexible (0.5 to 3 seconds) depending on a number of factors: context, fatigue, physical condition, age of subject, and so on. Furthermore, the integrating synchronization is dynamically unstable and will constantly and successively give rise to new assemblies, such transformations defining the trajectories of the system.

This 1-scale integration process corresponds to the experienced present, describable in terms of the RIP structure discussed above (Varela 1999; Thompson 2008). Whatever falls within this window counts as happening 'now' for the system, and this 'now' integrates (retains) some indeterminate sequence of the basic 1/10 scale neuronal events that have just happened. The system dynamically parses its own activity according to this intrinsic temporality. Each emerging present bifurcates from the previous one determined by its initial and boundary conditions, and in such a way that the preceding emergence is still present in (still has an effect on) the succeeding one as the trace of the dynamical trajectory (corresponding to, or causally constituting *retention* on the phenomenological level). The initial conditions and boundary conditions are defined by embodied constraints and the experiential context of the action, behavior, or cognitive act. They shape the action at the global level and include the contextual setting of the task performed, as well as the independent modulations (i.e., new stimuli or endogenous changes in motivation) arising from the contextual setting where the action occurs (Gallagher and Varela 2003, 123; see also Varela 1999, 283). The outcome of this neuronal integration thus manifests itself at a global level as an experience, action or behavior (Thompson 2008; Thompson and Varela 2001; Varela and Thompson 2003).

Intentional action takes time; it begins and ends, and takes up some duration in between. The time frame of intentional action may vary from very short to very long, depending on the degree of complexity involved in the action. This is an unremarkable observation in terms of objective measurable time. What is remarkable is the temporal structure of action, which both contributes to and derives from intention. An occurent action is, *per se*, ongoing towards the future, specifically towards its future end, and this feature is not reducible to the fact that this action requires more time to be complete. As Heidegger (1962, 236) would put it, action is always 'ahead-of-itself'. Moreover, as a way of being-in-the-world, my action is always and already situated in a particular set of circumstances, and these circumstances are shaped by what has gone before, which includes my own action up to this point. What I *can* do (what my possibilities are) is shaped by those circumstances. Yet my actions always transcend these circumstances in so far as I act for the sake of something other than the action itself. At the same time, at the same stroke, my action incorporates the situation that has been shaped by *past* actions, and the projected *future* toward which it is moving, in the *present* circumstances that can both limit and enable it. This is a temporal structure that is not captured by objective time. It's not enough to say that action takes time; there is a time *in* action, an intrinsic temporality or a temporal structure in action.

This intrinsic temporal structure is tied to the meaning of the action, which is tied to its goal, and reflects its significance to the agent. It also contributes to my ability to perceive meaning in the actions of others. The meaning of an action is not determined simply by how long it takes, as measured by the clock. For example, person A is five feet away from a door; person B is 15 feet away. There comes a knock on the door. Person A strolls over to the door to answer it; person B dashes to the door arriving at the same time as A. In one respect A and B's actions are equivalent actions; both of them answered the knock. Both actions took exactly the same amount of time. I can see, however, that B's action was hurried in a way that A's was not. The kinematics of this movement conveys meaning (see Berthoz 2000, 137). What the meaning is, of course, depends on many other circumstances to which I may or may not have access. But the hurriedness, and its meaning, are not simply a matter of covering more ground in less than normal time. The meaning of B's action in contrast to A's, is shaped by how motivated B is by what he already knows, or by what has already happened, by his specific expectation of who is knocking, by the present circumstances that either enable him or hinder him from reaching the door, and by his intention to reach the door as fast as possible. These factors are ordered in the intrinsic temporality of the action, and they manifest themselves in that action as meaningful.

If we treat action as a physical event stretched out and confined to objective time, we are naturally led to questions about causality, a concept that is defined in the framework of objective time. A cause always precedes its effect; an effect always follows its cause. What causes me to perform this particular action? To answer this question we naturally look to something that precedes the action. Perhaps I have a certain belief and a desire that 'cause' me (or motivate me) to act the way I do, or that at least give me reasons to do so (and if I do act on this basis this is often referred to as mental causation). Perhaps, however, my physical (brain) state or the social circumstances cause me to act the way I do (accordingly we can easily arrive at some version of physical or social determinism). These are the terms of the traditional discussion. If, however, we reframe the question in terms of the intrinsic temporality of action, it is not something in the past that causes or determines my action; it is some anticipated possibility of the future, some goal that draws me out of my past and present circumstances and allows me to transcend, and perhaps to change, all such determinations. Kant's antinomy concerning freedom and determinism may be deflated by this distinction between two different time frames. The scientific analysis of physical causes in objective time draws the conclusion that our actions are always determined by prior events. The practical analysis of possibilities as they are outlined in the intrinsic temporality of action opens the door to the possibility of freedom.[2]

6.4 One more time: primal impression and enactive structure

The idea that perception is enactive means that perception (and experience more generally) is characterized by a structural coupling between the agentive body and its environment in a way that generates action-oriented meaning. When I perceive something, I perceive it as actionable. That is, I perceive it as something *I can* reach, or not; something *I can* pick up, or not; something *I can* hammer with, or not, etc. Such affordances for action (even if I am not planning to take action) shape the way that I actually perceive the world (Gibson 1977; 1979). Although Merleau-Ponty (1962) is often cited as an inspiration for this idea, Merleau-Ponty himself points us back to Husserl's analysis of the 'I can' in *Ideen* II (Husserl 1989), and to his analysis of the correlation between kinaesthetic activation and perception (1997; see Zahavi 1994 and Gallagher and Zahavi 2012 for further discussion).

It seems right to suggest that the temporal structure that characterizes both consciousness and embodied action should in some significant way reflect or enable this enactive character. The question is this: if perception and action are enactive, then at a minimum, shouldn't their temporal structure be such that it allows for that enactive character? We can get a better perspective on this question by looking at a revision that Husserl (2001b) makes in his account of time consciousness in the *Bernau Manuscripts*, written around 1917–1918. The revision concerns the concept of primal impression. Rather than understanding primal impression as the origin and point of departure of the process of temporality, he considers it as the result of an interplay between retention and protention. The following quotations illustrate the difference between his earlier view and the one developed in the Bernau Manuscripts.

> The primal impression is something absolutely unmodified, the primal source of all further consciousness and being. Primal impression has as its content that which the word 'now' signifies, insofar as it is taken in the strictest sense. (Husserl 1991, 67)

> The now (i.e., the primal [impression]) is the boundary between two different [intentionalities], the retentions and protentions. (Husserl 2001b, 4)

Whereas the retention and protention in the early lectures were defined vis-à-vis primal impression, in his later writings, Husserl argues that the primal impression must be considered a line of intersection between the retentional and protentional processes that make up every momentary phase of consciousness. The primal impression by itself is not self-sufficient, rather its presenting occurs only in connection with retentions and protentions. But in addition, Husserl seems to suggest that the complicated interlacing of retentions and protentions is constitutive of the primal impression. The primal impression is not only non-self-sufficient, it is a constitutive product rather than something with a constitutive contribution of its own. This more radical claim is expressed in Husserl's idea that the point of departure rather than being the primal impression, is the empty anticipation.

> First there is an empty expectation, and then there is the point of the primary perception, itself an intentional experience. But the primary impression comes to be in the flow only by occurring as the fulfillment of contents relative to the preceding empty intentions, thereby changing itself into primal presenting perception. (Husserl 2001b, 4)

The primal impression is thus conceived as the fulfilment of an empty protention; the now is constituted by way of a protentional fulfilment (Husserl 2001b, 4, 14). Occasionally, Husserl even describes the matter in a way that doesn't mention the primal impression at all.

> Each constituting full phase is the retention of a fulfilled proten-
> tion, which is the horizonal boundary of an unfulfilled and for its
> part continuously mediated protention (Husserl 2001b, 8)

If we remain with a static phenomenology, the notion of the pri-mal impression plays an important role in the structure of time-consciousness. If, however, we take a more genetic/dynamic view, the notion of an isolated primal impression seems to be an abstraction and not something that exists in itself. If, experien-tially there is no such thing as an isolated primal impression, still, one could argue that there must be something like a limit or div-ision between retention and protention, aspects which do charac-terize our experience, but which need to be differentiated.

We've seen in the previous section how this temporal model applies to action. This gives us a hint of how to think of primal impression. When we look at action we can say that at any one moment the body is in some precise posture – as captured by a snapshot, for example; but that posture is a complete abstraction from the movement since in each case the body is not posturing from moment to moment, but is constantly on the way, in the flow of the movement such that the abstract postural moment only has meaning as part of that process. One could argue that *object-ively speaking*, at any moment the body actually is in a specific posture. But if that postural moment is anything, it is the prod-uct of an anticipated trajectory, of where the action is heading. Furthermore, we can define that abstract postural moment only when it is already accomplished – but that means, only in reten-tion, and as an end point of what had been a movement character-ized primarily by anticipation.

The suggestion is that we should think of consciousness in the same way, as a flow, where it is intentionally directed in such a way that when I am hearing the current note of a melody I'm already moving beyond it, and such protentional/anticipatory moving beyond is already a leaving behind in retention. What we have as the basic datum of experience is a process, through which the primal impression is already collapsing into the retentional stream even as it is directed forward in protention. Hearing a melody (or even a single note in some context) never involves hearing a currently sounded note (or part of a note), *and then* moving beyond it; rather, the 'and then' is already effected, already implicit in the experience.

Accordingly talk of any one of the three components in isolation runs into an abstraction. Our experience of the present is always dynamic. Pre-reflectively, consciousness has this structure. There is no impression of the present taken as a knife-edge; rather, as Husserl suggests, primal impression is already fulfilling (or not) protentions that have already been retained, and in doing so is already informing the current protentional process. This structure constitutes, in William James' (1890) term, a *specious* present, and our experience of that is what one might call a *secondary* impression – i.e., not a primary impression of a knife-edge present, but a secondary (constituted) impression of a specious present. What I experience in this immediate now is a complex presence.

The proposal is that we should abandon the idea that primal impression is a direct, straight and simple apprehension of some now-point of a stimulus that is unaffected by retention and protention. If I perceive a currently sounding note, for example, what I perceive is already modified by my just past and passing awareness of whatever came directly before. In that sense, primal impression is already modified by the retentional performance of consciousness. There is no primal impression that is not already qualified by retention. It is not that in a now phase of consciousness I have a retention of a past phase *plus* a primal impression of a current stimulus. It is not an additive function. The full experience of a melody is not well described by saying that I first experience (in primal impression) note A, and then (in a new primal impression) note B, as I retain note A. Or more precisely, the full experience is not given by

... iA ... followed by ... iB plus r[iA] ...

(where i = primal impression and r = retention). Rather, iB is already qualified (modified) by the just previous experience. For example, in Bach's *Concerto in B minor* the note B-minor sounded at a certain point will sound different from the note B-minor sounded at a certain point in Vivaldi's *Concerto in B minor*. Accordingly, the primal impression of B is never simply iB; it is iB that works its way through r[iA], that is, through the relevant retentional train of experience. That means that iB would be a different experience if it were preceded not by iA, but by i[~A], just as much as r[iA] would have to be different if in fact it were r[i{~A}].

Protention (p) also has an effect. First, the primal impression of A, (iA), when occurrent, is producing a determination of what my protentional horizon is – e.g., a protention of B...C...D...and so on. That is, whatever I anticipate must be modified by what I am currently experiencing. Furthermore, the primal impression of B, (iB), when occurrent, is already qualified by the previous protention (currently retained), whether that was a protention of B (now fulfilled), or something else (now unfulfilled). Generally speaking, then, primal impression constrains the current protention, and is constrained by the previous protention. This means that the occurrent primal impression is partially either the fulfillment or lack of fulfillment of the previous protention, and that the primal impression provides partial specification of what I am anticipating. Primal impression includes a protentional specification. My occurrent primal impression of B would be different if instead of a protention of B...C...D in the previous phase of experience I had anticipated silence or a different note. The primal impression of B confirming a previous protention of B is different from the primal impression of B disconfirming a protention of ~B.

Someone could object that we have confused the content of experience with the formal temporal properties of the experience. The analysis of time consciousness, which is about how one experienced note follows another, is not about the difference between how we hear Bach and Vivaldi. But this objection ignores the fact that *what* I experience has an effect on the temporality of my experience. If, for instance, I am bored by Bach and find Vivaldi vivacious, then Bach's *Concerto in B minor* will seem to drag on – time will seem to slow down – in contrast to my listening to Vivaldi's concerto. If I'm hungry, or mad, or in pain, the

retentional and protentional aspects of experience will be different from my satiated, happy, pain-free listening experience. To
that extent, content has an effect on the specifications of the formal structure. As Merleau-Ponty suggests, there is an 'influence
of the "contents" on time which passes "more quickly" or "less
quickly," of *Zeitmaterie* on *Zeitform*' (1968, 184). This is demonstrated in studies of temporal masking where, for example, the
tonal arrangement of sounds presented in a sequence can affect
the perception of that sequence (see Bregman and Rudnicky
1975). If in the sequence of sounds ABCDBA, the tones A and B are
of a particular low frequency, the order of C and D will be masked.
That is, you will not be able to distinguish the order of C and D.
You can also vary the tones A and B, so that C will appear to come
before D, or so that D will appear to come before C. It's not simply
that the conscious retention of A and B determines the phenomenal order of C and D, since the later sounds of B and A are also
required to get these effects. That is, the sounds that follow C and
D in the objective sequential order will also determine the way C
and D play out on the conscious level.[3]

Of course one can still say that there is some level of formal
temporalization that remains invariant – whatever the content,
or whatever the phenomenological velocity or experienced serial
order, or the implicit temporality of the object itself, I do experience a sequence in which some stimulus precedes another. But
what stimulus that happens to be, and what order it comes in, and
how fast it happens to swim by in the stream of consciousness –
these things make all the difference in experience.

If we say that primal impression is part of the structure of the
living present – that's true, but it's not enough. We also have to say
that the primal impression is itself structured by its very dynamic
participation in its relations to retention and protention (and vice
versa, of course). My primal impression of the current moment
is influenced by the retentional train – it's not just the abstract
beginning point of that train as if the business of retention was
strictly about the past and had no influence on the present. And,
my primal impression of the current moment is already influenced
by protention – not only the current protention (although perhaps
that one especially), but also by previously retained protentions.

Time-consciousness, in this sense, has a fractal character (see Gallagher and Zahavi, in press). Having distinguished primal impression from retention and protention in RIP structure, any closer examination of primal impression (or retention or protention) finds that same structure repeated – again, not in an additive way, but in a kind of fractal effect. This is not an overlap, but an effect that multiplies itself in such a way that any attempt to define primal impression in itself always finds the effects of retention or protention already included. But each element also reflects this structure again – primal impression, by itself, is an abstraction, but to think it *in* this structure is to think it *with* (or *having*) this structure – primal impression, in its intentional functioning, reflects the retentional and protentional components, and vice versa.

What this amounts to is that there is no primal impression – no current intuition of the present stimulus – without it already being anticipatory (on the basis of what has just occurred), so that my primal impression of the present is already involved in an enactive anticipation of how the stimulus will work out. Protention, primal impression, and retention are in an *enactive* structure in regard to the stimulus in the sense that a certain anticipatory aspect (already shaped by what has just gone before) is already complicating the immediacy of the present. Consciousness is not simply a passive reception of the present; it enacts the present, it constitutes its meaning in the shadow of what has just been experienced, and in the light of what it anticipates.

What the primal impression is, then, and how it relates to retention and protention, are not independent from the intentional nature of consciousness and action, or from the specific content that we experience. This means that the temporal structure of consciousness should be considered, in very pragmatic terms, as in-the-world. This account lines up well with Husserl's conception of embodied experience as an 'I can', as an *enactive* phenomenon. My hearing of the melody, for example, is not a passive reception of the sound. My hearing of any one note is a hearing directed toward the next note – that is, I only hear one note as the anticipation of the next note, or the next bit of silence – as something that is leading somewhere – and I never hear it just on its own. Primal impression, retention, and protention are not elements that simply add themselves to each other. They are rather in a genetic relation; they have a self-constituting effect on each other.

Moreover, together, they constitute the possibility of a broader enactive engagement with the experienced world (the object, the melody, etc.). Just as I perceive the hammer as affording the possibility of grasping it, or in a different circumstance, as affording the possibility of propping open my window, I likewise perceive the melody as affording the possibility of dancing or sitting in peaceful enjoyment, etc. The point, however, is not about hammers versus melodies. It's about the temporality of affordances and enactive engagements. Nothing is an affordance for my enactive engagement if it is presented to me passively in a knife-edge present; that is, nothing would be afforded if there were only primal impressions, one after the other, without protentional anticipation, since I cannot enactively engage with the world if the world is not experienced as a set of possibilities, which, by definition, involves the not-yet. Thus, the enactive character goes all the way down, into the very structure of time-consciousness, and one doesn't get this enactive character without an integration of all three components.

6.5   Further reading

Husserl (1991) consists of his lectures (from 1905) and later writings on the concept of time-consciousness. Brough (1972) and Kortooms (2002) trace the development of Husserl's thinking on time-consciousness in detail. Gallagher (1998) examines Husserl's analysis of time-consciousness and shows how it avoids some of the perplexities associated with James' concept of the specious present. Rodemeyer (2006) focuses on Husserl's later manuscripts and the relation between temporality and intersubjectivity. Miller (1984) and Dainton (2000) connect Husserl's analysis to discussions of perception and temporality in analytic philosophy of mind.

7 Self and First-Person Perspective

7.1 A tradition of disagreements

The only consistent theme to be found in the phenomenological literature on the concept of self is constant disagreement. Husserl begins the discussion by disagreeing with a certain tradition concerning the concept of the ego, and then later comes to disagree with himself. Heidegger challenges the entire tradition, including Husserl, by deconstructing the notions of self, soul, ego, person, etc., although he too reconsiders his analysis. Sartre and Gurwitsch reject the Husserlian analysis and propose an account that is closer to Hume and Buddhist doctrine, while Scheler develops a transcendental account similar to the later Husserl. Merleau-Ponty, in turn, rejects such transcendental accounts and argues for an embodied self. More contemporary debates about the self in phenomenology develop more complex, plural concepts of self. We'll see, however, that throughout all of this disagreement there is one thing that all phenomenologists do agree upon, although this is in disagreement with most philosophers of mind.

Husserl's initial disagreement is voiced in his *Logical Investigations*. Initially Husserl thought of the ego much in the same way as Hume – that is, he could find no such thing within the stream of consciousness. In this regard he goes against the Cartesian tradition, which endorses a substantial ego as the ground of subjectivity, and the Kantian tradition which posits a transcendental ego. Thus, he voices his disagreement with the neo-Kantian, Paul Natorp, indicating that he simply cannot find a pure ego as a 'primitive necessary center of relations' in experience (2001, 549). After approximately a dozen years, however, in the 1913 revision of the *Logical Investigations*, he is able to spot it, and admits, in a footnote, that 'I have since managed to find it, i.e., have learnt not to be led astray from a pure grasp of the given through corrupt forms of ego-metaphysic' (Ibid). That is, he learns not to be led astray by someone like Descartes who thinks of the ego as a substantial thing (a *res cogitans*). Like Kant, Husserl distinguishes the transcendental ego from the empirical ego; the latter, as the self that appears as part of the world, is bracketed in the phenomenological reduction, but the former remains as the formal, pure principle of unity in consciousness. In *Ideas I* he describes it as a 'subject pole', a 'ray of regard' that accompanies all experience. The ego is pure, formal, 'empty of content', a principle of unity. Husserl's thought about the ego soon becomes more complex as he thinks of it as a perspectival zero-point, and in this way can link it up with embodied aspects of experience. Dermot Moran summarizes this aspect of Husserl's thought.

> The ego is a 'zero point' (*Nullpunkt*), a center of reference and orientation, from which distances, times, etc., radiate outwards. Something is over there, to the left, on top, far away, near, all as mapped out taking myself as the centre of space (*Ideas II* § 41). As such the ego requires a bodily orientation and spatial location. The transcendental ego becomes embodied in a living body. (Moran 2000, 172)

Moran goes on to point out that Husserl starts to consider the ego as less formal, less pure, something that can be passively affected by its experiences, and as capable of maintaining attitudes and habits and capabilities (of the practical sort summarized by his concept of the 'I can'). The ego does not remain worldless or unaffected by experience or by the meaning it constitutes. This sends us back to considerations about temporality. Husserl's account of the temporal structure of consciousness, especially the longitudinal intentionality of retention, helps to explain how the self is built up (self-constituted) as a conscious center of experience (see Chapter 6). As Moran (173) points out, in line with Scheler's idea of a transcendental person, Husserl goes on to talk about the ego as 'person' and about 'intersubjective communal groupings' of persons.

Heidegger, in contrast, rather than entering more deeply into the analysis of ego-structures, rejects the concept of ego altogether, as well as all the traditional characterizations of the 'I', self, soul, subject, person. All of these concepts are metaphysically suspect in the sense that although human existence (*Dasein*) is specifically not something present-at-hand, all of these concepts suggest something present-at-hand. In other words, even if someone like Husserl brackets all metaphysical conceptions of the self and is not concerned with an empirical ego, a certain metaphysical way of thinking about the ego still characterizes his thought, in the same way that it characterizes all traditional ways of thinking about the self. This kind of thinking takes the self to be an identifiable and unified entity that we can characterize using the same categories that we use to characterize objects and things (things that are 'present-at-hand') that we find lying around the environment. We can say, of course, that the self is not such a thing, or that it is transcendental, but our ways of characterizing it derive from just the way we talk about such present-at-hand things.

We are naturally led to the standard philosophical answers of self, subject, soul, mind, ego, the 'I' ... etc., when the question is '*What* is Dasein'? Heidegger instead asks, '*Who* is Dasein'? – and he entertains the following answer: 'It could be that the "who" of everyday Dasein just is *not* the "I myself"' (150/115). His more positive answer is that Dasein is *Das Man* – which doesn't mean 'the man'. It means 'the they', where the 'they' is everyone and no one. On Heidegger's view, Dasein's kind of existence is such that it too easily falls into the anonymity of the crowd to the extent that Dasein does what everybody else does. That is, Dasein is so taken up by the world, its projects, and by dominating social practices, that it gets lost in a social inauthenticity in which it understands itself as being the same as everyone else. Adolescent Dasein comes home and whines to its Dasein parents – 'I want to do X; Billy Dasein is doing X, why can't I do X?' Dasein doesn't want to stand out; Dasein tends to conformity – it does what everyone else does, it reads what everyone else reads, it watches the same television shows, goes to the same movies, listens to the same music, plays the same video games, wears the same jeans, etc. Dasein tends to get lost in the world, taken up by every task, every responsibility, everything that everybody wants and expects Dasein to do. Dasein ought to graduate; Dasein ought to pick a career; Dasein ought to make as much money as possible; Dasein ought to buy this and that, consume this and that; Ms. Dasein, especially, ought to get married. Also, make sure you try to look presentable. Buy some nice clothes. If you happen to be a female Dasein (although for Heidegger Dasein is relatively neuter), do spend lots of money and time on cosmetics and try to look sexy; try to look different, the same as everyone else. If you're getting older, spend lots of money and time on cosmetics and try to look like you're not dying. Certainly Dasein should not worry about death. *They* are very quiet about death – it's not something people want to talk about. After all, you're alive; you should go shopping. In other words, we need to think of Dasein, in-the-world, by default, as *not itself*, as inauthentic. In this regard Heidegger characterizes social relations as the occasions of inauthenticity, whereas the possibility of authenticity seems to be tied to a being-towards a possibility that is said to involve no intersubjectivity at all – i.e., being-towards-death.

Existentially, Dasein is 'thrown' into worldly and social contexts, into time and place, into a history. At the same time, Dasein's existence is said to be in each case its own – '*in each case mine*' (1962, 67) – in such a way that its existence is an issue for it. Heidegger in this regard gives Dasein some control over its life.

> Dasein always understands itself in terms of its existence – in terms of a possibility of itself: to be itself or not itself. Dasein has either chosen these possibilities itself, or got itself into them, or grown up in them already. (1962, 33)

Heidegger, in later disagreement with himself, however, considers his analysis of Dasein to remain too Cartesian, in a way similar to the problematic metaphysical views of self that he had criticized. In his later philosophy, Dasein seems to be much less an agent, and much more a plaything of larger forces – or more precisely, the larger force of Being.

The idea that Dasein's own existence is an issue for it, with some deep agentive ability to make itself who it is, is something that the early Sartre takes over from the early Heidegger. Sartre also offers a critique of Husserl's notion of transcendental ego. In a famous essay, *The Transcendence of the Ego*, Sartre (1957) outlines a non-egological conception of consciousness. He argues that Husserl was mistaken to think that there is some ego-structure to consciousness, or some ego in consciousness. Whatever self exists, according to Sartre, is external to consciousness. Thus, for Sartre, the self is an empirical self, something objectified, something present-at-hand. To think of ourselves as such, however, is the product of certain inauthentic ('bad faith') attitudes that we take toward ourselves, and in which we deny our true nature – which is to not have a nature, to *not* be a something or constituted self. For Sartre, human subjectivity is a no-thingness, a freedom, a collection of possibilities, but not an actual thing. When we start to think of ourselves as something – a lawyer, a doctor, a husband, a wife, a student, a surfer – we close off possibilities and deny our freedom, and we thus inauthentically treat ourselves as some determinate thing. Following in the phenomenological tradition of self-disagreement, however, the later Sartre (1960) revises this early strong emphasis on free agency, and acknowledges the effects of larger cultural and historical forces on shaping our inauthentic existence.

Sartre's self-correction may in part be due to Merleau-Ponty, who regarded Sartre's characterization of subjectivity to be extreme since it suggested that authentic life would in some way involve a free-floating, unsituated, unhistorical subject. The fact that our existence is a bodily existence is necessarily reflected in our phenomenology. Thus Merleau-Ponty proposes the concept of a tacit *cogito*. Merleau-Ponty understands the body as 'a natural self', 'the subject of perception' (1962, 239). The body, however, to a great extent, does its work in a tacit and even anonymous way, and as such is 'another subject beneath me, for whom a world exists before I am here, and who marked out my place in it. This captive or natural spirit is my body' (1962, 294). Who we are, then, is never entirely transparent, as Sartre might want it. Rather, there is a kind of 'thickness and an opacity' involved in our existence

(1962, 56n.). One's body, with its non-conscious processes, and its emerging emotions, situates oneself in the world. Yet there is a certain truth to the cogito: 'The primary truth is indeed "I think," but only provided that we understand thereby "I belong to myself" while belonging to the world' (1962, 466). The cogito on this view is not the product of an introspective act of reflection, but of a tacit awareness that accompanies our experience of the world. And yet, again, in the spirit of phenomenological self-disagreement, Merleau-Ponty later thinks that 'what I call the tacit cogito is impossible. To have the idea of "thinking"...to return to immanence and to the consciousness of ___, it is necessary to have words' (1968, 224). There is, we might say, a hermeneutical complication since this pre-predicative existence of embodied experience never comes to consciousness unless it is already in some way predicative – put into words. The tacit cogito is either something that we do not experience – in which case positing its existence would not be phenomenological – or it is experienced only as expressed in a linguistically shaped awareness, in which case it already involves a metaphysical distortion.

7.2 Pre-reflective and minimal aspects of self

One thing that all of these phenomenologists consistently agree on, despite their various inter-and intra-disagreements, concerns the existence of pre- (or non-) reflective self-awareness. In contrast to a second-order, reflective, introspective examination of one's experience, the idea of a pre-reflective self-awareness is that it runs along with first-order experience. If you ask me to reflect on the pain I feel in my right foot, or to report on what I was just thinking about, I would engage in a reflective act and take up a certain perspective one order removed from the pain or the thought. In contrast, pre-reflective self-awareness is an awareness I have before I do any reflecting on my experience; it's an implicit, first-order awareness rather than an explicit or higher-order form of self-consciousness. Phenomenologists claim that an explicit reflective self-consciousness is possible only because there is an ongoing pre-reflective self-awareness built into experience.

Sartre, for example, maintains that pre-reflective (non-thetic) self-consciousness is not simply a quality added to the experience, an accessory; rather, it constitutes the very mode of being of the experience (Sartre 1956, liv)

Not all philosophers accept this concept of pre-reflective self-awareness. A significant number of analytic philosophers of mind, for example, question the idea. Yet there are philosophers in that tradition who hold a view that is close to and consistent with this phenomenological conception. Alvin Goldman, for example, describes the concept as follows:

> [Consider] the case of thinking about x or attending to x. In the process of thinking about x there is already an implicit awareness that one is thinking about x. There is no need for reflection here, for taking a step back from thinking about x in order to examine it…. When we are thinking about x, the mind is focused on x, not on our thinking of x. Nevertheless, the process of thinking about x carries with it a non-reflective self-awareness (Goldman 1970, 96)

Owen Flanagan defends a similar view. He argues that consciousness involves self-consciousness in the weak sense that there is something it is like for the subject to have the experience, and that this self-awareness is related to the fact that my experiences are experienced *as mine* (1992, 194).

To call this pre-reflective awareness a form of self-consciousness is not to make it equivalent to reflective self-consciousness, but rather to point to multiple (at least two) forms of self-consciousness, and multiple (at least two) conceptions of how we can characterize the self. On this basis, we can distinguish between a pre-reflective minimal aspect of self, and a reflective, higher-order self, which is sometimes called the narrative self. In this regard, reflective self-consciousness presupposes both conceptual knowledge and narrative competence. It requires maturation and socialization, and the ability to access and issue reports about the states, traits, and dispositions that make one the person one is. The pre-reflective minimal aspect of self may be nonconceptual in a way that is 'logically and ontogenetically more primitive than the higher forms of self-consciousness that are usually the focus of philosophical debate' (Bermúdez 1998, 274).

The notion of pre-reflective self-awareness, as Flanagan points out, relates to the idea that experiences have a subjective 'feel' to them, a certain (phenomenal) quality of 'what it is like' or what it 'feels' like to have them (Nagel 1974). There is something it is like to experience the pain in my left foot, for example, and it feels different from the itch in my right hand. There is something it is like to taste a lemon in contrast to what it is like to taste chocolate. It seems that there is also something it is like to remember what it is like to taste a lemon, or to run, or sit, or stand still, to feel envious, nervous, hungry, depressed or happy (see Chapter 5 and the concept of hyletic experience). Throughout these phenomenal contrasts, however, as I live through these differences, there is something experientially the same, namely, the distinct first-person character of these experiences. All these experiences are characterized by a quality of *mineness*, the fact that it is *I* who am having these experiences, a 'sense of ownership' for the experiences (Gallagher 2000). All the experiences are experienced (pre-reflectively or tacitly) as *my* experiences, as experiences *I* am undergoing or living through. Pre-reflective self-awareness, then, as a minimal form of self-consciousness, presents me with an immediate and non-observational sense of self in the *what it is like* quality of experience. If there were no pre-reflective self-awareness implicit in experience there would be nothing it is like to undergo it, and in effect, there would be no experience.

Pre-reflective self-awareness is a non-observational self-acquaintance. Heidegger, for example, describes it as follows:

> Dasein [human existence] as existing, is there for itself, even when the ego does not expressly direct itself to itself in the manner of its own peculiar turning around and turning back... The self is there for the Dasein itself without reflection and without inner perception, *before* all reflection. Reflection, in the sense of a turning back, is only a mode of self-*apprehension*, but not the mode of primary self-disclosure. (1982, 159)

Brentano had defended a different conception of self-awareness, although on some points he and the phenomenologists are in agreement. According to him, as I listen to a melody I am aware that I am listening to the melody. In this, however, I do not have two different mental states: my consciousness of the melody is one and the same as my awareness of perceiving it; they constitute one single psychical phenomenon. But for Brentano, in contrast to the phenomenologists, by means of this unified mental state I have an awareness of two objects: the melody and my perceptual experience.

> In the same mental phenomenon in which the sound is present to our minds we simultaneously apprehend the mental phenomenon itself. What is more, we apprehend it in accordance with its dual nature insofar as it has the sound as content within it, and insofar as it has itself as content at the same time. We can say that the sound is the *primary object* of the *act* of hearing, and that the act of hearing itself is the *secondary object* (Brentano 1995, 127–128)

Husserl disagrees on just this point, as do Sartre and Heidegger: my awareness of my experience is not an awareness of it as an object. That a psychological state is experienced, 'and is in this sense conscious, does not and cannot mean that this is the object of an act of consciousness, in the sense that a perception, a presentation or a judgment is directed upon it' (Husserl 2001, I, 273). Rather, it is non-objectifying in the sense that I do not occupy the position or perspective of a spectator or in(tro)spector who attends to this experience in a thematic way. In pre-reflective self-awareness, intentional experience is lived through (*erlebt*); it does not appear in an objectified manner, although, of course, we can objectify it if we take it as an object in reflection.

On this view, there is no separate self alongside our experiences that is different from them. To be aware of one*self* is not to be aware of a pure self that exists separately from the stream of experience. When Hume (1739) declares that he cannot find anything resembling a self when he searches his experiences, but finds only a series or bundle of particular perceptions or feelings, he overlooks the fact that he was looking only among his *own* experiences, and seemingly recognized them as his own, and could do so only on the basis of that immediate self-awareness that he seemed to miss. The minimal self is not a substance, nor some kind of ineffable transcendental precondition, nor a social construct that gets generated through time; rather it is an integral part of conscious life, with an immediate experiential character. In this regard, the phenomenological view accounts for psychological self-identity – the experience of self-identity through time – without positing anything like a self as a separate entity over and above the stream of consciousness (see the discussion of time-consciousness in Chapter 6). What remains constant and consistent across these changes is the sense of ownership constituted by pre-reflective self-awareness. Only a being with this sense of ownership or *mineness* could go on to form concepts about herself, consider her own aims, ideals, and aspirations as her own, construct stories about herself, and plan and execute actions for which she will take responsibility.

7.3   The sense of ownership

Ever since William James (1890) categorized different senses of the self philosophers and psychologists have refined and expanded the possible variations of this concept. James' inventory of physical self, mental self, and spiritual self has been variously supplemented. Ulrich Neisser (1988), for example, suggested important distinctions between ecological, interpersonal, extended, private and conceptual aspects of self. By the beginning of the 21st century one could add to the list: autobiographical self, cognitive self, contextualized self, core self, dialogical self, narrative self, embodied self, fictional self, gendered self, minimal self, neural self, etc. (Damasio 1999; Strawson 1999). All of these terms pick out certain aspects that point to the complexity of the notion of self. The concepts of minimal and narrative aspects of self, however, cut across a good number of these dimensions and have been used as general terms to organize recent discussions (Gallagher 2000; 2011c). The minimal aspects of self, as discussed in the previous section, involve a pre-reflective self-awareness of oneself as an embodied subject of experience. This includes a sense of ownership (or *mineness*), a sense that this experience is *my* experience.

Pre-reflective self-awareness also includes a sense of agency – a sense that I am in control of my actions.

> *Sense of self-agency (SA):* The pre-reflective experience that I am the one who is causing or generating a movement or action or thought process.
>
> *Sense of self-ownership (SO):* The pre-reflective experience that I am the one who is moving or undergoing an experience.

This is a phenomenological distinction that can be easily understood in the experience of involuntary movement. If someone pushes me from behind, I experience the initial movement as something happening to me, as something that I am experiencing, and so have an experience of ownership for the movement. I do not claim that it is someone else who is moving, since I have an immediate multi-modal (kinaesthetic/proprioceptive, vestibular, and visual) sense that I am the one moving. At the same time, however, I can say that I have no experience of self-agency for this movement. I did not cause it; someone else pushed me. Accordingly, in the case of involuntary movement (as well as in reflex movement) SA and SO come apart. In the case of voluntary action, on the other hand, SA and SO seem tightly fitted and indistinguishable in pre-reflective experience.[1]

In contrast to these *minimal* aspects of self, conceptualized as involving very short experiential time periods – that is, what James called the 'specious present', an extension of time that can be characterized in terms of Husserl's retentional-protentional structure, or what we called the integration temporal scale of seconds (Chapter 6) – *narrative* aspects of self are extended over longer periods. Narrative aspects of self involve a more or less coherent self (self-image, self-concept) constituted with a past and a future in the stories we tell about ourselves, and that others tell about us. Narrative competency plays an important role in a phenomenological account of intersubjectivity (as we'll see in Chapter 9), and here it signals the idea that individual selves are never constituted outside of social contexts. The narrative aspects of self are also closely tied to the concepts of action and agency, which will be discussed in the next chapter (Chapter 8). Here, in the present chapter, we will continue to focus on minimal aspects of self, and especially issues pertaining to the sense of ownership.

When I experience an occurrent pain, perception, or thought, the experience in question is given immediately and noninferentially. I do not have to judge or appeal to some criteria in order to identify it as *my* experience. There are no free-floating experiences; even the experience of freely-floating belongs to someone. As James (1890) put it, all experience is 'personal'. Although minimal aspects of self that involve senses of ownership and agency in the context of both motor action and cognition are relatively stable, it is also the case that they can be disrupted both in experimental contexts and in cases of psychopathology. One sign of their everyday stability can be seen in the use of the first-person pronoun in a self-referring way. Specifically, it's difficult to see how we can ever make a mistake in this regard. This kind of self-reference has a feature that some philosophers call 'immunity to error through misidentification relative to the first-person pronoun' (IEM) (Shoemaker 1984). IEM suggests that when a speaker uses the first-person pronoun ('I') to refer to herself *as subject*, she cannot make a mistake about the person to whom she is referring. As Wittgenstein (1958) first explained it, IEM applies to any use of the first-person pronoun *as subject*. He distinguished use of the first-person pronoun *as subject* from its use *as object*, by examples. On the one hand, 'as subject' means any first-person reference I make to myself as an experiencing subject. For example, if I experience a toothache, it would be nonsensical to say 'Someone has a toothache, is it I?' On the other hand, 'as object' means any reference I make to myself on the basis of an objectifying perception or thought. For example, looking in the mirror and seeing a sunburned arm, I might say 'I have a sunburn'. It's possible that I see someone else's arm in the mirror and mistake it for my own, and in that sense I would seem to be misidentifying myself. This first-person character, *as subject*, however, entails an implicit experiential self-reference. If I feel hungry or see my friend, I cannot be mistaken about who the subject of that experience is, even if I can be mistaken about it being hunger (perhaps it's really thirst), or about it being my friend (perhaps it's his twin), or even about whether I am actually seeing him (I may be hallucinating).

IEM is not simply a grammatical principle; it seemingly depends on the kind of experiential access that I have to myself. Shoemaker indicates that in cases of introspection, for example, misidentification is not possible precisely because the subject is not involved in a process of identification. In such cases I do not pick out an object and then ask whether this object fits a set of criteria that would allow it to count as being me. Rather, I have a non-observational introspective access to my experience. Accordingly if I am not trying to identify myself I cannot make an error of misidentification.

Discussions of IEM are usually framed in terms of introspective access, as we see in Shoemaker. It seems necessarily the case that I can only introspect my own thinking, and that I cannot find myself in the position of asking, 'Someone is thinking this, but is it I?' Introspection, however, is a reflective operation in which I think about my own thinking. In this respect the phenomenologist suggests that whether a certain experience is experienced as mine, or not, does not depend upon something apart from the experience, but depends precisely upon the pre-reflective structure of experience.

As we've seen, the phenomenological view maintains that when we consciously think, or perceive, or act, we are *pre-reflectively* aware that we are doing so, and this pre-reflective awareness is something built into experience itself. On this view I do not need a further reflective introspection to confirm that my thoughts are my own – I do not need access to them in that sense. Rather, what makes my thoughts accessible in reflective introspection is precisely an already operating pre-reflective self-awareness that is part of the concurrent structure of any conscious process and that provides a basic (minimal) sense of ownership. This suggests that the sense of ownership is very stable with respect to my thinking or stream of consciousness. James thought this was obvious but difficult to explain: 'Every thought is part of a personal consciousness …. The universal fact is not "feelings and thoughts exist," but "I think" and "I feel," [yet] to give an accurate account of [this] is the most difficult of philosophic tasks' (1890, I, 225).

The sense of ownership holds not only with regard to the stream of thinking, but also to experiences of my body or my body parts, and my actions. For example, when I reach and grasp something, I have a sense that it is my arm that is reaching and my hand that is grasping, but also in regard to my experiences of self-movement and action, this is not only my arm, but also *my* action. My sense of my own posture and movement are given by proprioception and kinaesthesia, respectively. Proprioception is the sense I have of the position of my limbs 'from the inside'. For example, if I ask you to close your eyes and then point to your knee, you are able to do this without vision because you have a proprioceptive sense of where your leg is and how it is postured. Kinaesthesia is the proprioceptive sense I have of my own movement. If, when my eyes are closed, someone moves my arm, I not only feel their touch on my arm, but I kinaesthetically feel the movement of my arm, and I know proprioceptively precisely the posture in which it ends up.

Gareth Evans (1982) argued that IEM extends to the kind of access I have to my own body by means of somatic proprioception and kinaesthesia. Although it is possible to make a mistake in identifying one's body via sense-perceptual modalities such as vision, it seems questionable whether it would be possible to have a proprioceptive sense of a body other than one's own (Evans, 1982; also see Cassam 1995; 2011). That proprioception is IEM means simply that via proprioception I cannot misidentify my own body. Likewise, it seems possible that passive touch is also IEM since it would be odd to ask: 'Someone is being touched, is it I?' This suggests that in this kind of experience, whether in the case of involuntary movement or voluntary action, the pre-reflective sense of ownership cannot be wrong, that is, I cannot be wrong with respect to *who* is moving, or standing, or sitting with legs crossed, etc. This does not mean that proprioception cannot be in error in other respects, however.

Proprioception/kinaesthesis provides information about posture, limb position, and how I am moving – and it can be wrong or be misled about these things. Experiments that involve vibrating certain muscles, thereby manipulating proprioception, for example, can lead me to believe that my arm is extended out in front of me when in fact it is not (e.g., Lackner 1988; Longo et al. 2009). The claim about IEM does not extend to the specifics of posture or movement. It pertains only to the question of *whose* body is in question. I might be misled to proprioceptively feel that my legs are crossed when they are not, but IEM states that I cannot be misled about them being *my* legs, or that *I* am the one crossing them.

Evans, however, does suggest a thought experiment in which the nervous system of Subject A is connected to the nervous system of Subject B in such a way that Subject A receives the proprioceptive input from Subject B's body. When Subject B's legs are crossed, Subject A reports that he (Subject A) feels that his (Subject A's) legs are crossed. In this case, it seems, he is mistaken in a way that violates IEM, since, via proprioception, he misidentifies B's legs for his own. We may be able to get a better idea about how to deal with this thought experiment by considering some actual empirical cases. Questions about IEM and the sense of ownership are raised by many empirical experiments that involve passive touch and proprioception. And further questions can be raised about the kind of misidentification that occurs in pathologies such as schizophrenic delusions and somatoparaphrenia.

7.3.1 Schizophrenia

John Campbell (1999) proposed that experiences involving delusions of control and thought insertion in schizophrenia might count as counterexamples to IEM. A schizophrenic patient who suffers thought insertion, for example, might claim that she is not the one who is thinking a particular thought, when in fact she is the one who is thinking the thought. The following example of a schizophrenic's account of her own thought processes illustrates this: 'Thoughts are put into my mind like "Kill God". It's just like my mind working, but it isn't. They come from this chap, Chris. They're his thoughts' (from Frith 1992, 66). In such cases the schizophrenic patient misidentifies the source of the thought and seemingly violates IEM.

Campbell suggests that Chris Frith's (1992) neurocognitive model of the breakdown of self-monitoring in schizophrenia turns out to be a good candidate for explaining IEM and how it breaks down. The model attempts to identify which mechanisms fail at the cognitive or neurological level when the schizophrenic patient suffers from delusions of control – that is, when he claims that someone other than him is causing his actions or bodily movements. To explain delusions of control Frith appeals to the notions of efference copy and comparator mechanisms involved in motor control. In the language of neuroscience, *efference* is a non-conscious signal sent from the brain to the body, for example, a command to move a muscle. *Afference*, in contrast, is a signal sent from the body to the brain. It includes sensory feedback, such as kinaesthetic information that indicates that my body has moved in a certain way. According to the comparator model when the motor system issues a motor command to move a body part, a copy (efference copy) of that command is sent to an area of the brain that compares it to the motor intention. This constitutes a non-conscious pre-motor or 'forward model' that allows for rapid, automatic error corrections (Frith et al. 2000). This forward comparator process anticipates the sensory feedback from movement and generates a sense of agency (SA) for the action, while afferent, sensory-feedback processes, including proprioception, that result from the movement, generate the sense of ownership (SO). If the forward model fails, or efference copy is not properly generated, sensory feedback may still produce SO ('I am moving') but SA will be compromised ('I am not causing the movement'), even if the actual movement matches the intended movement.

It turns out that schizophrenic patients who suffer from delusions of control have problems with the forward, pre-action monitoring of movement, but not with sensory feedback (Frith and Done 1988; Malenka et al. 1982). While control based on sensory feedback is thought to involve the cerebellum (Frith et al. 2000), problems with forward monitoring are consistent with studies of schizophrenia showing abnormal pre-movement brain potentials associated with supplementary motor, premotor and prefrontal cortexes (Singh et al. 1992). Experimental brain-imaging studies suggest involvement of the anterior or posterior insula in generating SA (Farrer and Frith 2002; Farrer et al. 2003). On this account, problems in precisely these brain areas may therefore result in the lack of SA, characteristic of these kinds of schizophrenic delusions of control. This is a bottom-up, neuroscientific explanation of why first-order (pre-reflective) experience may be disrupted

(Hohwy 2004; Mundale and Gallagher 2009). Such delusions, however, include an additional aspect: the schizophrenic typically attributes the action to someone else. On a bottom-up account this may be due to disruptions in brain processes responsible for differentiating self and other in action (see e.g., Georgieff and Jeannerod 1998). Given such disruptions the subject could actually experience the action as alien – as not generated by him but by someone else. Accordingly, this explanation stays at a level that concerns pre-reflective self-awareness, in contrast to top-down explanations that would look to disruptions at the level of higher-order, reflective (introspective) cognition and their expressions in narrative (e.g., Graham and Stephens 1994; Stephens and Graham 2000).

Bottom-up approaches thus point to possible neurological explanations of the immediacy involved in the senses of self-ownership, self-agency and IEM. Given this account, however, it is not at all clear that, as Campbell suggests, there is a violation of IEM in delusions of control. As noted above, in the case of action, SA and SO are normally indistinguishable. In the case of delusions of control, however, where the schizophrenic patient claims that he is not the agent of a particular action, SA is not present, but SO is still present. This is similar to the case of involuntary action. Indeed this is necessarily the case if the patient's complaint is to make any sense, since it is his own body that he is describing: '*my* body has engaged in an action; *my* body has been moved'. He claims that he, rather than someone else, is being moved, or being made to act, and that the action is not something he intended. SO is still intact for his body and for his movement, even as SA is not. This is precisely why he feels that this movement or action is *his* concern rather than someone else's; it's not happening to someone else, it's happening to him. His sense of self is *as subject* – he is the one who is experiencing this alien control. When he reports on his proprioceptive experience, or when he says '*I*' have experienced this alien control, or this alien thought (in the case of thought insertion), he is not mistaken about who is experiencing these things; his sense of self remains IEM and his SO remains intact.

Even if we accept this solution to delusions of control,[2] however, there are a significant number of other pathologies and experiments that challenge IEM in regard to bodily experience. I'll discuss a number of such challenges and try to refine this account and identify precisely what aspect of experience delivers IEM. First, however, let's return to Evan's thought experiment.

Jeannerod and Pacherie (2004), relying on neurological evidence, suggest that, with respect to determining who the agent of the action is, the ways that we come to know this 'are not entirely reliable and cannot be a source of identification-free first-person knowledge' (2004, 137). On this basis they conclude:

> In a nutshell, then, the bad news for philosophers is that self-identification is after all a problem. In the domain of action and intention, at least, there is no such thing as immunity to error through misidentification, whether for the self as object (sense of ownership) or for the self as agent (sense of agency). The mechanisms involved in self- and other-attribution may be reasonably reliable in normal circumstances, but are not infallible. (2004, 141)

Of course, this would be bad news for non-philosophers too! It's not clear, however, why Jeannerod and Pacherie associate the sense of ownership with the self *as object*. One distinction to be made here is between SO for a body part (I feel this to be my arm) and SO for movement (I am the one moving, even in the case of involuntary movement). The experience of my arm as mine can be based on proprioceptive/kinaesthtetic awareness – a pre-reflective sense of arm position or movement – or it may be based on actually seeing that my arm is there in its usual place, attached to my body. In the first case, as Wittgenstein defined it, we have a sense of our body *as subject*; in the second case we have a sense of our body *as object*. I can be mistaken about the second, as when I see an arm in the mirror and mistake it for mine when it is not; in this case, however, IEM is not an issue. Wittgenstein and other philosophers would claim that IEM pertains only in the first case. Jeannerod and Pacherie, however, suggest that even if proprioception delivers an awareness of my body (my self) *as subject*, providing a sense of ownership for it, this does not guarantee IEM. They cite Evans' thought experiment, where A receives B's proprioceptive input, which seems to suggest that I can be wrong about whose limbs are whose.

The thought experiment is a difficult case with respect to IEM, since proprioception (or a quasi-proprioception in which I am receiving signals from someone else's body) is involved. In this case I'm not only wrong about the position of my legs, but it also seems I'm wrong about whose legs they are, and that, seemingly violates IEM. Thus, Pacherie and Jeannerod suggest, at best we have only *de facto* immunity, but not *in-principle* immunity to this kind of misidentification.

> Proprioception and passive touch are *de facto* immune to error through misidentification. Although it seems conceivable that one could be hooked up to other bodies in such a way that one had proprioceptive and tactile access to their states as well, in the actual world proprioception and passive touch only carry information about one's own body. (Jeannerod and Pacherie 2004, 117)

Again, however, to get clarity on this issue, it will help to look at actual, empirical cases. Both SA and SO are easily shown to be fallible to the extent that efference and afference processes, including proprioception, are open to experimental manipulation, or neurological disruption.

7.3.2 Somatoparaphrenia

Somatoparaphrenia is a condition that sometimes manifests itself after stroke and damage to the right parietal cortex. In somatoparaphrenia the stroke victim may claim that her left arm is not *her* arm, but, for example, belongs to her niece. It seems that she misidentifies her body part, and clearly has a problem with SO for that body part. In this case, however, the question of IEM doesn't actually come up, since the subject has no proprioception for the limb. Patients with spared proprioception do not exhibit somatoparaphrenia (Vallar and Ronchi 2009). Accordingly, the somatoparaphrenic subject's access to the limb is *as object*, and there is no claim made for IEM in such cases; somatoparaphrenia cannot be considered a violation of IEM.

Katerina Fotopoulou (private communication) at the University of London, reports an interesting case that suggests further complications. Fotopoulou has a post-stroke patient with somatoparaphrenia. Her left arm (paralyzed and without proprioception or sensation), she claims, belongs to her grand-daughter. This is her response when she is asked about her arm and made to look at it. But when she is shown her full image in a mirror, and asked about her left arm as it appears in the mir-ror, she correctly identifies it as her own. When asked about her granddaughter's arm she looks down, directly at her left arm. Whenever she looks directly at her arm, she identifies it as her granddaughter's; whenever she looks at it in the mirror she iden-tifies it as her own.[3]

This case suggests that there may be different kinds of percep-tion of body-*as-object*. The difference might be described as the difference between visual perception of the limb in the experien-tial canonical positions (as I usually see my limbs without a mirror), and visual perception of the limb in experiential non-canonical positions, which includes perception in the mirror, which is closer to the way that others perceive my body. Experimental studies show that different brain areas may be responsible for these two different perceptions. Thus one possible explanation is that the area of the parietal cortex damaged by stroke involves (or connects to) an area responsible for registering the experiential canonical limb positions, but not for our perception of non-canonical limb position, or the perception of other's bodies.[4] In neither case, how-ever, is IEM an issue, since both are visual perceptions of the body as-object.

Experiential canonical positions – the positions of my limbs as I usually perceive them – are often associated with the egocentric (body-centered) spatial framework (e.g., Petkova and Ehrsson 2008, emphasize the importance of the egocentric framework in this regard) or first-person perspective (see, e.g., Fotopoulou et al. 2009). On this view, my perception of myself in the mirror would be termed allocentric (object-centered), or third-person. But I think this latter way of expressing it is misleading since all of my perceptions are ordered in the egocentric spatial frame-work (that is, they all have a spatial point of origin in my body), even my perception of my image in the mirror, in the sense that the mirror and the image in the mirror are either in front of me, to my right or to my left, etc. As Merleau-Ponty (1962) makes clear, the allocentric spatial framework is an abstraction from perceived space. If, for example, I visually perceive that object X is to the North of object Y, object X and object Y are still, necessarily located for me in some egocentric framework – X is either to my right or left or in front of me, etc. The egocentric framework applies clearly to the visual, tactile, and olfactory modalities of perception – they all involve a certain direction relative to my body or body part.

This is not the case for proprioception, however. Proprioception does not register in the egocentric framework. The proprioceptive position of my right hand is not relative to my body – it *is* my body's posture; it's not relative to a perceptual point of origin – it is that point of origin (e.g., in the case of haptic perception which involves my right hand touching something else). On the proprioceptive map, and in any experiential canonical position, my left foot isn't closer to me than my right hand (see Gallagher 2003). This may help to explain one difference between seeing my hand in an experiential canonical position and seeing it in the mirror. Seeing my hand in an experiential canonical position normally involves a consistent integration of proprioception in a non-relative, non-egocentric framework (call this the *non-relative bodily framework*) and vision (which operates in the relative, egocentric framework). Seeing my hand in the mirror involves a conflict between these two frameworks; I feel my hand proprioceptively here, but I see it there. In such cases I visually perceive my hand *as object* in egocentric space. To experience oneself *as subject*, in this context, is to experience oneself in the non-relative bodily framework, as the origin of the egocentric spatial framework. I do not, so to speak, make an entrance into this non-relative framework; I *am* it, or I *live* it. The integration of the non-relative bodily framework (the perceptual origin, which involves the complex organization of my body rather than a literal zero point) and the egocentric spatial framework constitutes the first-person perceptual point of view or perspective. This conception of the first-person perspective will help to clarify some of the following cases.

7.3.3 Rubber hand illusion and whole body displacement

Evans' thought experiment about A and B motivates the idea that IEM is *de facto* (i.e., that IEM is contingent rather than absolute). Even if cases of Somatoparaphrenia do not confirm this, it does seem to be reinforced by recent empirical experiments on the rubber hand illusion (e.g., Botvinick and Cohen, 1998; Tsakiris and Haggard 2005), and whole body displacement (in experimental situations, see Lenggenhager et al. 2007); or in out-of-body experiences (see Blanke and Arzy 2005; Blanke et al. 2002), which also place certain limits on passive touch and SO.

In the rubber hand illusion (RHI), you sit at a table with your left hand placed under a cover. A rubber arm-hand is placed on the table in front of you, close to the canonical position of your left hand. Your left hand undergoes passive tactile stimulation (e.g., a brushing of the fingers), and simultaneously you see the similar stimulation of the rubber hand. In short order you start to feel as if the rubber hand is your own, and that is where you feel the stimulation. Your sense of ownership for your body extends into the rubber hand. Does IEM, based on proprioception or passive touch, thereby break down?

Olaf Blanke's experiments with whole body displacement (Lenggenhager et al. 2007) operate on a similar design but are even more dramatic. You wear virtual reality goggles and view the live video of your own back, which is being tactilely stimulated. You thus see your own (virtual) back several feet in front of you being stimulated as you simultaneously feel the tactile sensations on your back. The effect is that you start to feel the tactile stimulation on the virtual body several feet in front of your actual location, and you feel yourself displaced to the location of the virtual body. The same effect can be created when a mannequin is substituted in the video and the tactile stroking of your back and the mannequin's back are simultaneous. The sense of ownership then shifts to the mannequin's body.

To the extent that SO is disrupted or displaced in these experiments, they seem to challenge IEM. But in both kinds of experiments, notice that visual perception of the body comes to dominate the tactile sensation – SO shifts, along with your tactile experience, to where you *see* the stimulus applied. Close your eyes and the effect disappears. If we assume that SO is the result of intersensory coordination of proprioceptive, vestibular, tactile, and visual signals, then, in the experiments the tactile/proprioceptive information is remapped onto the visual – the position of one's own hand, for example, is remapped onto the position of the viewed hand, and the viewed hand feels like one's own.[5] Vision hijacks proprioception and one might argue that in this case we are referring to or identifying ourselves visually *as object,* in a similar way to the mirror example mentioned by Wittgenstein. And yet one's immediate proprioceptive sense of where precisely one's arm is, or where one is being stimulated, is involved, albeit in a distorted way.

One also has to consider the precise situation that the subject is in when she agrees to do the experiment. The subject may in fact alter her perspective from a non-observational one with respect to her body (which may or may not be IEM) to an observational one, where she is reflecting on her body as object (which is definitely not, and is not claimed to be IEM). Anthony Marcel (2003) in a discussion of Anarchic Hand Syndrome – a condition in which one's hand seems to have a mind of its own and engages in intentional actions that the subject does not control due to damage in certain brain areas – notes that

> [T]he pathological condition makes the person an observer of their own action... this suggests that one only has observational knowledge of one's actions in particular states. In the pathological case, it is due to a restriction caused by removal of normal control. In the non-pathological case(s) [as in the experimental conditions], it is by adoption of a certain attentional attitude, namely, by taking a detached stance in inspecting one's proprioceptive feedback. (2003, 87)

Taking an observational or detached stance involves reframing the non-relative proprioceptive bodily perspective so that my body appears as an object in egocentric space. This happens quite easily when our attention is directed towards our body (or body part) rather than towards the task at hand.

On the one hand, to the extent that vision hijacks proprioception, and to the extent that the RHI and full body displacement
experiments put the subject in an observational stance with
regard to the self-as-object, one could argue that IEM is not meant
to apply, and that therefore there is no violation of IEM. On the
other (probably rubber) hand, if we take proprioception to be the
basis of IEM, and my proprioception (hijacked or not) is leading
me astray, then it might seem that IEM fails. In the latter case,
the strategy suggested by Jeannerod and Pacherie is to acknowledge the unusual or experimentally induced nature of these
phenomena, and argue that IEM is *de facto* (or contingent). Even
in this regard it still seems reliable enough for our everyday circumstances. Since in most everyday actions proprioception is not
misled, and SA and SO are not dissociated, and indeed are difficult to distinguish, the anchor of our pre-reflective embodied self-
awareness is relatively stable.

Before considering another type of experiment, it will be help-
ful to take a different look at the rubber hand illusion and to see
how SA modulates SO and produces a more holistic sense of self.
Tsakiris and Haggard (2005) demonstrated that during the RHI
there is a proprioceptive drift toward the rubber hand. That is, the
passively stimulated finger (of one's real hand) was judged to be
significantly closer to the location of the rubber hand than it really
was. But this effect was localized only for the stimulated finger and
not for the whole hand, which suggests a fragmented SO for body
parts. Tsakiris and Haggard then hypothesized that a more holistic body (motor) schema, engaged when in action, and thereby
involving SA, would contribute to a more coherent or holistic SO.
In a further experiment, subjects viewed live video of their hands
under two conditions: when the subject moves his own index finger, and when the subject's index finger is moved by the experi-
menter. In the first case of self-generated movement there is SA;
in the second, passive movement, no SA. Tsakiris and Haggard
show that while the proprioceptive drift in the passive movement is just for the one finger, the drift is for the whole hand in
self-generated movement. They conclude that, 'The active body is
experienced as more coherent and unified than the passive body'
(2005b; see Tsakiris, Bosbach, and Gallagher 2007). Agency and the

corresponding efferent signals involved modulate afferent feedback, and more generally bodily awareness, and thereby modulate the SO for one's actions. In the case of action, SO is integrated into the more holistic body-schematic processes of motor control.

7.3.4 The NASA robot experience

We can take this idea one step further and suggest that in instances when we are engaged in action or in doing some task, and are not attending (observationally) to the body in any explicit way, and when sensory feedback (including proprioception and visual information pertaining to our bodily posture and movement) is attenuated, SO and SA are both holistically integrated and pre-reflectively recessive. Just in such normal cases, when experience of the body is non-observational and pre-reflective, if I happen to be working with certain kinds of equipment, that equipment may be experienced as incorporated into my body schema, and both SO and SA may extend to the equipment. Just as the blind man's cane feels like an extension of his body, as Merleau-Ponty noted, following an observation made by the neurologist Henry Head (see Merleau-Ponty 1962, 143), the carpenter's hammer may also feel as if it were part of the carpenter's body.

Cole, Sacks and Waterman (2000) describe their experiences of controlling robotic arms using virtual reality goggles and gloves at the NASA Space Center. Every move they made with their hands caused the robots hands to move in the identical way, and they were viewing the robotic hands from the robot's perspective (i.e., they saw the robot's arms through the robot's camera eyes). In these circumstances they report that they had an immediate sense that the robot's arms were their own. For the agent who is controlling the robotic arms in this way, both their SO and SA shift to things and movements that do not *objectively* belong the agent's body. One might say that the robotic arms become extensions of the agent's body schema – part of the lived and experienced body-as-subject. If I, as agent, then experience the robotic arm as mine do I commit an error of misidentification?

Here there is a double ambiguity that needs to be resolved to gain a clear answer. First, there is the ambiguity between *experiencing* the robotic arm as mine and *identifying* it as mine. Second there is the ambiguity between what is objectively the case in regard to one's body, and the way that the subject lives the body in action. (a) If I am asked to reflectively judge whether I would identify the robotic arm as objectively part of my body, my answer will likely be 'No, this robotic arm is not part of my body'. Regardless of my answer, however, IEM is not at stake since IEM applies to neither explicit judgments of identification nor the body-as-object. But (b), as in the case of the NASA robot, I may actually experience the robot's arm as part of my (lived) body. In this case IEM is at stake, since it pertains to the subject of experience. When I say, expressing this experience: 'I am [or my arm is] grasping the tool', when it is actually the robotic arm that is grasping the tool, have I not misidentified myself in a way that violates IEM?

To clarify the difference between (a) and (b), which depends on the distinction between *as object* and *as subject*, consider a different kind of case where vision and visual kinaesthesia, override somatic proprioception and generate a sense of self-movement when there is none. Visual kinaesthesia involves visual information generated by my real or apparent movement. The optic flow and visual kinaesthesia that occur when the train next to mine is moving, but when my train is not moving, can lead to the mistaken experience that I (along with my train) am moving, even though I am not moving. If on this basis I say, 'I (rather than the guy in the other train) am moving' one could argue that I have made a mistake about who is moving, or, alternatively, that I am not mistaken about the person I am referring to (I am clearly referring to myself), I am simply mistaken about moving. In either case, however, there is arguably no violation of IEM, since somatic proprioception is not involved (assuming that I am sitting still and not moving my limbs) and the claim of IEM is for somatic proprioception and not for visual kinaesthesia.

This example of the train helps us to stay on track with the Wittgensteinian distinction between *as subject* and *as object*. (a) On the one hand, if in the case of sitting in a train I say, based on visual kinaesthesis, 'I am moving', we could interpret this as a use of the first-person pronoun *as object*, and as an objective claim about my physical state, which is dependent on the state of the train. That is, I am moving if the train is moving. And it is perfectly sensible to ask, 'Someone is moving, is it I?' Just as in the mirror case, I am right or wrong about who has the sunburn depending on certain contingencies with regard to the position of the mirror vis à vis myself, so also, whether in the train I am right or wrong about who is moving depends on certain contingencies with regard to what the train is actually doing. If my train is not moving, I am definitely mistaken about who is moving, but not in violation of IEM. (b) On the other hand, and closer to expressing the actual experience, if I said '*I feel like* I'm moving' (which is the basis for my inference that I'm moving) it seems clear that I am not mistaken about *who* is having the experience (the feeling), even if I were not moving. It would not be sensible to ask, 'Someone is having this experience, is it I?' Returning to the case of the NASA robot, if I say: 'I have the tool in my hand', there are two ways to understand that statement: (a) as a mistaken statement of objective fact where I make an error about whose hand is involved, in which case IEM is not violated since this is a statement about self-as-object. Or (b) as a statement about my experience: '[I feel like] I have the tool in my hand'. But this suggests that the 'I' about whom I am talking is indeed myself, even if objectively speaking the hand to which I refer is the robot's hand. In this case I am not misidentifying myself.

Through all of these examples – Evan's thought experiment about A and B, Somatoparaphrenia, rubber hand illusion, whole body displacement, the NASA robot, the non-moving train – one can still claim for proprioception a *de facto* IEM. For most of our ordinary and everyday experiences and actions, we do have a sense of ownership and a sense of agency that is immune from error through misidentification. Which is to say, our bodily experiences and our actions are in almost all instances directly and reliably anchored to a pre-reflective sense of self. But, as I'll make clear in the next section, the example of the NASA robot suggests that it is possible to make an even stronger claim for IEM.

7.4 First-person perspective

As we've seen, proprioception may be disrupted or distorted by various pathologies and experiments. Likewise, both SO and SA may disappear or be derailed in various instances and to varying degrees. Can we maintain, however, despite such modulations of experience, even in such cases IEM is more than a contingent fact? My experience may lack a proprioceptive dimension, it may lack SA, it may lack SO for a certain limb, or it may mistakenly incorporate SO for a limb that really isn't mine. But even when I'm missing SA for an action that I am generating, or when I'm experiencing a limb that isn't mine as mine, etc., it is still I who am experiencing (even if I am experiencing something in a mistaken way), and it still seems that I cannot be mistaken about that. Accordingly, there must be something more basic than proprioception, SA, or SO in which to anchor IEM.

Pre-reflective self-awareness includes a basic self/non-self discrimination. It also includes a basic sense of mineness for whatever experience I have, even if SO for specific body parts or bodily movements is disrupted. I may lack proprioception for specific parts of my body, I may think that my left hand belongs to someone else (as in Somatoparaphrenia), or my proprioception may be distorted by visual experience, as when under certain conditions I experience the rubber hand as part of my body, or I may even experience my whole body as somehow displaced or alien (in whole body displacement experiments), but in all of these cases I nonetheless have a sense that *I* am experiencing these things. The self-specificity of these experiences is tied to something that survives all of these situations. In regard to bodily experience, what survives (even when proprioception does not) is the non-relative bodily framework that acts as the origin point (or more precisely the complex bodily origin) of the *first-person perspective*, which, in terms of perception and action, is manifested in the integration of the non-relative bodily framework and the egocentric spatial frame of reference.

Indeed, we could say that this first-person perspective is self-specific in a strict sense. Here I follow Legrand and Ruby (2009) in defining self-specificity as (1) exclusive and (2) non-contingent.

> A given self, S, is constituted by a self-specific component C only if C characterizes S exclusively (i.e., C does not characterize non-S) and noncontingently (i.e., changing or losing C would amount to

changing or losing the distinction between S and non-S). (Legrand and Ruby 2009, 272)

On this definition, the first-person perspective that is implicit in all perception is self-specific. The reliability of our bodily self-awareness in this minimal sense is anchored in the non-relative bodily framework that is the point of origin for my first-person perspective on the world. I can never experience anything, even a loss of SA or SO, except from this perspective, since it is pre-reflectively part of the structure of my experience.

On this basis it seems possible to make an even stronger claim about IEM, namely, that even if both SA and SO are disrupted or shifted there is nonetheless something in our self-experience that remains IEM, namely, the embodied, first-person perspective on the world. Indeed, if, as phenomenologists claim, all experience has this pre-reflective structure, then even when I am reflectively aware of myself *as object*, even when I am looking into Wittgenstein's mirror and misidentifying myself *as object*, I am not wrong about who it is that I am misidentifying – I am misidentifying myself. To say it oddly, but precisely: to be able to misidentify myself *as object*, I cannot be misidentifying myself *as subject*.

In this respect, one should not confuse IEM with 'guaranteed self-reference' of the sort argued for by P. F. Strawson (1994). Guaranteed self-reference is tied to the grammatical use of the first-person pronoun. Whoever says 'I' cannot help but refer to himself or herself. Even use of first-person pronoun *as object* cannot be mistaken in this sense. When I look in the mirror and say 'I have a sunburn', I may be wrong about who has a sunburn, but the word 'I' refers to no one other than myself, the speaker – and that's precisely why my judgment is mistaken.

IEM mirrors guaranteed self-reference, so to speak, but is more basic because it is based on the first-person perspective, which is what allows me to generate first-person *as-subject* statements in the first place. IEM is even more pervasive than guaranteed self-reference, since it pertains even to experience that is not expressed using the first-person pronoun. Rather, it pertains to any experience that involves the first-person perspective – which arguably includes all of my experiences. When I see the sunburned arm in the mirror, and mistakenly say 'I am sunburned', not only does the 'I' not refer to anyone other than myself for reasons pertaining to guaranteed self-reference, but it refers to myself as a subject who is more than the speaker since I also occupy the first-person perspective of the person who sees the arm in the mirror, even as I mistakenly attribute something to myself *as object*. This first-person perspective anchors me unmistakably to myself and underwrites my pre-reflective awareness of myself as subject. I'm not wrong about *who* it is to whom I attribute the sunburn; I attribute it to myself, and it is precisely for that reason that I make a mistake. But that is a mistake about who has the sunburn; it is not a mistake about who is making the (incorrect) attribution, or who is having the experience of looking in the mirror. I am not only the person who is using the first-person pronoun, but also, and more basically, I am the person who is looking in the mirror – I am the percei*ver*, even if I am not the percei*ved* in this case. To *be* is clearly more than to be perceived (the self as-object); it is to be the perceiver (the self as-subject), and this is more than being just the speaker who uses the first-person pronoun. I can only identity or misidentify myself-as-object, because I (as the one who perceives, or acts, or judges) can never misidentify myself-as-subject, and in any case where I do identify or misidentify myself-as-object, I am always acting and experiencing, and making the misidentification, as-subject. This makes IEM more than simply *de facto*.[6]

This also gives us a different answer to Evans' thought experiment which links A's body to B's proprioceptive information. A states that his legs are crossed and supposedly misidentifies himself, since it's really B's legs that are crossed. In this case, however, the claim that A misidentifies himself on the basis of proprioception is based on objective considerations about what constitutes the identity of A's body. That is, objectively speaking, we distinguish between A's body and B's body. But from the first-person perspective, that is, as A experiences it, this distinction doesn't hold. In the non-relative bodily framework, and from A's first-person perspective, the body in question is A's lived body – the body that A experiences proprioceptively, regardless of whether proprioception delivers veridical objective knowledge about bodily position. The lived body, as phenomenologists like Husserl and

Merleau-Ponty understand it, can include things like phantom limbs (which one might say are not objectively there), and can incorporate things into its body schema like the blind man's cane or rubber hands or robotic arms, which are not objectively part of the body. The body, as experienced or lived from the first-person perspective, can extend into the environment, in a way that the objective body cannot. Objectively it makes sense to say that A's body does not include B's legs. Once we re-engineer A's proprioceptive system to incorporate B's legs (or more generally, B's body), however, then the problem of A saying 'my legs are crossed' when the reference is to B's legs, is not a problem of misidentification. A is precisely in a relation to B's legs in which A does *not* have to identify them in order to say they are crossed. And this, as we know from Shoemaker (1984), is just what characterizes IEM. That is, in such cases, we are immune to error through misidentification not because we are so good at identifying ourselves, but because no process of identification is involved.

Is it a complication for this strong claim about IEM that the first-person perspectival source itself can shift? This is said to be what happens in an experiment on body swapping reported by Petkova and Ehrsson (2008). In this experiment the subject wears VR goggles and sees the image projected by a video camera that is worn headtop by another person who is standing facing the subject. The video image, which the subject sees, is a frontal view of the subject himself. When the subject reaches out to shake hands with the other person, the experience is one of shaking hands with himself, notably accompanied by a felt shift of perspective.

> In the present illusions, the visual, tactile, proprioceptive information and the predicted sensory feedback from these modalities during active movements were temporally and spatially congruent in an ego-centric reference frame centred on a new body. Thus, the matching of multisensory and motor signals from the [shifted] first person perspective is sufficient to create a full sense of ownership of one's own entire body. (Petkova and Ehrsson 2008, 6)

Does the fact that the first-person perspectival source can 'travel' have implications for the strong claim of IEM?

In some regard the NASA robot experiment is a clear example of this. If, for example, I mistakenly say 'I am sitting in front of a table' and I'm wrong about that because I'm actually looking through virtual goggles and I'm seeing the table from the perspective of the robot, am I misidentifying myself? It is clearly I (as the perceiving subject) who am experiencing this. My visual perspective has been technologically shifted (and perhaps has taken my proprioceptive sense with it) – but that perspective is still mine – even if it no longer (objectively) coincides with the canonical perspective of my bodily location – and even if what I experience I experience, as subject, from that shifted perspective. The 'I' refers to that subject, who I am, and whose experience is in that perspective.

Let's consider one final case in which the link between IEM and first-person perspective is seriously challenged. The case, involving anonymous vision, is reported by Zahn, Talazko and Ebert (2008). They describe a disorder with selective loss of the sense of self-ownership specifically for visual perception of objects. Notably, the subject (DP, a 23 year old male) has an intact SO in the proprioceptive domain and an intact sense of self-agency. DP's initial complaint was that he had 'double visions', the onset of which followed a long overseas flight after a holiday during which he engaged in ocean diving. Examination revealed that he did not literally have double vision, i.e., he did not see objects in double. Rather he described a two-step process involved in seeing.

> When looking at or concentrating on a new visual object, he is able to see the object as a single object, but...the way he perceived had markedly changed in a way which he had never experienced before. It appeared to him that he was able to see everything normally but that he did not immediately recognize that he was the one who perceives and that he needed a second step to become aware that he himself was the one who perceives the object. (Zahn et al. 2008, 398)

Despite this problem with vision, DP reports no problems with action; his actions feel no different from normal and he is immediately aware that he is acting. SA for actions remains intact, and he needs no second step to identify himself as the agent of his actions. Moreover, even as his visual perception of objects is problematic in the sense just explained, his perception of other people and their movements are normal, as are his social interactions and communications. He shows no schizophrenic signs and has never manifested psychiatric or medical conditions. Imaging studies showed abnormal (hypometabolic) functioning in inferior temporal, parieto-occipital and precentral regions. Standard neuropsychological testing showed nothing abnormal; the researchers excluded attention and executive deficits using reactive cognitive flexibility and divided attention subtests from the Test Battery for Attentional Performance and other tests.

Zahn et al. claim that this case challenges IEM because DP's access to his first-person experience is not direct or non-observational. It seems that DP is sensibly able to ask the Wittgensteinian nonsensical question: 'Someone is seeing this object, is it I?' As far as we know, however, in every case where the correct answer is 'yes', DP answers that question in the affirmative. Even if his sense of ownership for vision depends on reflective introspection and he actually has to make a judgment about the identity of the seeing subject, he so far has not made an error of misidentification. The fact that he has to make a judgment at all, however, is an issue. As Shoemaker explains, when we are required to make a judgment of identification we implicitly or explicitly appeal to criteria. One question in DP's case concerns what criteria he uses to make the correct judgment. That is, why does he answer the question in the affirmative? What aspects of his experience does he consider in order to answer the question? This is not clear from Zahn et al.'s report; and it may not be clear to DP.

Is it possible that just this issue of how the reflective judgment is made could defeat the threat to IEM? Zahn et al. resist this suggestion. If a critic suggests that for DP self-ownership is simply delayed but still intact, Zahn et al. rightly note that DP's reversion to reflective judgment is simply not the way that IEM is supposed to work. For clarity, however, let's set the question of self-ownership aside. As we've seen, the critical factor for IEM is not SO (or SA, or even proprioception), but the first-person perspective. Tim Lane (2012), in a recent paper, makes it clear that this is just what is at stake in the case of DP. Lane suggests that when DP sees an object the seeing is not anchored in the first-person perspective. But this is *not* at all clear. That is, it is not clear that DP's vision is a free-floating, non-positional seeing. If DP's vision of the object is literally the view of no one, this does not mean that it is a view from nowhere; it is of necessity (i.e., it is part of the essence of vision to be) perspectivally situated, and this may be the very thing that allows DP to *judge* it to be *his* view. Indeed, we could easily predict, as Shoemaker would predict regarding DP's introspection, that DP will never make a mistake in this regard since it is never the case that he finds himself having someone else's visual experience.

One might object that perspective may be non-conscious. In cases of non-conscious visual perception, for example, the vision is still determined by the perspectival orientation of the perceiving mechanism. I'm thinking here not only of masked priming effects, where a timely subsequent stimulus masks an earlier one, but of the relatively rich (but non-conscious) information provided by the dorsal visual system for motor control which necessarily includes information about where the object is located vis à vis one's potential reach, for example. Now someone may want to say that if the perspective of DP's vision is non-conscious then it is hardly a 'first-person' perspective – perhaps it would be better to say that it is sub-personal. But this is clearly not the case for DP since the vision he describes is conscious vision. DP does not describe, for example, a case of blindsight, that is, a case where damage to the visual cortex causes blindness but where some non-conscious visual information can still inform the subject's choices and behavior. He does not complain that he does not see. Indeed, to make the kind of judgment he makes about it being *his* vision, the vision must be conscious. To say that his vision is conscious and perspectivally situated (i.e., DP consciously sees the object from a certain spatial perspective) implies that there is an embodied perceptual origin, and that the object appears in an egocentric spatial frame of reference. Everything that anyone would want for there to be a first-person perspective is present in DPs vision. That seems to go with the idea that a first-person perspective is built into the very structure of perception, and that there can be no perception from nowhere.

If it's not a problem with first-person perspective, however, what explains DP's experience? One possibility is that the problem is on the level of reflective introspection or report. There are some instances in which first-order pre-reflective experience remains intact, but reflective processes break down and interfere with the subject's ability to report that first-order experience. Anthony Marcel's experiments on the speed and mode of report of visual perceptual experience, for example, shows that a perceiving subject may have a veridical visual perception but may be unable to provide a veridical report of it, or may provide contradictory reports, e.g., that he did see something and simultaneously that he did not see it (Marcel 1993). One mode of reflective report may in fact mask the perception while the other confirms it. Another example is the hyperreflection that sometimes accompanies schizophrenic alien experiences (Sass and Parnas 2003). An overly reflective, and sometimes obsessive attention to aspects of experience that usually remain tacit or recessive introduces a distorted and alien sense for those processes. Indeed, this kind of distortion may be involved in or lead to delusions of control.

Zahn et al. screened DP for schizophrenia and ruled that out. More generally, however, the likelihood that DP's problem is somehow to be located at the level of first-order, first-person perspective is no greater than that it is a problem with reflective processes.[7] His description, which was first expressed in terms of double vision, ends up being somewhat neutral between these two possibilities. It is explicated in terms of a two-step process – visual perception plus reflective self-identification. But if it is difficult to conceive of a conscious visual perception lacking a first-person perspective (it's not clear what that would look like, and there is no description provided by DP in Zahn et al.), it is not so difficult to conceive of a reflective process that can interfere with first-order experience to the point that it might seem ambiguous in regard to being the subject's experience, although that same reflection cannot avoid judging (in contrast to the schizophrenic) that it can be no one else's. On this interpretation, although the subject comes to think of the question, 'Someone is seeing the object, is it I?' as a sensible one, it's only because his reflective cognition leads him in that direction, and away from what remains implicit in his first-person perspective, and that, regardless of everything, manifests itself every time he correctly judges that it is indeed his perception.

Another way to look at this is that DP doesn't select a set of visual object perceptions among a large variety of such experiences that belong perhaps to others or perhaps to himself. Standing next to me, he doesn't pick out my visual experience as a possible candidate for his own. He, quite normally, like Hume and the rest of us, finds only his own visual experiences available, characterized already and without exception as experiences from a first-person perspective. That should be the end of the story since we do not normally, in contrast to DP, initiate a reflection to ascertain whether such experiences are our own. What's different in DP's case is that he does initiate a reflection in which he attempts to identify such experiences as his own. The researchers have not ruled out the possibility that the problem is just with the fact that this unnecessary but consistently veridical reflection introduces a second step that masks and then correctly verifies the first-person perspective implicit in his visual object perception.

The view that the true anchor for IEM is the self-specific first-person perspective that characterizes every experience is clearly challenged by the case of DP and by the possibility of shifting perspectives in the body swapping experiment. I think the jury is still out with regard to the case of DP (we need more evidence), but there is at least one reasonable interpretation that leaves IEM intact even in that case, namely that it is just as likely a problem with reflective introspection as with the first-person perspective of first-order experience. In regard to the shifting perspectives experiment, it seems that IEM is rigorous enough to follow wherever the first-person perspective leads.

7.5   Further reading

Sartre (1957) criticizes Husserl's concept of the transcendental ego and argues for a non-egological conception of consciousness. Henry (1973) gives a detailed phenomenological account of the ego and its self-constitution in passive auto-affection. Zahavi (2005) provides a comprehensive look at different conceptions

of the self in phenomenology. Carr (1999) defends phenomenological accounts against both post-structuralist and scientistic
conceptions. Crowell (2001b) discusses the concept of first-person
subjectivity in Heidegger. Gallagher (2011c) contains essays by
Legrand, Thompson, and Zahavi that explore the phenomenological conceptions of self.

8 Lifeworld, Action, Narrative

Considerations about the senses of ownership and agency in regard to the embodied minimal aspects of self are only a small part of a larger story. The sense of agency, and action itself, scale up to more narrative aspects of self and into realms that are better described in terms of intentions, reasons for acting, freedom and responsibility. Narratives about ourselves and others are not about the minimal dimensions of perceptual experience, the pre-reflective details of motor control, or the elemental or integrative timescales of milleseconds or seconds. They are about actions and events that occur over time and in the larger contexts of the world.

8.1 The lifeworld

The world in which we act is something more than the physical environment in which we move around. The world is a set of experienced meaningful contexts that are irreducible to the purely physical objects that surround us. The 'world of immediate experience', the world 'already there', 'pregiven', the world as experienced in our everyday and natural attitude, is what Husserl calls the 'lifeworld' (*Lebenswelt*). There are two things to note about Husserl's characterization of the lifeworld. First, it retains the somewhat intellectualist character of his early conception of act-intentionality, although Husserl is always pointing towards something like a non-intellectual, more pragmatic relation with the world. Here are some of Husserl's intellectualist descriptions: we are 'conscious of the world as universal horizon'; the world is 'valid for our consciousness'; the world is 'pre-given with ontic meaning'. This last phrase, however, starts to point to the non-intellectual aspects. The lifeworld is not 'given' to consciousness, but 'pre-given'. For Husserl, a perceived object is 'given' to consciousness – it appears at the end point of a relation of noetic intentionality. The lifeworld, however, is pre-given – it's there before you know it, prenoetically. It's always and already there for you as a horizon in which things are given. The non-intellectualist, more pragmatic aspects are expressed as follows: we 'belong to the world'; in which we are 'constantly active on the basis of our passive having of the world'.

Second, Husserl emphasizes the fact that we are in this together – that being in the lifeworld is always a matter of being in a world with others – 'all of us together' are in the lifeworld. For Husserl, the world is intersubjectively constituted in its meaning. In the next chapter we will see how the objectivity of the world depends on an open or transcendental intersubjectivity. For now we can note that the lifeworld exhibits certain pervading structures and normative styles which derive from specific social and cultural arrangements and which can be studied phenomenologically. We can discover universal features of the lifeworld, but also identify certain features in the lifeworld that are culturally determined.[1]

The more pragmatic aspects of the lifeworld are distinguished from any theoretical attitude we might take towards life; the lifeworld involves our pre-theoretical attitude to life – our un-contemplated life of action, which turns out to be the life on which all theorizing is based and from which all theorizing is ultimately derived. When we do science, for example, we do it as a scientist (along with other scientists) with two feet firmly planted in the lifeworld. Yet, the world as science explains it is not the lifeworld. It's the world of particles, atoms, molecules, or it's the world of stars and distances and events that we never see or experience, and find it difficult even to conceive. The scientific world is a theory about the world – in the same way that metaphysics offers theories about the world. But before we try to explain the world in any kind of theoretical fashion, we are living in the world.

One way to understand the difference between the lifeworld and the 'true' world as portrayed in science, is to think about Eddington's tables. Arthur Eddington, a well-known physicist, delivered the Gifford Lectures at the University of Edinburgh in 1927. At the beginning of the lecture he gave the following example. His own words best describe it, so I include them here as a longish quote.

I have settled down to the task of writing these lectures and have drawn up my chairs to my two tables. Two tables! Yes; there are duplicates of every object about me – two tables, two chairs, two pens. This is not a very profound beginning to a course which ought to reach transcendent levels of scientific philosophy. But we cannot touch bedrock immediately; we must scratch a bit at the surface of things first. And whenever I begin to scratch the first thing I strike is my two tables.

One of them has been familiar to me from earliest years. It is a commonplace object of that environment which I call the world. How shall I describe it? It has extension; it is comparatively permanent; it is coloured; above all it is substantial. By substantial I do not merely mean that it does not collapse when I lean upon it; I mean that it is constituted of 'substance'.... I do not think substantiality can be described better than by saying that it is the kind of nature exemplified by an ordinary table. And so we go round in circles. After all if you are a plain commonsense man, not too much worried with scientific scruples, you will be confident that you understand the nature of an ordinary table....

Table No. 2 is my scientific table. It is a more recent acquaintance and I do not feel so familiar with it. It does not belong to the world previously mentioned, that world which spontaneously appears around me when I open my eyes, though how much of it is objective and how much subjective I do not here consider. It is part of a world which in more devious ways has forced itself on my attention. My scientific table is mostly emptiness. Sparsely scattered in that emptiness are numerous electric charges rushing about with great speed; but their combined bulk amounts to less than a billionth of the bulk of the table itself. Notwithstanding its strange construction it turns out to be an entirely efficient table. It supports my writing paper as satisfactorily as table No. 1; for when I lay the paper on it the little electric particles with their headlong speed keep on hitting the underside, so that the paper is maintained in shuttlecock fashion at a nearly steady level. If I lean upon this table I shall not go through; or, to be strictly accurate, the chance of my scientific elbow going through my scientific table is so excessively small that it can be neglected in practical life.

Reviewing their properties one by one, there seems to be nothing to choose between the two tables for ordinary purposes; but when abnormal circumstances befall, then my scientific table shows to advantage. If the house catches fire my scientific table will dissolve quite naturally into scientific smoke, whereas my familiar table undergoes a metamorphosis of its substantial nature which I can only regard as miraculous. There is nothing substantial about my second table. It is nearly all empty space – space pervaded, it is true, by fields of force, but these are assigned to the category of 'influences', not of 'things'. (Eddington 1927, ix–x)

There are two important points to take from Eddington's descriptions. First, Husserl would be happy with the distinction between the first table and the second, as reflecting the difference between the lifeworld and the scientific world. But we can start to see some complications that Husserl saw, and that perhaps Eddington did not see. The complications have to do with the latter's characterization of the first table as 'substantial', and his description of what that means. The idea that the table is constituted as a substance is surely a piece of metaphysical theory. There is a sense in which I do, in my everyday life, think of the table as something substantial. To the extent that this metaphysical concept (which certainly goes back to Aristotle) has more or less invaded commonsense notions of the world, then that piece of metaphysical theory has invaded my lifeworld – the world that I live in pre-theoretically. But then, the same can be said of scientific theory, although this seems less likely in regard to the table. That is, I might become so familiar with science that I start to think of the table, even in my everyday pre-theoretical attitude towards it, as something composed mostly of space, or as something composed of atoms, particles, and forces.

We can borrow a phrase from Habermas, who uses Husserl's concept of lifeworld to talk about certain social ideas – although we'll bracket the social issues for now. Habermas talks about the 'colonization of the lifeworld'. The lifeworld is sometimes invaded and taken over by certain systems and concepts that don't actually belong to the lifeworld – but then, to the extent that the lifeworld is colonized in this way, these concepts actually find a place in it. One can perhaps find better examples than the table, since most of us don't go around thinking about tables as processes composed of atoms. A good example might be the way we think of depression. A hundred years ago people thought about depression as melencolia – a kind of prolonged mood that some people get into. Today, although in the lifeworld we encounter depression in this same way – i.e., in terms of people being in certain depressed states – we may also think of depression in scientific terms as a kind of illness that involves serotonin levels in the brain. That's a scientific way of thinking about depression, even if we don't think of serotonin in its chemical terms as 5-Hydroxytryptamine (5-HT). Ever since Prozac, scientifically educated cultures have been familiar with serotonin receptor reuptake inhibitors (SRRIs), and this way of thinking about depression has more or less invaded the lifeworld. Whether this scientific way of thinking about depression is correct or not, that's a different question.

Even if certain aspects of scientific explanations invade the lifeworld, we should note that, for Husserl, the scientific world is actually the result of a kind of abstraction from the lifeworld. At the same time, we can see another relation between lifeworld and science. Husserl suggests not only that scientific conceptions can invade the lifeworld, while still being abstractions from the lifeworld, but also that scientific theories appear as cultural objects in the lifeworld. Thus,

> we become aware that we scientists are, after all, human beings and as such are among the components of the life-world which always exists for us, ever pre-given; and thus all of science is pulled, along with us, into the merely 'subjective relative' life world... [Scientific theories as] logical constructs, are of course not things in the life-world like stones, houses, or trees. They are logical wholes and logical parts made up of ultimate logical elements... But this... ideality does not change in the least the fact that they are human formations, essentially related to human actualities and potentialities, and thus belong to this concrete unity of

the life-world, whose concreteness thus extends further than that of 'things'. (1970, 130)

The second thing that we should notice about the two tables is that really there are three tables. Very much like Husserl's concept of the lifeworld, Eddington only hints at the third table, when he mentions practical life.

1st table: call it Husserl's lifeworld table: described as 'a commonplace object of that environment which I call the world. How shall I describe it? It has extension; it is comparatively permanent; it is coloured; above all it is substantial.' Eddington could have simply gone back to Descartes to find such a description. The first table is the one that we take as a commonsense object – a piece of furniture in the world.

2nd table: call it Eddington's scientific table: The table described in scientific terms – somewhat removed from the lifeworld.

3rd table: call it Heidegger's table: this is actually the table that we see when we first walk into the room looking for a place to write our lecture. It goes along with the chair that we see as a place to sit. That is, our primary encounter with the table is not as an object with extension, color, and substance, but as something that offers practical opportunities – as something that indicates a place to sit and write, or to sit and eat, etc.

8.2 Turning the tables

Heidegger published *Being and Time* the same year Eddington gave his Gifford lectures. As Heidegger makes clear in that work, the third table is actually the primary sense of table. You discover this table when you walk into a room and see a table and chair. What do you see? Heidegger suggests that you don't see them as two *objects* – a table and a chair positioned in geometrical proximity. You don't see them in a contemplative manner, where you start thinking about them as such. Rather, you see the table and chair in a pragmatic way. Moreover, you see them in one way if you are looking for a surface to write upon, or a place to put something down, but you see them in a different way if you need something for the blockade you are building outside on the street. That is, our primary way of encountering the table and chair is not to encounter them as objects with extension, color, and substance, but in terms of a situation that offers practical opportunities – as things I can sit and write on, or as things that I can use to bolster my defenses.

The chair, the table, the various things and instruments that we find in our environment have a certain kind of being in relation to us. They are, Heidegger says, ready-to-hand (*Zuhanden*). The particular relation that we have to them, moreover, characterizes our way of being-in-the-world. Our relation to the world around us is primarily this kind of pragmatic relation. We are in the world in such a way that we are grabbing things before we know it; picking them up to use them; arranging them so that we can sit or lean on them. Indeed, we design a built environment, and we dwell in such an environment, and we see the world in such ways because we tend to always be involved in some project or other.

Heidegger distinguishes this primary way of being in-the-world, where things are ready-to-hand, from what he thinks is a secondary or derivative mode of being that we attribute to things, which he calls 'present-at-hand' (*Vorhanden*). When we take the table or chair, not as a practical instrument to use, but rather as an object to be explained, by metaphysics or by science, for instance, we are treating it as an object present-at-hand. Heidegger uses the example of a hammer to clarify the distinction. If you happen to be a carpenter making something, you reach for your hammer and start hammering. As you hammer you might be thinking about going out to the beach next weekend with your friends. Or you might be planning a trip to the museum to see a new exhibit. In any case, you are not thinking about the hammer. You're using the hammer in such a way that the hammer is not an object for you. Perhaps you are focused on the design of what you are building. You put the hammer down, line something up, pick up the hammer again and drive a nail with one swift swing. For you the hammer is ready-to-hand. What happens, however, if the hammer suddenly breaks? Perhaps the head comes off, or the handle splits. Something goes wrong. Now you start looking at the hammer trying to figure out what the problem is. Now the hammer is no longer ready-to-hand; it has turned into something Heidegger calls 'unready-to-hand'. Even more abstractly we can consider the hammer as something present-at-hand, as a mere object or substantial thing that is unusable.

The world that you live in is first of all, in terms of how you experience, how you live in it, a network of ready-to-hand entities. Heidegger calls this a network of involvement. One thing is connected with another; one thing refers to another. The hammer involves nails to drive; the nails hold together the frame you just built; the frame holds the painting which you've just hung on the wall; the wall is part of a house you live in. This network of things that you use also points to the involvement of other people – the person who created the painting, the person who built the house, the landlord, the carpenter who fixes it, and so on. The world hangs together in these practical meanings, and all of these involvements come back to you as an agent who is pragmatically engaged with the things that you see around you. Dasein *has* a world, or is in-the-world, in the sense that the world is disclosed in perception and action in a meaningful way.

One of the curious aspects of the ready-to-hand is that it withdraws. In other words, we tend not to notice such things – we don't think about them – as tools or instruments, or things. We just pick them up and use them. When we walk into the room, we just sit down in our chairs and start writing at the table, without having to consider that this is a chair or this is a table. In other words, we don't have to have a theory about what a chair is before we can sit down.

Heidegger argues that this primary or primordial way of being-in-the-world is missed when we treat things theoretically. But that's precisely what philosophy has always done, and explicitly so. If we ask Plato, or Aristotle, or a modern metaphysician like Descartes or Locke, what is the best form of knowledge to have, the consistent answer will be theoretical knowledge (*theoria*). Aristotle is very explicit about this; for him, practical knowledge is second best, and *techne* (technical knowledge) is the lowest kind of knowledge to have. Heidegger challenges this idea with respect to his larger project of trying to answer the question of Being. In other words, metaphysics has always started with things understood as present-at-hand and treated that as fundamental. Heidegger challenges this phenomenologically – that is, simply by looking at the way that we do experience the world. This has implications for how we understand nature, for example.

> Hammer, tongs, and needle, refer in themselves to steel, iron, metal, mineral, wood, in that they consist of these. In equipment that is used, 'Nature' is discovered along with it by that use – the 'Nature' we find in natural products. Here, however, 'Nature' is not to be understood as that which is just present-at-hand, nor as the power of Nature. The wood is a forest of timber, the mountain a quarry of rock; the river is water-power, the wind is wind 'in the sails'. As the 'environment' is discovered, the 'Nature' thus discovered is encountered too. If its kind of Being as ready-to-hand is disregarded, this 'Nature' itself can be discovered and defined simply in its pure presence-at-hand. But when this happens, the Nature which 'stirs and strives', which assails us and enthralls us as landscape, remains hidden. The botanist's [i.e., theorist's] plants are not the flowers of the hedgerow; the 'source' which the geographer establishes for a river is not the 'springhead in the dale'. (1962, §15)

Heidegger goes a bit poetic at the end of this passage, and this portends his later philosophy where there is something of a re-thinking about how much our ready-to-hand attitude (or way of being) should be treated as primordial (see especially Heidegger 1993).

Heidegger's analysis of the priority of pragmatic engagement in our everyday understanding of the world has been taken up by the American philosopher Hubert Dreyfus (1991; 1992). Dreyfus draws from Heidegger's analysis implications for the possibility (or impossibility) of developing artificial intelligence, and for an understanding of what constitutes expertise. In regard to AI, for example, he suggests that standard computational-programming approaches to AI would not be able to capture the ready-to-hand aspect of how we understand and act in the world. Rather it would only be able to treat the world as a collection of present-at-hand entities. Accordingly, AI, or, for example, any robot that would be designed using standard AI principles, would never be able to have a pragmatic grasp on the world. For this critique Dreyfus also draws on Merleau-Ponty's phenomenology of embodiment, and he further offers an account of expertise not as an intellectual capacity – where we intellectually understand what to do – but as a pragmatic capacity. We have expertise in the way that we proficiently can engage with the world as a network of ready-to-hand involvements. Being-in-the-world means, for the most part, being-in-the-flow.

Heidegger's table is one that Husserl and Eddington only hint at when they hint at the pragmatic or practical. Later, around the mid-20th century, the psychologist J. J. Gibson (who was influenced by Merleau-Ponty, who in turn was influenced by Husserl and Heidegger) described this feature of the practicality of things under the concept of 'affordance'. We perceive the world as a set or series of affordances – the chair affords sitting; the table affords writing, etc. This, he suggests, is actually how we perceive the world – we don't perceive the world as a set of objects with certain properties that allow us to infer use-value; we perceive it as a set of affordances that we can act upon. Earlier I suggested that this is one way that we might understand the concept of noema (Chapter 4). In that case, perception is, at least in most cases, action-oriented. As we've seen, contemporary philosophical discussions of enactive perception and intentionality derive from and build on this view.

8.3 Action and agency

What we defined as the sense of agency (Chapter 7), at the pre-reflective level, is either enhanced or diminished by the fact that action is characterized in terms of a higher-order intentionality. The sense of agency is, in fact, phenomenologically complex, involving different levels of experience, from the basic aspects of sensory-motor processing to the higher levels of intention formation and retrospective judgment.

The idea that the sense of self-agency (SA) is pre-reflective means that it is neither equivalent to nor dependent on the agent taking an introspective reflective attitude. Nor does it require the agent to engage in an explicit perceptual monitoring of bodily movements. Just as I do not attend to the details of my own bodily movements as I am engaged in action, my sense of agency is not normally something that I attend to or something of which I am explicitly aware. As such, SA is phenomenologically recessive.

If we are thinking of action as physical, embodied action that involves self-generated movement, then motor control processes are necessarily involved. The most basic of these are efferent brain processes involved in issuing motor commands. Sensory suppression experiments suggest that SA arises at an early efferent stage in the initiation of action and that awareness of the initiation of my own action depends on efferent signals, which precede actual bodily movement (Tsakiris and Haggard 2003). Experiments with subjects who lack proprioception but still experience a sense of effort reinforce this conclusion (Lafargue, Paillard, Lamarre and Sirigu 2003; see Marcel 2003).

This pre-reflective SA does not arise simply when I initiate an action; as I continue to control my action, continuing efferent signals, and the kind of afferent feedback that I get from my movement, contribute to an ongoing SA. To the extent that I am aware of my action, however, I tend to be aware of what I am doing rather than the details of how I am doing it, e.g., what muscles I am using. Even my recessive awareness of my action is struck at the most pragmatic level of description (e.g., 'I'm getting a drink') rather than at a level of motor control mechanisms. That is, the phenomenal experience of my action already involves an intentional aspect. Body-schematic processes and basic bodily movements involved in what I am trying to accomplish in the world take their meaning from my intentions and are constrained thereby.

The intentional aspects of what I am trying to do and what I actually accomplish in the world enter into (reinforcing or diminishing, depending on my success) SA. This is clear phenomenologically, but is also verified by brain experiments that help to distinguish between the purely motor control contributories (the sense that I am moving my body) and the most immediate and perception-based intentional aspects of action (the sense that I am having an effect on my immediate environment) (see Tsakiris, Bosbach and Gallagher 2007 for summary).

Over and above the sensory-motor processes that involve motor control and the perceptual processes that allow us to monitor and guide the intentional aspects of our actions (corresponding to motor intentions and intentions-in-action, respectively), there are higher-order cognitive components involving intention formation that contribute to SA. Pacherie (2007; and others like Bratman 1987 and Searle 1983) distinguish between future (F-) intentions and present (P-) intentions. F-intentions relate to prior deliberation processes that allow us to formulate our relatively long-term goals. For example, I may decide (form my intention) to purchase a car tomorrow (or next week, or next month, or at some undetermined time). At the appropriate time I may then go out and engage in that action. Not all actions involve prior intention formation, however. For example, I may decide right now to get a drink from the kitchen and find myself already moving in that direction. In that case I have not formed an F-intention, although my action is certainly intentional. In that case, my intention (P-intention) is in my ongoing action (what Searle calls an 'intention-in-action'). My P-intention to get a drink from the kitchen may involve an actual decision to get up and to move in the direction of the kitchen – and in doing so I may be monitoring what I am doing in an explicitly conscious way. It may be a rather complex action. At my university office the kitchen is located down the hall and it is locked in the evening. If I want to get a drink I have to walk up the hall, retrieve the key for the kitchen from a common room, and then proceed back down to the kitchen, unlock the door, retrieve the drink, relock the door, return the key and return to my office. Although I may be thinking of other things as I do this, I am also monitoring a set of steps that are not automatic.

In other cases I may be so immersed in my work that I don't even notice that I'm reaching for the glass of water on the table next to me. In such cases, I would still have a minimal SA, consisting of the pre-reflective sense generated in motor control processes and a rather recessive intentional aspect (which I may only notice if I knock over the glass or spill the drink). In such cases there is still what Merleau-Ponty calls motor intentionality or what Pacherie calls an M-intention.

It is likely that when there is an F- and/or P-intention involved, such intentions generate a stronger SA. Certainly, if I form an F-intention to buy a new car tomorrow, and tomorrow I go to the car dealership and purchase a car, I will feel more in charge of my life than if, without prior intention I simply find myself lured into a car dealership by a red Mustang convertible, and purchasing the car without prior planning. In the latter case, even if I do not deny that I am the agent of my action, I might feel a bit out of control. So, it seems clear that part of the phenomenology of agency may be tied, in some cases, to the formation of a prior intention. We should distinguish, however, between the cognitive level of intention formation – which may involve making judgments and decisions based on beliefs, desires, or evaluations, such elements that can fit into a narrative account of what we are doing or are planning to do – and a first-order level of experience where we find the pre-reflective SA. SA is not itself a judgment, although I may judge that I am the agent of a certain action based on my sense of agency for it. But what is clear is that intention formation may generate a stronger SA than would exist without the formation of F- or P-intentions.

The effect of the formation of a prior intention is clearly prospective. But there are also post-action processes that can have a retrospective effect on the sense of agency. Graham and Stephens (1994; Stephens and Graham 2000) distinguish between two kinds of self-attribution.

> *Attributions of subjectivity*: where the subject reflectively realizes and is able to report that he is moving. For example, he can say, 'This is my body that is moving'.
>
> *Attributions of agency*: where the agent reflectively realizes and is able to report that he is the cause or author of his movement. For example, he can say 'I am causing this action'.

According to Graham and Stephens SA originates at this higher-order level of attribution. They propose an explanation of SA in terms of 'our proclivity for constructing self-referential narratives' which allow us to explain our behavior retrospectively: 'such explanations amount to a sort of theory of the person's agency or intentional psychology' (1994, 101; Stephens and Graham 2000, 161).

In that case, whether I take myself to be the agent of some action 'depends upon whether I take the occurrence of [the action] to be explicable in terms of my underlying intentional states' (1994, 93). On this view SA for a particular action depends on whether I can reflectively explain my action in terms of my beliefs, desires, and intentions. Accordingly, whether I count something as my action 'depends upon whether I take myself to have beliefs and desires of the sort that would rationalize its occurrence in me (1994, 102).

From a phenomenological perspective, this reflective, retrospective and overly rational view does not provide the best explanation of SA since it does not account for the contribution of pre-reflective, motoric and intentional aspects of action. Yet it does seem right to suggest that, together with the prospective, motoric, and intentional aspects, a retrospective awareness of what we have done and an ability to attribute action to ourselves can further reinforce SA and contribute to a sense of responsibility for action. The prospective and retrospective contributories to SA – such is the stuff that carries action into the narrative scale while it is still firmly grounded on the elementary scale of motor control processes and the integrative scale of intentional performance.

8.4 The narrative scale

One's own sense of self and personal identity over time is something that goes well beyond the concept of minimal self. We surely think and speak of ourselves as entities extended in time. It is undeniable that we have memories, form intentions, and make plans, and that there is continuity between our past and our future. Hume (1739) famously suggested that the self consists of a bundle of momentary impressions that are strung together by the imagination. On his view an extended self is simply a fiction, albeit a useful one because it lends a practical sense of continuity to life, but a fiction nonetheless. Several narrative theories of self read it this way. Dennett (1991), for example, offers a theory of the narrative self that seems consistent with the Humean view, and consistent with the current scientific understanding of how the brain functions. Neurological processing, for the most part, is distributed across various brain regions, and it cannot be said that there is a real, neurological center of experience. Thus, Dennett concludes, there is no real simplicity of experience at one time nor real identity across time that we could label the self. At best, we might refer to a minimal biological self as something real. But the latter is nothing more than a principle of organization involving the distinction between self and non-self which is not sufficient for constituting a coherent continuity or identity over time. As humans, however, we do have something more than this – we have language. And with language we begin to make our experience relatively coherent over extended time periods. We use words to tell stories, and in these stories we create what we call our selves. We extend our biological boundaries to encompass a life of meaningful experience.

Two things are to be noted from Dennett's account. First, we cannot prevent ourselves from 'inventing' our selves. We are hardwired to become language users, and once we are caught up in the web of language and begin spinning our own stories, we are not totally in control of the product. Dennett, not unlike some phenomenologists, suggests that 'for the most part we don't spin them [the stories]; they spin us' (1991, 418). Second, an important product of this spinning is the narrative self. According to Dennett, however, the narrative self is nothing substantially real. It is, rather, an empty abstraction. Specifically, Dennett defines the self as an abstract 'center of narrative gravity', and likens it to the theoretical fiction of the center of gravity of any physical object. In the case of narrative gravity, however, an individual self consists of the abstract and movable point where the various stories (of fiction or biography) that the individual tells about himself, or are told about him, meet up.

Galen Strawson goes further in the direction of denying reality to the narrative self by challenging the very notion of a narrative self, even one with a fictitious nature. He questions the relevance of narrative as a way to characterize his own experience. In part, his claim is phenomenological insofar as it is based on his own experience. He reports that he has 'absolutely no sense of [his] life as a narrative with form, or indeed as a narrative without form. Absolutely none'. He also suggests that thinking of the self in terms of narrative may 'close down important avenues of thought, impoverish our grasp of ethical possibilities, needlessly and wrongly distress those who do not fit their model, and [may be] potentially destructive in psychotherapeutic contexts' (Strawson 2004, 429).

It's not clear, however, that in explicating this position Strawson does not rely on a specific metaphysical conception of the self, which he outlines in a number of his other essays (Strawson 1997; 2011). Specifically, he draws a distinction between 'one's experience of oneself when one is considering oneself principally as a human being taken as a whole, and one's experience of oneself when one is considering oneself principally as an inner mental entity or "self" of some sort' (Strawson 2004, 429). He consistently characterizes the self* (a designation he uses to signify the inner mental entity) as a minimal self – a self that 'in the living moment of experience' (2011, 253) does not persist for longer than about 3 seconds, and that should not be characterized as an agent (Strawson 1997). Accordingly, he admits that he, as self*, has a special relation to the other selves* that have inhabited his body, but currently is a different mental entity than those other selves*. 'I'm well aware that my past is mine *in so far as I am a human being*, and I fully accept that there is a sense in which it has special relevance to me* [my current self*] now. At the same time I have no sense that I* [the current self*] was there in the past, and think it is obvious that I* was not there, as a matter of metaphysical fact' (Strawson 2004, 434; emphasis added). It seems clear, however, that whatever he can say about his relation to his past selves*, *in so far as he is a human being*, would necessarily take a narrative form. On his view this would be a trivial conception of how narrative applies to self. Nonetheless, if we accept his story about the self*, then he seems to be in agreement with phenomenologists and narrative theorists, that the minimal self, as he characterizes it, i.e., as a 3-second, non-agentive, mental thing, is simply not a narrative self.

In contrast to Strawson, Ricoeur (1994) conceives of the self as a longer-term phenomenon, and in contrast to Dennett, Ricoeur conceives of the narrative self, not as an abstract point at the intersection of various narratives, but as something richer, more concrete, having a gravity of its own, so to speak. Beyond what one might take to be one unified life narrative, following Ricoeur we can think of the self as the sum total of many narratives, which includes within itself all of the equivocations, contradictions, conflicts, struggles and subtexts that find expression in personal life. In contrast to Dennett's center of narrative gravity, this extended self is decentered, distributed and multiplex. At a psychological level, this view allows for conflict, moral indecision and self-deception, in a way that would be difficult to express in terms of an abstract point of intersection. For Ricoeur, moreover, one's own self-narrative is always entangled in the narratives of others.

Most importantly, narratives are essentially linked to actions. The argument about the reality of the self should not be that the self simply floats on its own self-constituting narrative processes, no matter how rich and complex such processes might be. Rather, the self is real, not because it is constituted by a narrative, but because it engages in actions which have real consequences. What I refer to when I refer (and when 'I' refers, and when my narrative refers) to a self, is the embodied agent engaged in action projects in a highly contextualized lifeworld. Such an agent is intelligible to me and to others, as such, because actions are meaningful and significant in ways that are irreducible to any set of neuronal activations, isolated motor processes, muscle contractions, or basic movements – phenomena that can be characterized in purely naturalistic terms. Actions are performed by a bodily agent who consists of more than a collection of mechanisms. They have a meaningful intentionality and we interpret them and their agents in narrative terms.

Actions, as Ricoeur (1992) and others such as Alistair MacIntyre (1984) and Charles Taylor (1989) suggest, can be narrated because they have a narrative form. MacIntyre (1984, 206) indicates that an action can be interpreted with 'equal truth and appropriateness' as digging, gardening, taking exercise, preparing for winter, or pleasing one's spouse. The very same digging behavior may have different meanings and fit into different, sometimes intersecting stories, depending on complex pragmatic and social contexts, so that the meaning of any action is not purely intrinsic to its motoric aspects. Actions flow 'intelligibly from a human agent's intentions, motives, passions, and purposes. ...' (MacIntyre 1984, 209), but their full significance depends on the particular context in which they occur, and to capture that one requires what we might call a *full dress* narrative – not simply the agent's narrative, although that might be the most immediate available, but the narrative that would result by integrating what others could say about the action. Actions are intelligible in the first place insofar as they are tied to the agent's purpose or goal. Intention formation, as in the formation of one's F-intentions, is subject to normative pressures for consistency and coherence relative to the agent's beliefs and other intentions (Pacherie 2007). This is clearly the case with retrospective attributions as well. In addition, actions can go beyond their intended consequences. Narrative accounts thus include normative or evaluative dimensions which also go beyond the single action and pertain to the agent herself. They apply not just to individual intentions and actions but also to the agent's life as a whole as her actions and her life fit into certain traditions and conceptions of the good (MacIntyre 1984, 219; Taylor 1989, 3).

As Mayra Schechtman (2011) points out, on some views, specifically those which are skeptical about the reality of the narrative self, selves/agents are regarded as merely the products, the protagonists, of narrative. End of story. Other views, however, link 'selfhood to the capacity to think in narrative terms and to offer narrative explanations' (2011, 398).

Agents who act are also agents who provide narratives that explain or justify their actions to others. To be able to do this, that is, to be able to generate self-narratives, real agents require capacities for (1) temporal ordering, (2) minimal self-reference; (3) episodic/autobiographical memory; and (4) metacognition.

(1) Capacity for temporal ordering. Narrative involves a twofold temporal structure. First, there is a timeframe that is internal to the narrative itself, a serial order in which one event follows another. This internal timeframe contributes to the composition of narrative structure. In narrative, Ricoeur (1992) notes, there is a dialectic of 'discordance' and 'concordance'. Each event, as it emerges in the narrative, is something new and different (discordance); yet

in another way each event is part of a series (concordance), determined by what came before and constraining what is to come. Configurations of concordance and discordance compose basic plot structures in stories. Even if there is no plot, however, there is always a serial order in the narrative.

One can think of the internal serial order of the narrative in terms of what McTaggart (1908) called a B-series, in which one event follows another. Once established, this is an unchanging order. That is, if event X predates event Y, then it always does so. The American revolutionary war happened before the French revolution, and this fact does not depend on how long ago these events happened. Within narrative, however, a series of events that have a certain objective order may be presented out of order, which may happen in several ways and for several reasons, e.g., to create a dramatic effect, or a reasoned explanation, by presenting event Y first, and then moving back (flashing back) to event X; or it may be the case that the narrator simply does not know (or misremembers) the objective order of events and thinks that event Y did happen before event X – a simple mistake rather than an intended dramatic effect. If the narrative references real events in this way, then it does so in a non-veridical way.

In contrast to the internal time frame, there is an external temporality that defines the narrator's temporal relation to the events of the narrative. We can think of this as McTaggart's A-series, which is a perspectival or relative time frame. That is, from the narrator's current perspective (the present), the narrated events happen either in the past, the present, or the future. Even if this relation is left unspecified ('Once upon a time...') it is usually open to specification that these events happened in the past, or will happen in the future, relative to the narrator's present. In the case of fictional events, of course, the events may never have happened and never will happen. We might think of them precisely as not having a specifiable place in time relative to the narrator. With respect to self-narrative, however, this cannot be the case. Even if the event in question never did happen (for example, an event falsely remembered) or never will happen (for example, a planned event that never comes to be actualized) in self-narrative it is still set in a temporal relation to the narrator.

By the capacity for temporal ordering I mean simply the ability to work in these time frames without serious confusion. These are learned capacities that are based on a more fundamental temporal ordering of experience described by Husserl (see Chapter 6). The basic temporal structure of experience that we characterized in terms of elemental and integrative scales is not only a prerequisite for the proper temporal ordering found in narrative, but, as we saw, is also a necessary condition for the development of a minimal sense of self, for our ability to remember our experience, for our ability to engage in action, and for our ability to reflect on our action.

(2) *Capacity for minimal self-reference.* As Husserl showed in his analysis of this basic temporal structure of consciousness, the retentional function retains not only an intentional sense of the just-past object but it does so only by retaining the consciousness of that object. Retention gives us an experience of ourselves experiencing the world. This is the pre-reflective sense of the 'mineness' of experience which we called the sense of ownership (Chapter 7) – the ground for my use of the first-person pronoun, and the basis for my ability to issue reports about my experience. To begin to form a self-narrative one must be able to refer to oneself by using the first-person pronoun. Without the basic sense of differentiation between self and non-self I would not be able to refer to myself with any specification, and self-narrative would have no starting point. The minimal sense of self is what gets extended and enhanced in the self-narrative, and, as we've seen, immunity to error through misidentification (IEM) makes the minimal self an extremely secure anchor for self-narratives.

(3) *Episodic/autobiographical memory.* A necessary condition for anchoring narrative in non-fictional events is the proper working of episodic memory. Both the capacity for temporal ordering and the capacity for minimal self-reference are necessary for the proper working of autobiographical memory, which involves the recollection and specification of a past event and when it took place, for example, the self-attribution of a past action. Building on a long philosophical tradition, starting with Locke (1690), which holds that just such memories form the basis of personal identity, narrative theorists contend that personal identity is primarily

constituted in narratives that recount past autobiographical events. If there is any degree of unity to my life, it is the product of an interpretation of my past actions and of past events that happened to me, all of which constitute my life history (Ricoeur 1992). If I were unable to form memories of my life history, or were unable to access such memories, then I would have nothing to interpret, nothing to narrate sufficient for the formation of self-identity.

It should be noted that self-narrative is not simply something that depends on the proper functioning of autobiographical memory, but in fact contributes to the functioning of that memory. Just to the extent that the current contextual and semantic requirements of narrative construction motivate the recollection of a certain event, that recollection will be shaped, interpreted and reconstructed in the light of those requirements. In addition, autobiographical memory depends on, but also reinforces a more objective sense of self. One can see this in terms of development. Around the same time that the capacity for autobiographical memory starts to form, 18 months to 24 months, the child gains capability in mirror self-recognition, which generates an objective sense of self, as well as capability in language, which is essential for the construction of narrative (Howe 2000, 91–92).

(4) *Capacity for metacognition.* Another important cognitive capacity required for narrative competency is an ability to gain a reflective distance from one's own experience. The process of interpretation that ordinarily shapes episodic memories into a narrative structure, depends on this capacity for reflective metacognition. To form a self-narrative, one needs to do more than simply remember life events. One needs to reflectively and selectively consider them, deliberate on their meaning, and decide how they fit together. A life event is not meaningful in itself; rather it depends on a narrative structure that reflects its complex context and sees in it significance that goes beyond the event itself.

Metacognition is clearly essential for the interpretive process that produces the self-narrative. As Merlin Donald (2006) puts it, metacognition provides the 'cognitive governance' that allows for disambiguating and differentiating events within the narrative. It not only allows for reporting on one's experience, but also for an enhancement of that experience. It is possible, for the sake of a unified or coherent meaning, to construe certain events in a way that they did not in fact happen. To some degree, and for the sake of creating a coherency to life, it is normal to enhance (and even confabulate) one's story. As Ricoeur points out, narrative identity 'must be seen as an unstable mixture of fabulation and actual experience' (1992, 162). Deception, and often self-deception are not unusual.

In the formation of a self-narrative or a narrative self, there is always a certain narrative distance that opens up between the narrator (i.e., the narrating self) and the narrated self. That is, the self never fully coincides with itself. This narrative distance, which is greater in deceptive than in non-deceptive self-narratives (see Bedwell et al. 2011), is present even in what we would consider veridical self-narratives. It is still the case that, as Katherine Nelson suggests, in narrating our actions we gain in self-understanding in a way that 'integrates action and consciousness into a whole self, and establishes a self-history as unique to the self, differentiated from others' experiential histories' (Nelson 2003, 7). That the integration may never be complete simply means that the 'whole self' is really an imperfect whole, and perhaps never completely differentiated from the intentions, actions, and histories of others.

In this respect it is important to note that narratives are not just retrospectively about the past. In prospective intention formation, for example, I form a narrative of future actions which may or may not happen. As David Velleman notes, this ability makes the narrator an agent. The agent's narrative motivates and provides reasons to engage in actions and to follow a course that he has set. Narrative competency provides the agent with different possible ways to complete the story and this gives him some degree of free will, some degree of agential control (Velleman 2006, 218–21). In this sense, narrative not only reports on or reinforces our sense of agency, but, in a kind of self-fulfilling prophesy, self-constitutes ourselves as agents who have degrees of freedom and responsibility.

The latter concepts, we note, would be meaningless in a world that did not include others. As we'll see in the next chapter, neither our possibilities for action nor our self-narratives are ever completely distinguished from the actions and narratives of others;

moreover, they play an important role in how we understand others. Just on this basis, we can say, with Taylor, 'one is a self only among other selves. A self can never be described without reference to those who surround it'. He adds: 'this obviously cannot be just a contingent matter' (Taylor 1989, 35).

8.5 Further reading

Arendt (1958) develops a theory of action informed by the phenomenological tradition. Ricoeur (1966) explains how decisions and actions involve self-constitution; Ricoeur (1994) engages in dialogue with analytic and traditional philosophies of personal identity and self from a phenomenological and narrative perspective. In Berthoz and Petit (2008) a neuroscientist and a phenomenologist, argue for a non-representationalist account of action. Dreyfus (2000), following Merleau-Ponty, also presents a non-representationalist view of action and motor intentionality.

9 Intersubjectivity and Second-Person Perspective

At various points in the preceding chapters I started to draw arrows that were directed at this topic of intersubjectivity. I'm not sure that this is the best topic to save until last. It's implicated in many ways in the various topics covered in previous chapters, so it might seem that I've been dancing around something important. Now it's time, in this chapter to engage in a serious tango, that is, to step into a hands-on, face-to-face encounter with the issue of intersubjectivity. An account of intersubjectivity is needed to support various claims about phenomenological methodology – specifically claims about the possibility of intersubjective validity. It's also needed to motivate the enactive conception of intentionality outlined in Chapter 4, and the accounts of action and narrative in Chapter 8. Most importantly, however, phenomenology requires an account of intersubjectivity simply, but also significantly, because it is a central theme and phenomenon of human experience.

9.1 Transcendental intersubjectivity

In Husserl's Fifth Meditation (1960), he develops a transcendental analysis of how we experience the other person. The analysis claims a universal validity insofar as it is proposed as an eidetic insight into the structure of any possible experience of others.

Husserl makes several important claims in his analysis. First, a primary and non-intersubjective experience of the difference between my psychophysical body and 'external things' is presupposed by any intersubjective experience of empathy. In a subject's experience one animate organism is *'uniquely* singled out' (Husserl 1960, 97) due to the fact that the subject can ascribe hyletic experiences (e.g., tactile sensations or sensations of warmth and coldness) only to the subject's own body. This uniqueness is also supported by the fact that the subject has the ability to *'rule and govern'* this body *'immediately'* (Husserl 1960, 97), which gives the subject a basic sense of the 'I can'. In earlier texts Husserl had pointed out that every bodily movement is accompanied by kinesthetic sensations that belong only to the organism undertaking the movement. All such experiences, later analyzed by Merleau-Ponty in terms of the body schema, help to distinguish the subject's organism from everything else. As we saw in Chapter 7, this capacity is modulated in some circumstances, such as in the rubber hand illusion and the robot experiment.

Second, the experience of the other person is based on an apperception (Husserl 1960, 110). Apperception is a mode of experience in which something that is not explicitly presented is nonetheless perceived in a certain way. For example, when I visually perceive the apple on the table in front of me, I literally see only one side of it, and I can never see it in its entirety all at once. Nonetheless, I experience it as a whole apple, and not just as a one-sided façade of an apple. Accordingly, I have some kind of experience of the parts of the apple that I do not literally see – the apple as a whole is 'appresented'. In a similar way, the other person is presented incompletely, not only in regard to her body, which I can see in any one instance only incompletely, but also in regard to her inner experiences, which I cannot literally see at all. And yet, when I do perceive another person, that person is experienced as having her own experiences, an inner mental life. I perceive the other as an *animate* organism – not as an organism that simply behaves in a certain manner, but as an organism that has an inner life. That inner life is appresented, experienced in some way, although different from the way I experience my own inner life. The other is not given to me in the first-person way that my own experience is give to me. My self-experience is asymmetrical with my experience of the other. This is an important difference between myself and the other. The incompleteness of the other, in this regard, is precisely her presence *as other* (see Levinas 1969).

Third, this apperception of the other as animate organism is based upon a passive association, a 'pairing' between my experience of the other's body and that of my own. The concept of *pairing* is central to Husserl's analysis. Pairing is based on a perceived similarity between myself and the other. This similarity, however, is not something discovered in an act of comparison where, for example, I look at myself and then at the other, and then conclude that we are similar in appearance. It is not the result of a kind of analogy that I make between myself and another, where I analogically infer that the other must be similar to me. Nor is it a similarity based on the appearances of our bodies. Phenomenologists claim that a similarity in this sense fails, since my awareness of my own body, in proprioceptive and agentive terms, is quite different from my awareness of the other person's body, visually and from the outside. One could argue, based on recent psychological research, that perception is cross-modal and that visual and proprioceptive systems code things in the same 'language' (see Gallagher and Meltzoff 1996), so that there is a certain similarity that crosses over from what I visually see to what I proprioceptively feel. One could think of this also in Husserl's own terms of a kinaesthetic similarity, or in contemporary neuroscientific terms of an elicited motor resonance – an activation of my own system when I see another person's actions, facilitated by mirror neurons.[1] Merleau-Ponty would again talk about processes that involve body schemas and what he referred to as an *intercorporeity*, which he describes in this way: 'between this phenomenal body of mine, and that of another as I see it from the outside, there exists an internal relation which causes the other to appear as the completion of the system' (1962, 352). In any case, Husserl interprets this kind of pairing to be a form of empathy: an experience in which the other person's inner mental life is apperceived automatically, before any voluntary decision or any interpretation happens.

Finally, Husserl maintains that the apperception of the other person is verified in a continuous experience characterized by harmonious or consistent behavior, on what is clearly the narrative scale. My experience of the other as an animate organism, that is as an organism with an inner life, breaks down if her behavior (or, we would add, the narrative) is too discordant (Husserl 1960, 114). It would make sense to think that the pairing process, and empathy as Husserl defines it, can be disrupted by such behavior.

One important thing to notice in this analysis is that in apperception or pairing no inference is necessary. That is, we do not enter into any extra-perceptual cognitive process where we attempt to discover what the other person's mental states are. Of course Husserl intends this to be a transcendental analysis, and not necessarily an attempt to explain how we come to understand any particular other. As we saw in Chapter 2, however, Husserl suggests that 'every analysis or theory of transcendental phenomenology [...] can be produced in the natural realm, when we give up the transcendental attitude' (1960, §57). This move to a non-transcendental or natural attitude would constitute the beginning of a phenomenological psychology. Instead of pursuing this kind of analysis, however, we should note another important aspect in Husserl's notion of transcendental intersubjectivity.

Husserl holds that intersubjectivity has direct relevance to the concept of intentionality. My intentional experience of the world gives me a sense of objectivity that cashes out in terms of intersubjective accessibility. The world does not exist for me alone, and this speaks of a certain undeniable sense of the intersubjective.

> Transcendental intersubjectivity is the absolute and only self-sufficient ontological foundation out of which everything objective (the totality of objectively real entities, but also every objective ideal world) draws its sense and its validity. (1977, 344)

The objectivity and transcendence of the world – its otherness, the fact that it does not reduce to just a set of ideas in my mind – is constituted by this intersubjective dimension. The world is not just my world since it is experienced by others in ways that do not reduce to my own experience of it. The world escapes my complete perception and is something that is necessarily beyond my own existence since it opens onto other perspectives that I can only apperceive.

> Thus everything objective that stands before me in experience and primarily in perception has an apperceptive horizon of possible experiences, my own and those of others. Ontologically speaking, every appearance that I have is from the very beginning a part of an open endless, but not explicitly realized totality of possible appearances of the same, and the subjectivity belonging to this appearance is open intersubjectivity. (Husserl 1973, 289)

Sartre is well known for drawing dramatic existential themes out of these insights. He summarizes Husserl's view in this way: '[E]ach object, far from being constituted, as for Kant, by a simple relation to the subject, appears in my concrete experience as polyvalent; it is given originally as possessing systems of reference to an indefinite plurality of consciousnesses' (1956, 229). Whereas for Husserl this is a transcendental truth that we hardly notice, for Sartre it's an oddly felt ontological shift in the experience of the world. He suggests that my relationship to things undergoes a fundamental change when I experience somebody else observing these very same things. When another person walks into the park where I am sitting, for example,

> [...] suddenly an object has appeared which has stolen the world from me. Everything [remains] in place; everything still exists for me; but everything is traversed by an invisible flight and fixed in the direction of a new object. The appearance of the Other in the world corresponds therefore to a fixed sliding of the whole universe, to a decentralization of the world which undermines the centralization which I am simultaneously effecting. (1956, 255)

The power of the other's perspective becomes even more angst motivating when the other's gaze falls on me. We'll return to the importance of the other's ability to see me – to take me as an object – when we turn our attention to the question of social cognition, below.

9.2 Being-with others

Heidegger offers a different account of intersubjectivity, or what he calls 'being-with' (*Mitsein*), one that moves away from the seeming immediacy of body-to-body paring or the sense that the other might be the occasion of an existential anxiety. Instead, for Heidegger, the other ends up being the source of an overly comfortable conformity. As for intersubjectivity as the transcendental source of objectivity, this could play only a derivative role rather than an instituting one.

There is no doubt that Heidegger understands being-with as an important dimension of human existence, and most commentators will insist on the centrality of his notion of being-with others (e.g., Wheeler 2005, 149). Being-with is an existential aspect of Dasein, equally primordial or co-original with Being-in-the world (1962, 149/114; also 153/117). Heidegger avoids the term 'intersubjectivity', since it seems to signify the traditional (and Cartesian) idea that there is one isolated individual subject, A, standing over against a second isolated individual subject, B, so that the problem then gets defined as how A can understand B, and vice versa. This is simply the wrong way to pose the problem (e.g., Heidegger 1988, 237–238). Likewise, Heidegger would not use the term 'social cognition' since that seems to define the problem as one that involves cognition or knowing. Consistent with his analysis of being-in-the-world he maintains that cognition, and associated worries about epistemic objectivity, are derivative issues. Being-with others is something more basic and existential than that – that is, it has an ontological significance more basic than what can be captured by the concept of cognition or the idea of knowing other minds. Despite these critical vocabulary issues, Heidegger's ontological analysis still has something important to tell us about basic inter-subjective processes and, derivatively, social cognition.

To say that being-with is equally primordial or co-original with being-in-the-world means that it is part of the existential structure of human existence (*Dasein*), not an add-on; not something supplemental to Dasein. Being-with does not signify that Dasein is in-the-world first, and then, because of that, it comes to be with others. Heidegger makes this point strong and clear.

Being-with as an originary existential structure of Dasein actually has nothing to do with the fact that there may be other people in the world. The fact that others are in the world only has significance because Dasein is being-with, not the other way around. If Dasein happens to be alone, Dasein is still being-with – and 'only as being-with can Dasein be alone' (1988, 238), or, indeed, lonely. Heidegger makes this point so strongly that it seems that being-with as such does not depend on there being others; Dasein 'is far from becoming being-with because an other turns up in fact' (239).

> This being-with-one-another is not an additive result of the occurrence of several such others, not an epiphenomenon of a multiplicity of Daseins, something supplementary which might come about only on the strength of a certain number. On the contrary, it is because Dasein as being-in-the-world is of itself being-with that there is something like a being-with-one-another (1985, 239)

Dreyfus, in his commentary on *Being and Time* (1991, 149) puts it this way: 'Being-with would still be a structure of my Daseining even if all other Daseins had been wiped out.'

For Heidegger, Dasein's encounter with others is 'by way of the world' (1988, 239/242). That is, it is through everyday pragmatic contexts that Dasein encounters the other. Dasein's dealings with its environment provide immediate reference to other Dasein. For instance, a piece of work by a craftsperson causes us to encounter not just the thing, but also the person who made it and the person for whom it is intended. This is the nature of the initial and original encounter with others. We come upon them as unavoidably involved in the same way that we are involved in pragmatic contexts: 'Here it should be noted that the closest kind of encounter with another lies in the direction of the very world in which [Dasein's] concern is absorbed' (1988, 241).[2] We come upon people who are already in-the-world in this sense of being involved in the pragmatic affairs of everyday life. And we, like them, seem to be already involved with things in the same way. Dasein thus understands itself, and others, 'proximally and for the most part in terms of its world' (1962, 156/120).

The fact that Dasein is in-the-world, and that the world is shared with others, helps to answer the question of 'who' Dasein is. As we saw in Chapter 7, Heidegger shifts the answer away from the traditional solutions of 'I', self, mind, and soul. 'It could be that the "who" of everyday Dasein just is *not* the "I myself"' (1962, 150/115). Rather, Heidegger suggests, the 'they' (*das Man*) constitutes an important part of Dasein's identity. That is, Dasein is so taken up by the social dimension, and by the dominance of others, that it gets lost in a social inauthenticity in which it understands itself as being the same as everyone else.

In contrast to Dasein's ready-to-hand 'circumspective' stance toward the world of 'proximal concern', Dasein's stance toward the other is one of 'solicitude' (1962, 155/119; 157/122). Heidegger explicates what he terms 'deficient modes of solicitude' which include the variety of ways that we pass by each other in our everyday comings and goings without much notice. Solicitude also has two positive, non-indifferent manifestations. In Heidegger's odd terminology these are 'leaping in' (*einspringen*) and 'leaping ahead' (*vorausspringen*) (158–159/122). When we 'leap in' we take over for another that with which he or she should be concerned. This is an act of domination leading to dependence, even if it is tacit and the other is not fully aware of what has taken place. As such it is equivalent to what Sartre later called 'bad faith' in our relations with others. To 'leap ahead', Heidegger says, 'pertains essentially to authentic care – that is, to the existence of the Other, not to a *"what"* with which he is concerned; it helps the other become transparent to himself *in* his care and to become *free for* it' (158/122; see 344/297–298).

Heidegger tells us that our everyday interactions take place between these two poles of positive solicitude. He goes on to indicate that leaping in often takes place between those who are 'hired for the same affair' where the relationship 'thrives only on mistrust'. Conversely, when they (ourselves and others) take up a common project they may become '*authentically* bound together' which creates the right kind of possibilities and 'frees the Other in his freedom for himself' (1962, 159/122). In any case, whether we leap in or leap ahead with others we are already involved with them because we are already pragmatically involved in the world (160/123).

Heidegger rejects the idea that we come to understand the other person first in an intellectual way, or that our relations to others are primarily cognitive. Because Dasein's existence is being-with, 'its understanding of Being already implies the understanding of Others. This understanding, like any understanding, is not an acquaintance derived from knowledge about them, but a primordial existential kind of Being, which, more than anything else, makes such knowledge and acquaintance possible' (160 /123).

The way that a transcendental analysis is set up has some import for how one can then think of the empirical. This becomes clear if we contrast the analyses of our relations with others in Husserl and Heidegger. Although both give a clear transcendental primacy to intersubjectivity or being-with, for Husserl the other is a necessary prerequisite for the experience of the world as real and objective, whereas this seems not to be the case for Heidegger. Dasein is being-with and is in-the-world even if there are no others in the world. In terms of how this gets cashed out in the analysis of our everyday encounters, on Heidegger's account, Dasein encounters others only in a world in which Dasein is already pragmatically involved, whereas on Husserl's account, in regard to ordering the world, intersubjectivity has a clear primacy over anything considered to be pragmatic, and certainly has primacy over object perception. While Heidegger can agree with this last clause, his analysis suggests that we encounter others only on a stage that has already been set by our pragmatic involvements; pragmatic coping with the world seems to be already in place before we come upon others, despite Heidegger's insistence on the equally primordial character of being-with and being-in-the-world (Gallagher and Jacobson, 2012). This prompts Gadamer to say that '*Mitsein*, for Heidegger, was a concession that he had to make, but one that he never really got behind.... [It] is, in truth, a very weak idea of the other.... (2004, 23).[3]

In wanting to give primacy to the intersubjective, Husserl ends up with the idea of a primal experience of the other. This idea is meant to solve a problem, most clearly outlined by Dan Zahavi. 'Under normal circumstances, I still experience that which I accidentally experience alone (for instance this computer that I am writing on now) as transcendent, objective, and real, although I am not simultaneously experiencing this object as being experienced by Others' (2003, 116). Husserl admits this and even suggests that if the entire population of the world were wiped out (to borrow Dreyfus's phrase), the lonely experiencing subject would still experience an objective world. This seems to put him in a similar position to Heidegger who suggests that Dasein's being-with does not depend on there being any other in the world. Husserl, however, insists that this can only be the case after a primary, instituting encounter. The problem is solved 'if one differentiates between our first primal experience of Others – which once and for all makes the constitution of objectivity, reality, and transcendence possible, thus *permanently* transforming our categories of experience – and all subsequent experiences of Others' (Zahavi 2003, 116). Apparently, even if I were prevented from having those subsequent experiences of others, I would still be able to experience the world as transcendent and objective due to an initial instituting or primal experience of the other.

How much do such transcendental thought experiments tell us about our actual encounters with others? Let me turn this question around. Can an examination of our everyday encounters with others – including phenomenological and empirical analyses – contribute anything to such transcendental considerations? Can they help to adjudicate the differences between Husserl and Heidegger on such issues, or at least clarify what these differences are? On some accounts, recent studies of social cognition may do just that.

9.3 Standard views of social cognition

There are two standard and dominant approaches to questions of social cognition in the philosophy of mind, psychology, and cognitive science disciplines: 'theory theory' (TT) and simulation theory (ST). Indeed, much of the literature on social cognition is taken up by a debate between these two theories. They both fall under the heading 'theory of mind' (ToM), which focuses on explaining our ability to 'mindread', i.e., to attribute mental states to others. The attribution of mental states such as beliefs and desires, according to ToM, allows us to explain and predict the other person's actions. TT claims that we understand others by making inferences to mental states based on our knowledge of folk psychology, that is, the commonsense theory about how people generally behave in light of their beliefs and desires (see, e.g., Carruthers 2009). ST, in contrast, claims that we have no need for folk psychological theory, because we have a model, namely, our own mind, that we can use to simulate the other person's mental states. We put ourselves in the other person's shoes and formulate what their beliefs or desires must be on the basis of what ours would be in that situation, and we then project those beliefs and desires to the other person (see, e.g., Goldman 2006). Here is Alvin Goldman's description of the simulation process.

> First, the attributor creates in herself pretend states intended to match those of the [observed] target. In other words, the attributor attempts to put herself in the target's 'mental shoes'. The second step is to feed these initial pretend states [e.g., beliefs] into some mechanism of the attributor's own psychology ... and allow that mechanism to operate on the pretend states so as to generate one or more new states [e.g., decisions]. Third, the attributor assigns the output state to the target ... [e.g., we infer or project the decision to the other's mind]. (Goldman 2005, 80–81)

Simulation is often considered a form of empathy, or a way to explain empathy (Gallese 2003; Goldman 2006; Steuber 2006). In this connection ST has received a boost from neuroscientific research on mirror neurons. Given that observation of the other person's action activates my own motor system, the claim is that this kind of mirror resonance is a form of empathy or simulation. Simulationists accordingly distinguish between low-level, automatic empathic processes based on subpersonal neural simulations, and high-level more explicit processes that require conscious or habitual simulation or empathy (Goldman 2006; Steuber 2006).

For both TT and ST, the problem is that we have no direct access to the other person's mind. We are primarily observers of behavior. When we attempt to understand the actions of others, using either theoretical inference or simulation, we do so by mindreading the other's mental processes, and on either theory, this is our primary and pervasive way of explaining or predicting what others have done or will do.[4]

As the problem of social cognition is defined within these approaches, it is, as Heidegger puts it, 'the phenomenon which proximally comes to view when one considers the theoretical problematic of understanding the "psychical life of Others"' (1962, 161 /124). From the perspective of phenomenology, this frames the problem in the wrong way. I don't encounter others as other minds or as theoretical problems that I need to explain; I encounter them in embodied interactions and often as agents with whom I am already engaged in meaningful projects. The meaning of the others' behaviors and my understanding of them are directly tied to my embodied interactions with them and to the instrumental or social situations in which I encounter them. In normal unproblematic circumstances there is no further mystery, nothing extra, hidden away, that I need to theorize about. Nor do I require a simulation process to bridge a gap between myself and others.

9.4 Phenomenological approaches to social cognition

Recent phenomenological approaches[5] to issues in social cognition have challenged these more established and standard ToM explanations. The phenomenological approaches have involved both a critique of various versions of TT and ST, and a positive twofold account of social cognition. The twofold account draws not only from phenomenology, but also from developmental science, social neuroscience and narrative theory, and includes:

(a) An account of basic forms of intersubjectivity that emphasizes embodied face-to-face interaction in pragmatic and social contexts – this is sometimes referred to as interaction theory (IT);

(b) An account of communicative and narrative practices that build on, but also modulate, basic forms of intersubjectivity, and can explain our more nuanced adult capacity for social cognition.

Phenomenological approaches challenge four basic suppositions that inform most standard ToM accounts of social cognition.

(1) *Hidden minds:* The problem of social cognition is due to our lack of access to the other person's mental states. Since we cannot directly perceive the other's beliefs, desires, feelings, or intentions, we need some extra-perceptual cognitive (mindreading) process (inference or simulation) to understand their mental states.

(2) *Mindreading as default:* These mindreading processes constitute our primary, pervasive, or default way of understanding others.

(3) *Observational stance:* Our normal everyday stance toward the other person is a third-person, observational stance. We observe their behaviors in order to explain and predict their actions, or to theorize or simulate their mental states.

(4) *Methodological individualism:* Understanding others depends primarily on cognitive capabilities or mechanisms located in an individual subject, or on processes that take place inside an individual brain.

Contra (1), phenomenological approaches maintain that the other person's emotions and intentions are normally and frequently apparent in their embodied and contextualized behaviors, including their vocalizations, gestures, facial expressions, eye gaze, and situated postures. For example, we can see that someone is sad or angry from their facial expressions, or that they intend to do something specific from their posture and movement. Intentions are not mental states hidden away, but embodied in the other's action in such a way that we can see what they intend – we can perceive their motor intentions and their intentions-in-action. Likewise, emotions are not pure mental states; they are constitutionally embodied and manifested in perceptible ways. Intentions and emotions and the meanings of actions are not abstractly embodied, but are always contextualized by situations. Often the circumstances in which we see and interact with others make it clear why they are sad or angry, what they intend to do, or what their precise action will mean. Moreover, *contra (2)*, in most everyday encounters our understanding of others does not need to go beyond what we can perceive in such behaviors and expressions. That is, mindreading is not usually required, although it is not ruled out, for example, in rare puzzling situations. *Contra (3)*, from a phenomenological perspective, we understand others, not by taking up observational positions, or attempting to work out explanations of their behavior in terms of their mental states, but in the contexts of shared situations where we work with, play with, or otherwise interactively engage with them. Nor is social understanding, *contra (4)*, reducible to mechanisms located in individual minds or brains (ToM mechanisms, mirror neurons, etc.). Rather, they are ultimately cashed out in interaction processes that take more than one person to accomplish.

Interaction (rather than observation) obviously plays a central role in IT. Here's a formal definition:

> *Interaction*: a mutually engaged co-regulated coupling between at least two autonomous agents where the co-regulation and the coupling mutually affect each other, constituting a self-sustaining organization in the domain of relational dynamics. (see De Jaegher et al. 2010)

This definition involves the strong claim that interaction in some cases (but not all cases) constitutes, and does not just causally contribute to intersubjective understanding. If interaction in such cases makes social cognition what it is, it is more than just a causal element. Evidence to support such a strong claim can be found across a number of different disciplines.

9.4.1 Developmental studies

IT appeals to evidence from developmental studies, starting with primary and secondary intersubjectivity (Trevarthen 1979; Trevarthen and Hubley 1978). Primary intersubjectivity consists of the innate or early-developing sensory-motor capacities that bring us into relations with others and allow us to interact with them. These capacities are manifested at the level of action and action-oriented perceptual experience – we *see* or more generally *perceive* in the other person's bodily movements, gestures, facial expressions, eye direction, vocal intonation, etc. what they intend and what they feel, and we respond with our own bodily movements, gestures, facial expressions, gaze, etc. In this respect perception is perception-for-action or perception-in-action, rather than off-line observation. From birth the infant is pulled into these interactive processes. This can be seen in the very early behavior of the newborn. Infants from birth are capable of perceiving and imitating facial gestures presented by another (Meltzoff and Moore 1977; 1994). Importantly, this kind of imitation is not an automatic or mechanical procedure; Csibra and Gergely (2009) have shown, for example, that the infant is more likely to imitate when the other person is attending to it.

Primary intersubjectivity can be specified in more detail as the infant develops. At 2 months, for example, infants are able to follow the gaze of the other person, to see that the other person is looking in a certain direction, and to sense what the other person sees (which is sometimes the infant herself), in a way that throws the intention of the other person into relief (Baron-Cohen 1995; Maurer and Barrera 1981). In addition, second-person interaction is evidenced by the timing and emotional response of infants' behavior. Infants 'vocalize and gesture in a way that seems [affectively and temporally] "tuned" to the vocalizations and gestures of the other person' (Gopnik and Meltzoff 1997, 131). Murray and Trevarthen (1985) have shown the importance of the mother's live (and lively) interaction with her 2-month old infant in a two-way video monitor experiment where mother and infant interact by means of a live television link. When presented with a recorded replay of their mother's previous actions, however, interaction fails; infants quickly disengage and become distracted and upset.

At 5–7 months, infants are able to detect correspondences between visual and auditory information that specify the expression of emotions (Walker 1982; Hobson 1993; 2002). At 6 months infants start to perceive grasping as goal directed, and at 10–11 months infants are able to parse some kinds of continuous action according to intentional boundaries (Baldwin and Baird 2001; Baird and Baldwin 2001; Woodward and Sommerville 2000). They start to perceive various movements of the head, the mouth, the hands, and more general body movements as meaningful, goal-directed movements (Senju, Johnson and Csibra 2006). All of this adds up, so that by the end of the first year of life, infants have a non-mentalizing, perception-based, embodied and pragmatic understanding of the emotions and intentions of other persons.

Secondary intersubjectivity begins with the advent of joint attention (likely even before 9 months). Attending with another to objects in the world and seeing how they are regarded and used provide the infant not only with information about the world, but specifically about the other's attitudes and actions. Thus, even before 1 year of age infants start to use pragmatic and social contexts (the surrounding environment and the various normative practices that define the social milieu) to enter a two-fold process. (1) They refer to others (in social referencing) and enter into joint actions where they learn how objects are used by using them and from seeing others use them, and they begin to co-constitute the meaning of the world through such interactions with others in a process of 'participatory sense-making' (De Jaegher and Di Paolo 2007); and (2) they build upon these interactions to make sense of the other's behavior in specific contexts. Thereby they gain a more nuanced understanding of others by situating their actions in contexts that are defined by both pragmatic tasks and cultural practices.

Aspects of secondary intersubjectivity and participatory sense-making have been explored in a variety of experiments. For example, Csibra and Gergely (2009) provide evidence that human infants are sensitive to ostensive signals (gestures, eye gaze, utterances) when addressed by another person and they develop referential expectations that the information conveyed (by showing or communication) in such contexts is kind-relevant and generalizable. Infants, as early as 8 months, expect to see a referenced object when they follow the gaze of the other, and at 13 months they expect to see a specific kind of thing behind a barrier when that thing is named by the person whose gaze they are following (Moll and Tomasello 2004). When 14-month-olds see another's emotional display directed towards a particular object, they take this to signify something about the valence of the thing rather than about the person's subjective attitude, and they generalize this to mean that others will also find the object to have the same valence (Csibra and Gergely 2009).These expectations and interpretations are apparent, however, only when the other person interacts with the infant in an ostensive way, that is, addressing or looking at the child first. Csibra and Gergely call this a 'natural pedagogy', and this is clearly a good example of participatory sense-making where objects take on a certain meaning through the intersubjective interaction.

Experiments with 18-month-old infants show they are able to understand the action intentions of another person who is playing with a toy but fails to complete some task (e.g., trying to separate two parts of the toy but failing). If given the chance, infants will go on to complete those intended actions (Meltzoff 1995). In this situation the infant is focused more on understanding what the other person wants to do. The understanding demonstrated in such a situation clearly depends on the pragmatic context as well as the bodily actions of the other person.

As Rakoczy et al. (2009, 445) suggest, starting around 1 year of age the actions that children learn 'are not just individual, idiosyncratic behaviours, but cultural conventional forms of action. And many of these forms of action are rule-governed and normatively structured...' In their experiments they show that by the time young children are 2 and 3 years of age they adopt strict norms about how to play a particular game, following rules arbitrarily set by the experiments. The children objected and strongly protested when a puppet played the game in the 'wrong' way, taking the puppet's actions as failing to conform to the social norm.

9.4.2   Behavioral and phenomenological evidence

Neither primary nor secondary intersubjectivity disappears after the first or second year of life. These are not stages that we leave behind. Rather, citing both behavioral and phenomenological evidence, IT argues that the embodied and pragmatic processes of primary and secondary intersubjectivity continue to be operative in adult social engagements and to characterize our everyday encounters even as adults. That is, we continue to understand others in strong interactional terms, facilitated by our recognition of meaning in facial expressions, gestures, postures, and actions situated in pragmatic and social contexts.

Scientific experiments bear this out. Point-light experiments (actors wearing point lights on their body joints, presenting abstract physical patterns of emotional and action postures in the dark), for example, show that not only children (although not autistic children) but also adults perceive emotion even in movement that offers minimal information (Hobson and Lee 1999; Dittrich et al. 1996). Detailed analysis of facial expression, gesture and action in everyday contexts shows that as adults we continue to rely on embodied interactive abilities to understand the intentions and actions of others and to accomplish interactive tasks (Lindblom 2007; Lindblom and Ziemke 2007).

Accordingly, meaning and emotional significance is co-constituted in the interaction – not in the private confines of one or the other's head. The analyses of social interactions in shared activities, in work situations, in communicative practices, and so on, show that agents most often unconsciously coordinate their movements, gestures, and speech acts (Issartel et al. 2007; Kendon 1990; Lindblom 2007). In the contextualized practices of secondary intersubjectivity timing and emotional attunement continue to be important as we coordinate our perception-action sequences; our movements, for example, are coupled with changes in velocity, direction and intonation in the movements and utterances of the speaker.

Husserl's notion of *pairing* finds some support in the developmental evidence and the continuing adult behavior. From birth our actions are coded in the same cross-modal, sensory-motor 'language', in a system that is directly attuned to the actions and gestures of other humans (Meltzoff and Moore 1994; Gallagher and Meltzoff 1996). In this kind of interaction, as Merleau-Ponty's notion of intercorporeity makes clear, there is a bodily (or motor) intentionality distributed across the interacting agents, an intentionality that could not be realized without there being actual interaction. The meaning, the intentionality of one's action, is *in the interaction*. That is, in cases of interaction, one's intentions are not just formed in one's individual body as the result of an isolated subjective process, but depend in a dynamic way on the other's elicitations and responses. Intercorporeity involves a mutual influence of body schemas, a reciprocal, dynamic and enactive response to the other's action, taking that action as an affordance for further action and interaction.

9.4.3 Evidence from dynamical systems modeling

As suggested in Chapter 3, dynamical systems modeling and the use of computer simulations can serve as useful technological supplementations to phenomenological methodology. Theorists have used such approaches to investigate minimally social behavior. Iizuka and Di Paolo (2007), for example, basing their model on Murray and Trevarthen's (1985) two-way video contingency study (discussed above), used an evolutionary robotics approach to show that the detection of social contingency emerges from the dynamics of the interaction process itself. In their simulation model the evolved agents successfully acquired the capacity to discriminate between 'live' (interactive) and 'recorded' (one-way, non-interactive) relations. Dynamical systems analysis demonstrates that this capacity cannot be reduced to the isolated individual agent, but that the dynamics of the interaction process itself play an essential role in enabling this behavior. When the agent attempts to interact with a non-responsive 'partner' whose movements are merely played back from a recording of a previously highly successful encounter, the interaction fails to materialize. Individual actors do *not* achieve their action performance by utilizing internal computational mechanisms, such as 'social contingency detection modules'. Rather, their successful performance constitutively depends on dynamical properties involved in their mutual coupling with the other. The give and take, back and forth mutual process makes the action on either side what it is.

On this view, social interaction can best be explained from an enactive perspective. That is, as embodied agents we do not passively receive information from our environment and then create internal representations of the world; rather, we actively participate in the generation of meaning, which is the result of pragmatic and dynamic interchanges between agent and environment

(Varela et al. 1991). In the intersubjective context, interaction involves processes that go beyond what any one individual brings to the interaction (De Jaegher et al. 2010). Indeed, much like dancing the tango, the interaction is not reducible to a set of mechanisms contained within the individual; it requires at least two embodied individuals who are dynamically coupled in the right way.

9.5   The narrative scale in social cognition

Phenomenological accounts of social cognition appeal to these different kinds of evidence to support a strong concept of interaction in primary and secondary intersubjective contexts. To get the full story of social cognition, however, one would need to add to these various processes of interaction *communicative and narrative (C&N) competencies,* which develop later and which bring along the more subtle and sophisticated aspects of social cognition that we find in adulthood. There is also a developmental story to be told here since young 'pre-verbal' infants are already involved in meaningful communicative practices that involve eye gaze, facial expressions, affective responses, gestures, pointing, and verbal communication (e.g., motherese). As Merleau-Ponty (1987) indicates, the infant is born into a 'whirlwind of language' since we never wait for the infant to 'acquire' language before we start talking to the infant. Moreover, in almost all cultures caregivers begin to tell stories (e.g., nursery rhymes, sing-song rhymes, children stories) to infants even before they can understand them. When children begin to verbalize, a caregiver will begin to elicit their self-narrative (which already involves others) by asking leading questions about, e.g., 'what we did yesterday at the zoo'.

Children also engage in narrative practices in the form of pretend play. 'Children's first narrative productions occur in action, in episodes of symbolic play by groups of peers, accompanied by – rather than solely through – language. Play is an important developmental source of narrative' (Nelson 2003, 28). This shows, importantly, that our C&N competencies emerge out of our interactions. Accordingly, as C&N practices develop, they carry primary and secondary intersubjective capabilities forward and put them into service in much more sophisticated social contexts (see Gallagher and Hutto 2008; Hutto 2008). These practices, however, not only inform our reflective abilities to understand and give reasons for our actions and the actions of others, they also loop back to implicitly inform our more primary and pre-reflective ways of understanding others and the situations they are in.

On the phenomenological accounts, the claim is that the majority of what happens in most of our everyday social-cognitive encounters with others can be accounted for in terms of primary and secondary intersubjective interactions and our communicative and narrative competencies. In most situations we are not trying to mindread the other person; we are not concerned about the other person's mental states, although such concerns may be motivated by relatively unusual behaviors, or by attempts to give reasons for or justify actions reflectively. Even in response to questions about *why* someone is doing something (as opposed to simply *what* is happening), however, narrative accounts in terms of actions and situations often suffice. Even when mental state concepts enter into the story, the story usually takes the form of a folk psychological *narrative* rather than a folk psychological *theory* (see Hutto 2008).

9.6 Revisiting transcendental intersubjectivity

Merleau-Ponty acknowledged a strong intersubjective shaping of experience, which, following Husserl, he called 'transcendental intersubjectivity'. His claim was that intersubjective processes, which are closely tied to our embodied, affective experience, shape the way that we perceive the world – and not just our perception of others. In terms of IT, part of what this means can be captured in the concept of participatory sense-making. We learn about the world, learn how to engage with things, by interacting and jointly acting with others. We learn what is important, what is relevant, what is acceptable, and so on, from just such interactions. The interaction itself is constitutive of such meaning.

Can participatory sense-making be considered the naturalized equivalent to something like Husserl's transcendental intersubjective constitution of the meaning and objectivity of the world? Whether the problem of transcendental intersubjectivity can be naturalized, is a controversial issue. In this regard, however, we might take guidance from Merleau-Ponty once again.

> Now if the transcendental is intersubjectivity, how can the borders of the transcendental and the empirical help becoming indistinct?...All of my facticity is reintegrated into subjectivity...Thus the transcendental decends into history. (Merleau-Ponty 1967, 107)

In this respect, one could argue that facticity is on Husserl's side in the transcendental contrast we pointed to between Husserl and Heidegger. To put it most succinctly, there is no room for primary intersubjectivity in Heidegger's account. His starting point is secondary intersubjectivity. It is only in terms of our involvement in some pragmatic project that we encounter others. Face-to-face embodied and affective engagements with others seem to be missing in Heidegger's *Mitsein*. Being-with others is not so much being *with* others as being involved in some project that involves them, and indeed, in ways that pull all of us into specific forms of inauthenticity. There is no doubt about the importance of this kind of analysis, but it may easily miss certain possibilities (perhaps even possibilities of authentic relations with others) if it leaves primary intersubjectivity out of account.

On Husserl's side, the concept of primary intersubjectivity may provide a better solution than Husserl himself does to the problem of the transcendental constitution of objectivity. He appealed to an instituting primal encounter which, as Zahavi puts it, '*once and for all* makes the constitution of objectivity, reality, and transcendence possible' (Zahavi 2003, 116, emphasis added) even if, for some reason, all further experiences with others were foreclosed. Surely the better story is that our instituting encounters are ongoing and are most adequately explained in the practices of primary and secondary intersubjectivity where the objectivity of entities and events are constantly being instituted and reinstituted. Participatory sense-making is the result of continuous interactions with others, and what counts as real is not determined entirely outside of the influence of history (as Merleau-Ponty notes) or culture. The meaning of the world, and the objectivity of entities and events within the world are not established once and for all, or forever guaranteed. Instances of perceptual illusion as well as pathological hallucinations and delusions all testify to the possibility of losing just such an objective and meaningful grasp on the world.

Whatever one thinks of these issues, phenomenological approaches to intersubjectivity that enlist the resources of developmental psychology, the behavioral and simulation sciences, as well as other sciences can certainly capture, at the very least, the empirical shadow of the transcendental.

9.7 Further reading

Husserl (1950), the *locus classicus* of his transcendental analysis of intersubjectivity, introduces the concept of pairing and apperception. Steinbock (1995) focuses on Husserl's later manuscripts on intersubjectivity and generative phenomenology. Stein (1964) provides a phenomenological account of empathy which involves imaginative transposal of myself into the place of the other. Gurwitsch (1979) extends Heidegger's analysis of being-with in terms of our pragmatic relations with others. Schütz (1967) develops a phenomenological account of social action. Merleau-Ponty (1964) presents a set of lectures on development and the embodied approach to intersubjectivity. Scheler (1954) explicates the notions of sympathy and fellow-feeling, love and other emotions. Levinas (1969) offers a critique of phenomenological accounts pointing to the irreducible ethical nature of the face-to-face relation. Zahavi (1999) defends a phenomenological account of alterity.

Notes

Introduction

1. In this respect, this volume offers something different from some of the recent introductions to phenomenology (e.g., Moran 2000; Sokolowski 2000), and something similar to but completely different from an older book with the same title, *Phenomenology*, written by Jean-Francois Lyotard (1991, first published in 1954). Lyotard also looked at classical concepts in phenomenology and then tried to apply them to issues that were of great contemporary concern. In his case, the concern was social and political thought in France (especially Marxism), which is not at all my concern in this book. I focus on questions that pertain to philosophy of mind and the cognitive sciences. For a more comprehensive account of classical phenomenology I highly recommend Moran's introduction.

2   Naturalism, Transcendendentalism and a New Naturalizing

1. Although Husserl studied mathematics in Berlin from 1878–1880, he wasn't in Berlin when Sartre studied there, and Sartre never met Husserl. Husserl's ideas about phenomenology likely originated when he went to Vienna in 1881 to finish his PhD in mathematics and started to attend Brentano's lectures. On Brentano's advice, he then went to study with the psychologist Carl Stumpf at University of Halle in 1886.

2. Similarly, see De Preester (2002), who suggests that if phenomenology accepts the assumptions of cognitive science concerning issues like computationalism and representation, then phenomenology self-destructs. 'A naturalized phenomenology is no longer phenomenology' (De Preester 2002, 645). This would only be the case, however, if we supposed a positive answer to Edelman's (2002, 125) question: 'Is a new phenomenology, which would completely eschew transcendentalism in favor of computational principles, possible?' The issue really goes the other way. That is, the introduction of phenomenology

into cognitive science has critically challenged the basic assumptions of cognitive science, including computationalism, and indeed the very concepts of nature and naturalism, and has moved cognitive science towards a view that is more consistent with the views of Husserl and Merleau-Ponty on intentionality, intersubjectvity, action, and embodiment. See Gallagher and Varela (2003); Thompson (2007); Varela, Thompson and Rosch (1991).

3. See Husserl 2001, 5th Investigation, §39, and Husserl 2005, Text No.14 (1911–1912): 363–377; Marbach 2010; Yoshimi 2007. Marbach 2010 also notes the connection with Frege's *Begriffsschrift*.

4. We note that Husserl, himself a trained mathematician, viewed mathematical formula as incapable of capturing phenomenological results. 'One cannot define in philosophy as in mathematics; any imitation of mathematical procedure in this respect is not only unfruitful but wrong, and has most injurious consequences' (Husserl 1982, 9). Roy et al. argue, however, that even if this was true of the mathematics of Husserl's time, the development of dynamical systems theory offers new possibilities in this regard (1999, 43). For some critical remarks see Zahavi (2004).

5. Jean Petitot also provides good examples of this approach in his analyses of spatial perception (Petitot 1999; 2008), as does Varela (1999) in his dynamical analysis of time-consciousness.

4 Intentionalities

1. Here is his original formulation. 'Here is how it works: first you decide to treat the object whose behavior is to be predicted as a rational agent; then you figure out what beliefs that agent ought to have, given its place in the world and its purpose. Then you figure out what desires it ought to have, on the same considerations, and finally you predict that this rational agent will act to further its goals in the light of its beliefs. A little practical reasoning from the chosen set of beliefs and desires will in most instances yield a decision about what the agent ought to do; that is what you predict the agent will do' (Dennett 1987, 17).

2. Cash (2010) describes it as follows: 'On this normative view... the paradigmatic cases of such ascriptions are made by another member of the agent's linguistic and normative community; the ascriptions abide by, and are justified by, the norms of that community's practice of giving intentional states as reasons for actions. This practice is firmly situated in and supported by that community's shared, public language, with its norms regulating the appropriate uses of words to give content to intentional states. ... This practice constrains what

ascriptions an observer is licensed to ascribe according to the agent's behavior. But they also normatively constrain the further actions of the agent. Agents who recognize that observers are licensed to ascribe particular intentional states to them ought to take themselves to be committed to further actions consistent with those intentional states. If I say to you that I intend to go for a walk, I should recognize that this utterance licenses you to ascribe to me the intention to go for a walk; I have licensed you to expect me to go for a walk, and thus I have placed myself under a commitment (ceteris paribus) to go for a walk.'

3. In recent debates about the extended mind hypothesis (Clark 2008; Clark and Chalmers 1998) critics have appealed to the Brentanian idea that non-derived (mental state) intentionality is the mark of the mental and that such non-derived intentionality is entirely in the head (Adams and Aizawa 2008;2009). If, in contrast, operative (embodied, enactive) intentionality is original and non-derived in the sense argued for here, this would present a possible response for defenders of extended mind (see Gallagher and Miyahara 2012).

5   Embodiment and the Hyletic Dimension

1. See Gallagher (1986) for a more detailed discussion.

2. One can see this idea in the inverted spectrum thought experiments which focus to a large extent on color; for example, the experiential redness of a red apple. One can also see this in Dennett's Chase and Sanborn example, and the acquired taste of beer example, where what is at stake is the experiential taste of the coffee or the beer.

3. To be as clear as possible, I am suggesting that enactivists should neither (1) go too wide and reduce experience to being enacted purely by sensory-motor contingencies understood in the logic of if-then bodily movements that constitute skilled sensorimotor behavior or know-how (Noë 2004), nor retreat to positions that either (2) deny phenomenal consciousness or think of it as purely epiphenomenal (as one might find in Dennett) or (3) go too narrow and attribute it to only neural activity (as one finds in Clark – but also e.g., Hutto and Myin (2013, ch. 1): 'Radical enactivists hold that phenomenality is nothing other than specifiable sorts of activity – even if only neural activity'.

6   Time and Time Again

1. There are interesting and complex historical and philosophical connections between James and Husserl that have been well

summarized in the scholarly literature. See Gallagher (1998) for a more complete account of the connections between Brentano, Stumpf, Stern, and James, and the history of philosophical-psychological reflections on time in the German tradition of Herbart, Lotze, Wundt, and Volkmann.

2. The role of narrative scale temporality is important in this regard. See Chapter 8 for further discussion.

3. Another example is when the meaning of a word in a sentence is deferred until a phrase or the sentence is complete, so that the word itself, as it is read or sounded, motivates a certain anticipation towards the fulfillment of its meaning. Such things often slow down our reading and make us go back over text to get clarification. See Gallagher (1998) for other examples of effects of content on experienced temporal sequence.

7   Self and First-Person Perspective

1. The logic of involuntary movement suggests that SA, in a minimal sense of having to do simply with control of bodily movement, may correlate with efferent brain signals (motor commands), since both SA and efferent signals are missing in the case of involuntary movement. SO, on the other hand, may be generated in part by sensory feedback, especially proprioceptive/kinaesthetic reafference generated in the movement itself, or the integration of sensory feedback from different modalities (Tsakiris and Haggard 2005).

2. Not everyone does. See, e.g., Billon (2011) and Bortolotti and Broome (2009).

3. A similar phenomenon of mirror correction has been found to cause immediate recovery from anosognosia for hemiplegia (Fotopoulou et al. 2009).

4. Farrer et al. (2003) showed differential activation in the inferior part of the parietal lobe, specifically on the right side, for perceived self-movement of limbs in non-canonical positions and in the insula for perception of self-movement in canonical positions in non-pathological subjects. Saxe, Jamal, and Powell (2006) found activation in the right extrastriate body area in response to images of body parts presented from a non-canonical perspective. Corradi-Dell'acqua et al. (2008) have shown activation of the right parieto-temporal-occipital junction during perception of the self as an external object (as in the mirror, or in a video game).

5. Mike Martin (1995) proposed that SO is bound to the somatosensory body boundaries – but it seems that the RHI and other phenomena

(phantom limb, personal neglect) go against that suggestion. Martin's proposal ignores the effect of vision. As in out-of-body experiences, the '[i]ntegration of proprioception, tactile, and visual information of one's body fails due to discrepant central representations by the different sensory systems. This may lead to the experience of seeing one's body in a position that does not coincide with the felt position of one's body' (Blanke and Arzy 2005).

6. Cassam (1997) suggests that IEM is based on one's *awareness of one-self* (or one's body, e.g., via proprioception) *as perspectival origin.* Bodily self-awareness is 'as subject' only if (1) it is an awareness of oneself as perspectival origin (e.g., proprioception) and (2) it is the basis for first-person statements that are IEM. But we've seen that to the extent that this sort of awareness is not reliable, IEM is only *de facto.* In contrast, the claim I'm making is not about my *awareness* of myself as perspectival origin – it's about *being* the perspectival origin of my awareness. Evans (1982, e.g. 222) also hints at this more than once, but maintains that IEM depends on mode of access or 'ways of gaining knowledge'.

7. The neuroscience in this regard is quite complex. Zahn et al. (2008) found abnormalities (hypometabolism) in the inferior temporal and parieto-occipital regions which they associate with visual object representation. Yet these are areas selectively activated for explicit (reflective) self-reference (Lou et al., 2004; also Fingelkurts and Fingelkurts 2011). Hypometabolism was also found in cerebellar and motor regions, areas involved in predicting the sensory consequences of one's own movements, and necessary for SA in the motor domain, although no problems were found in DP's experience of agency. Zahn et al. (2008, 9) rightly note that "a single case can never reveal whether abnormalities in a brain region are sufficient or even necessary to evoke abnormal experiences". Their study also does not make clear the timing involved in the reflective process described by DP, nor do they discuss any activity in the brain that might correlate to such reflective processes.

8 Lifeworld, Action, Narrative

1. The concept of lifeworld is taken up by sociology via the work of Alfred Schutz (one of Husserl's students) and Thomas Luckmann in their book *Structures of the Life-World* (1973; 1983). It also makes its way into critical theory, via Habermas (1987) and his distinction between system and lifeworld and the notion of the colonization of the lifeworld.

9 Intersubjectivity and Second-Person Perspective

1. Mirror neurons are neurons that activate both when (1) I engage in intentional action, such as reaching for a drink, and (2) when I see you engage in that action. For a good analysis of how Husserl's phenomenology relates to the neuroscience of mirror neurons, see Zahavi (2012b).

2. Heidegger goes on to further emphasize that this particular way of being-in-the-world co-determines all other modes of Dasein: 'By reasons of this *with-like* [*mithaften*] Being-in-the-world, the world is always the one that I share with Others. The world of Dasein is a *with-world* [*Mitwelt*]. Being-in is *Being-with* Others. Their Being-in-themselves within-the-world is *Dasein-with* [*Mitdasein*]' (1962, 155/118).

3. This is a controversial claim, but Gadamer is not alone. Heidegger's student, Karl Löwith (1928), for example, a year after *Being and Time* was published, suggested that Heidegger ignored the role of direct interpersonal contact in his account. Binswanger (1962) made similar criticisms and claimed that the idea that Dasein is being-with left him with 'a knot of unresolved questions' (1962, 6). Heidegger's (1989, 236–242) response was that Binswanger worked with an ontic, psychological interpretation, whereas Heidegger had been concerned with an ontological analysis. This motivated another Heidegger scholar, Otto Pöggeler to comment that 'it is certainly beyond doubt that Heidegger's inquiry into social being is some of the most unsatisfying questioning of his work. This must be said even if one considers that Heidegger never concretely worked out this question; that he dealt with it at all only with the intention of doing "fundamental ontology"' (1989, 251).

4. These are the terms of art in the TT and ST literature: 'mindreading', 'mentalizing', 'explaining', and 'predicting', rather than 'understanding'. Gaining the ability to use folk psychology, or the ability to employ explicit or habitual simulation routines has been standardly thought to occur around the age of 4 years. Prior to that children are thought to lack a full theory of mind, but may be capable of precursor abilities that allow them to understand actions or intentions (see, e.g., Baron-Cohen 1995).

5. I refer to phenomenological approaches in the plural to include those that draw not only from phenomenological philosophy, but also from enactive theories of perception, developmental studies of social

interaction, and/or narrative theory. There are a number of authors who take such approaches to social cognition, but who give different weight to these different aspects. They are in general agreement in their criticism of ToM approaches, but are not in full agreement in their positive accounts. See, for example, De Jaegher, Di Paulo and Gallagher (2010); Fuchs and De Jaegher (2009); Gallagher (2001; 2004; 2005; 2007b; 2008b); Gallagher and Hutto (2008); Gallagher and Zahavi (2008); Hobson (1993); Hutto (2008); Ratcliffe (2007); Reddy (2008); Trevarthen (1979).

References

Adams, F. and Aizawa, K. (2009). Why the mind is still in the head. In P. Robbins and M. Aydede (eds), *The Cambridge Handbook for Situated Cognition* (78–95). NY: Cambridge University Press.

Adams, F. and Aizawa, K. (2008). *The Bounds of Cognition*. Malden, MA: Blackwell.

Arendt, H. (1958). *The Human Condition*. Chicago: University of Chicago Press.

Babinski, J. (1899). De l'asynergie cérébelleuse. *Revue de Neurologie* 7, 806–816.

Baird, J. A. and Baldwin, D. A. (2001). Making sense of human behavior: action parsing and intentional inference. In B. F. Malle, L. J. Moses, and D. A. Baldwin (eds), *Intentions and Intentionality: Foundations of Social Cognition* (193–206). Cambridge, MA: MIT Press.

Baldwin, D. A. and Baird, J. A. (2001). Discerning intentions in dynamic human action. *Trends in Cognitive Science* 5(4), 171–178.

Baron-Cohen, S. (1995). *Mindblindness: An Essay on Autism and Theory of Mind*. Cambridge, MA: MIT Press.

Bedwell, J., Gallagher, S., Whitten, S. and Fiore, S. (2011). Linguistic correlates of self in deceptive oral autobiographical narratives. *Consciousness and Cognition* 20, 547–555.

Beer, R. D. (1997). The dynamics of adaptive behavior: a research program. *Robotics and Autonomous Systems* 20(2–4), 257–289.

Bergson, H. (1999). *Duration and Simultaneity*, R. Durie (ed.), Manchester: Clinamen Press.

Bermúdez, J. L. (1998). *The Paradox of Self-Consciousness*. Cambridge, MA: MIT Press.

Bernet, R., Kern, I. and Marbach, E. (1993). *An Introduction to Husserlian Phenomenology*. Evanston, IL: Northwestern University Press.

Berthoz, A. (2000). *The Brain's Sense of Movement*. Cambridge, MA: Harvard University Press.

Berthoz, A. and Petit, J-L. (2008). *The Physiology and Phenomenology of Action*. Oxford: Oxford University Press.

Bhalla, M. and Proffitt, D. R. (1999). Visual–motor recalibration in geographical slant perception. *J of Experimental Psychology: Human Perception and Performance* 25, 1076–1096.

Billon, A. (2011). Does consciousness entail subjectivity? The puzzle of thought insertion. *Philosophical Psychology* doi:10.1080/09515089.201 1.625117

Binswanger, L. (1962). *Grundformen und Erkenntnis menschlichen Daseins.* Ernst Reinhardt Verlag.

Blanke, O. and Arzy, S. (2005). The out-of-body experience: disturbed self-processing at the temporo-parietal junction. *Neuroscientist* 11(1), 16–24.

Blanke, O., Ortiguef, S., Landist, T. and Margitta Seeck, M. (2002). Stimulating illusory own-body perceptions. *Nature* 419, 269–270.

Boden, M. A. (ed.) (1996). *The Philosophy of Artificial Life.* NY: Oxford University Press.

Bortolotti, L. and Broome, M. (2009). A role for ownership and authorship in the analysis of thought insertion. *Phenomenology and the Cognitive Sciences* 8(2), 205–224.

Botvinick, M. and Cohen, J. (1998). Rubber hands 'feel' touch that eyes see. *Nature* 391, 756.

Bourgine, P. and Varela, F. J. (1992). Introduction: towards a practice of autonomous systems. In F. J. Varela and P. Bourgine (eds), *Towards a Practice of Autonomous Systems: Proc. of the 1st Euro. Conf. on Artificial Life* (1–3). Cambridge, MA: The MIT Press.

Brandom, R. B. (2008). *Between Saying and Doing: Towards an Analytic Pragmatism.* Oxford: Oxford University Press.

Brandom, R. B. (2000). *Articulating Reasons: An Introduction to Inferentialism.* Cambridge, MA: Harvard University Press.

Brandom, R. B. (1994). *Making It Explicit: Reasoning, Representing, and Discursive Commitment.* Cambridge, MA: Harvard University Press.

Bratman, M. E. (1987). *Intention, Plans, and Practical Reason.* Cambridge, MA: Cambridge University Press.

Bregman, A. S. and Rudnicky, A. I. (1975). Auditory segregation: stream or streams? *Journal of Experimental Psychology: Human Perception and Performance* 1, 263–267.

Brentano, F. (1995). *Psychology from an Empirical Standpoint.* Trans. A. C. Rancurello, D. B. Terrell and L. L. McAlister. London and NY: Routledge.

Brooks, R. A. (1991). New approaches to robotics. *Science* 253, 1227–1232.

Brough, J. B. (1972). The emergence of an absolute consciousness in Husserl's early writings on time-consciousness. *Man and World* 5, 298–326.

Butterworth, G. and Hopkins, B. (1988). Hand-mouth coordination in the newborn baby. *British Journal of Developmental Psychology* 6, 303–314.

Buytendijk, F. J. J. (1974). *Prolegomena to an Anthropological Physiology.* Trans. A. I. Orr. Pittsburgh: Duquesne University Press.

Campbell, J. (1999). Schizophrenia, the space of reasons and thinking as a motor process. *The Monist* 82(4), 609–625.

Carr, D. (1999). The Paradox of Subjectivity: The Self in the Transcendental Tradition. NY: Oxford University Press.

Carruthers, P. (2009). How we know our own minds: the relationship between mindreading and metacognition. *Behavioral and Brain Sciences* 32(2), 121–182.

Cash, M. (2010). Extended cognition, personal responsibility, and relational autonomy. *Phenomenology and the Cognitive Sciences* 9(4), 645–671.

Cash, M. (2008). Thought and oughts. *Philosophical Explorations* 11(2), 93–119.

Cassam, Q. (2011). The embodied self. In S. Gallagher (ed.), *The Oxford Handbook of the Self.* Oxford: Oxford University Press.

Cassam, Q. (1997). *Self and World.* Oxford: Clarendon Press.

Cassam, Q. (1995). Introspection and bodily self-ascription. In J. Bermúdez, A. J. Marcel and N. Eilan (eds), *The Body and the Self* (311–336). Cambridge, MA: MIT Press.

Chemero, A. (2009). *Radical Embodied Cognitive Science.* Cambridge, MA: MIT Press.

Clark, A. (2009). Spreading the joy? Why the machinery of consciousness is (probably) still in the head. *Mind* 118, 963–993.

Clark, A. (2008). Supersizing the Mind: Embodiment, Action, and Cognitive Extension. Oxford: Oxford University Press.

Clark, A. (1997). Being There: Putting Brain, Body, and World Together Again. Cambridge, MA: MIT Press.

Clark, A. and Chalmers, D. (1998). The extended mind. *Analysis* 58(1), 7–19.

Clark, A. and Grush, R. (1999). Towards a cognitive robotics. *Adaptive Behavior* 7(1), 5–16.

Cole, J., Sacks, O. and Waterman, I. (2000). On the immunity principle: a view from a robot. *Trends in Cogitive Sciences* 4(5), 167.

Corradi-Dell 'acqua, C., Ueno, K., Ogawa, A., Cheng, K., Rumiati, R. I. and Iriki, A. (2008). Effects of shifting perspective of the self: an fMRI study. *Neuroimage* 40(4), 1902–1911.

Cosmelli, D. and Thompson, E. (2010) Embodiment or envatment? Reflections on the bodily basis of consciousness. In J. Stewart, O. Gapenne and E. di Paolo (eds), *Enaction: Towards a New Paradigm for Cognitive Science*. Cambridge, MA: MIT Press.

Cerbone, D. R. (2006). *Understanding Phenomenology*. Montreal: McGill-Queen's University Press.

Cliff, D., Harvey, I. and Husbands, P. (1993). Explorations in evolutionary robotics. *Adaptive Behavior* 2(1), 73–110.

Crowell, S. G. (2001a). *Husserl, Heidegger, and the Space of Meaning*. Evanston: Northwestern University Press.

Crowell, S. (2001b). Subjectivity: locating the first-person in *being and time*. *Inquiry* 44, 433–454.

Csibra, G. and Gergely, G. (2009). Natural pedagogy. *Trends in Cognitive Sciences* 13, 148–153.

Dainton, B. (2000). Stream of Consciousness: Unity and Continuity in Conscious Experience. London: Routledge.

Damasio, A. (1999). The Feeling of What Happens: Body and Emotion in the Making of Consciousness. NY: Harcourt Brace and Co.

Dansiger, S., Levavb, J. and Avnaim-Pessoa, L. (2011). Extraneous factors in judicial decisions. *PNAS* 108(17): 6889–6892.

de Biran, M. (1929). *The Influence of Habit on the Faculty of Thinking*. Trans. M. D. Boehm. Baltimore: Williams and Wilkins.

Dennett, D. C. (2001). The fantasy of first-person science. Private circulation, at http://ase.tufts.edu/cogstud/papers/chalmersdeb3dft.htm. (Accessed 24 July 2012).

Dennett, D. C. (1991). *Consciousness Explained*. Boston: Little, Brown.

Dennett, D. C. (1988). Quining qualia. In A. Marcel and E. Bisiach (eds) *Consciousness in Modern Science*. Oxford: Oxford University Press.

Dennett, D. C. (1987). *The Intentional Stance*. Cambridge, MA: MIT Press.

De Jaegher, H. and Di Paolo, E. (2007). Participatory sense-making: an enactive approach to social cognition. *Phenomenology and the Cognitive Sciences* 6, 485–507

De Jaegher, H., Di Paolo, E. and Gallagher, S. (2010). Does social interaction constitute social cognition? *Trends in Cognitive Sciences* 14(10), 441–447.

Depraz, N., Varela, F. and Vermersch, P. (2003). *On Becoming Aware*. Amsterdam: John Benjamins.

De Preester, H. (2002). Naturalizing Husserlian phenomenology: an introduction. *Psychoanalytische Perspectieven* 20(4), 633–647.

Dittrich, W. H., Troscianko, T., Lea, S. E. G and Morgan, D. (1996). Perception of emotion from dynamic point-light displays represented in dance. *Perception* 25, 727–738.

DiPaolo, E. A., Noble, J. and Bullock, S. (2000). Simulation models as opaque thought experiments. In M. A. Bedau, J. S. McCaskill, N. H. Packard and S. Rasmussen (eds), *Artificial Life VII: Proc. of the 7th Int. Conf. on Artificial Life* (497–506). Cambridge, MA: MIT Press.

Donald, M. (2006). An evolutionary rationale for the emergence of language from mimetic representation. Plenary paper presented at Language Culture and Mind Conference (17–20 July 2006), Paris.

Drummond, J. J. (1990). *Husserlian Intentionality and Non-Foundational Realism*. Dordrecht: Kluwer Academic Publishers.

Dreyfus, H. (2000). A Merleau-Pontyian critique of Husserl's and Searle's representationalist accounts of action. *Proceedings of the Aristotelian Society* 100, 287–302.

Dreyfus, H. (1992). *What Computers Still Can't Do*. Cambridge, MA: MIT Press.

Dreyfus, H. (1991). Being-in-the-world: A Commentary on Heidegger's Being and Time, Division I. Cambridge, MA: MIT Press.

Dreyfus, H. L. and Dreyfus, S. E. (1988). Making a mind versus modelling the brain: artificial intelligence back at a branch-point. *Daedalus* 117(1), 15–44

Eddington, A. (1927). *The Nature of the Physical World*. London: Kessinger Publishing, 2005. Also at http://www-history.mcs.st-and.ac.uk/Extras/Eddington_Gifford.html.

Edelman, S. (2002). Constraints on the nature of the neural representation of the visual world. *Trends in Cognitive Sciences* 6, 125–131.

Engbert, K., Wohlschläger, A., Thomas, R. and Haggard, P. (2007). Agency, subjective time, and other minds. *Journal of Experimental Psychology, Hum Percept Perform* 33(6), 1261–1268.

Evans, G. (1982). *The Varieties of Reference*. Oxford: Clarendon Press.

Farber, M. (1928). Phenomenology as a method and as a philosophical discipline. University of Buffalo Studies VI, Monographs in Philosophy, No. 1.

Farrer, C., and Frith, C. D. (2002). Experiencing oneself vs. another person as being the cause of an action: the neural correlates of the experience of agency. *NeuroImage* 15, 596–603.

Farrer, C., Franck, N., Georgieff, N., Frith, C. D., Decety, J. and Jeannerod, M. (2003). Modulating the experience of agency: a positron emission tomography study. *NeuroImage* 18, 324–333.

Fingelkurts, A. A. and Fingelkurts, A. A. (2011). Persistent operational synchrony within brain default-mode network and self-processing operations in healthy subjects. *Brain and Cognition* 75, 79–90.

Flanagan, O. (1992). *Consciousness Reconsidered*. Cambridge, MA: MIT Press.

Føllesdal, D. (1969). Husserl's notion of noema. *Journal of Philosophy* 66, 680–687.

Føllesdal, D. (1995). Gödel and Husserl. In J. Hintikka (ed.), *From Dedekind to Gödel* (427–446). Dordrecht, Boston: Kluwer Academic Publishers.

Fotopoulou, A., Rudd, R., Holmes, P. and Kopelman, M. (2009). Self-observation reinstates motor awareness in anosognosia for hemiplegia. *Neuropsychologia* 47, 1256–1260.

Frege, G. (1894). Rezension von E. Husserl: philosophie der arithmetik. *Zeitschrift für Philosophie und philosophische Kritik* 103, 313–332.

Frith, C. D. (1992). *The Cognitive Neuropsychology of Schizophrenia.* Hillsdale, NJ: Lawrence Erlbaum Associates.

Frith, C. D., Blakemore, S.-J. and Wolpert, D. M. (2000). Abnormalities in the awareness and control of action. *Phil. Trans. R. Soc. London. B* 355, 1771–1788.

Frith, C. D. and Done, D. J. (1988). Towards a neuropsychology of schizophrenia. *British Journal of Psychiatry* 153, 437–443.

Froese, T. and Gallagher, S. (2010). Phenomenology and artificial life: toward a technological supplementation of phenomenological methodology. *Husserl Studies* 26(2), 83–107.

Fuchs, T. and De Jaegher, H. (2009). Enactive intersubjectivity: participatory sense-making and mutual incorporation. *Phenomenology and the Cognitive Sciences* 8, 465–486.

Gadamer, H-G. (2004). A Century in Philosophy: Hans-Georg Gadamer in Conversation with Riccardo Dottori. NY: Continuum.

Gallagher, S. (in press). Phenomenology of intersubjectivity: transcendental and empirical perspectives [in Portuguese]. Trans. Diogo Ferrer. *Revista Filosófica de Coimbra*.

Gallagher, S. (2012a). Naturalized phenomenology. In D. Zahavi *Oxford Handbook of Contemporary Phenomenology* (70–93). Oxford: Oxford University Press.

Gallagher, S. (2012b). Multiple aspects of agency. *New Ideas in Psychology* 30, 15–31

Gallagher, S. (2012c). First-person perspective and immunity to error through misidentification. In S. Miguens and G. Preyer (eds), *Consciousness and Subjectivity* (187–214). Frankfurt: Philosophical Analysis Ontos Publisher.

Gallagher, S. (2012d). Ambiguity in the sense of agency. In J. Kiverstein and T. Vierkant (eds), *Decomposing the Will*. Oxford: Oxford University Press.

Gallagher, S. (2012e). In defense of phenomenological approaches to social cognition: interacting with the critics. *Review of Philosophy and Psychology* 3(2): 187–212. doi 10.1007/s13164–011–0080–1

Gallagher, S. (2011a). Phenomenology. *Oxford Bibliographies Online: Philosophy*. Oxford: Oxford University Press. (http://www.oxfordbibliographiesonline.com/view/document/obo-9780195396577)

Gallagher, S. (2011b). Time in action. In C. Callender (ed.), *Oxford Handbook on Time* (419–437). Oxford: Oxford University Press.

Gallagher, S. (ed.) (2011c). *The Oxford Handbook of the Self*. Oxford: Oxford University Press.

Gallagher, S. (2008a). Are minimal representations still representations? *International Journal of Philosophical Studies* 16(3), 351–369.

Gallagher, S. (2008b). Inference or interaction: social cognition without precursors. *Philosophical Explorations*, 11(3), 163–173.

Gallagher, S. (2007a). Pathologies in narrative structure. *Philosophy* (Royal Institute of Philosophy) Supplement 60, 65–86.

Gallagher, S. (2007b). Simulation trouble. *Social Neuroscience* 2(3–4), 353–365.

Gallagher, S. (2005). *How the Body Shapes the Mind*. Oxford: Oxford University Press/Clarendon Press.

Gallagher, S. (2004). Understanding problems in autism: interaction theory as an alternative to theory of mind. *Philosophy, Psychiatry, and Psychology* 11, 199–217.

Gallagher, S. (2003). Phenomenology and experimental design. *Journal of Consciousness Studies* 10(9–10), 85–99.

Gallagher, S. (2001). The practice of mind: theory, simulation or primary interaction? *Journal of Consciousness Studies* 8(5–7), 83–108.

Gallagher, S. (2000). Philosophical conceptions of the self: implications for cognitive science. *Trends in Cognitive Sciences* 4(1), 14–21.

Gallagher, S. (1998). *The Inordinance of Time*. Evanston: Northwestern University Press.

Gallagher, S. (1997). Mutual enlightenment: recent phenomenology in cognitive science. *Journal of Consciousness Studies* 4(3), 195–214.

Gallagher, S. (1986). Hyletic experience and the lived body. *Husserl Studies* 3, 131–166.

Gallagher, S. and Brøsted Sørensen, J. (2006). Experimenting with phenomenology. *Consciousness and Cognition* 15(1), 119–134.

Gallagher, S. and Hutto, D. (2008). Understanding others through primary interaction and narrative practice. In J. Zlatev, T. Racine, C. Sinha and E. Itkonen (eds), *The Shared Mind: Perspectives on Intersubjectivity* (17–38). Amsterdam: John Benjamins.

Gallagher, S. and Jacobson, R. (2012). Heidegger and social cognition. In J. Kiverstein and M. Wheeler (eds), *Heidegger and Cognitive Science* (213–245). London: Palgrave Macmillan.

Gallagher, S. and Meltzoff, A. N. (1996). The earliest sense of self and others. *Philosophical Psychology* 9, 213–236.

Gallagher, S. and Miyahara, K. (2012). Neo-pragmatism and enactive intentionality. In J. Schulkin (ed.), *Action, Perception and the Brain*. Basingstoke, UK: Palgrave Macmillan.

Gallagher, S. and Schmicking, D. (eds) (2010). *Handbook of Phenomenology and Cognitive Science*. Dordrecht: Springer.

Gallagher, S. and Varela, F. (2003). Redrawing the map and resetting the time: phenomenology and the cognitive sciences. *Canadian Journal of Philosophy*. Supplementary Volume 29, 93–132.

Gallagher, S. and Zahavi, D. (in press) Primal impression and enactive perception. In D. Lloyd and V. Arstila (eds) *Subjective Time: The Philosophy, Psychology, and Neuroscience of Temporality*. Cambridge, MA: MIT Press.

Gallagher, S. and Zahavi, D. (2012). *The Phenomenological Mind* (2nd edition). London: Routledge.

Gallese, V. (2003). The roots of empathy: the shared manifold hypothesis and the neural basis of intersubjectivity. *Psychopathology* 36, 171–180.

Georgieff, N. and Jeannerod, M. (1998). Beyond consciousness of external events: a who system for consciousness of action and self-consciousness. *Consciousness and Cognition* 7, 465–477.

Gibson, J. J. (1966). *The Senses Considered as Perceptual Systems*. Boston: Houghton-Mifflin.

Gibson, J. J. (1979). *The Ecological Approach to Visual Perception*. Boston: Houghton-Mifflin.

Goldman, A. I. (2006). Simulating Minds: The Philosophy, Psychology, and Neuroscience of Mindreading. NY: Oxford University Press.

Goldman, A. I. (2005). Imitation, mind reading, and simulation. In S. Hurley and N. Chater (eds), *Perspectives on imitation II* (80–91). Cambridge, MA: MIT Press.

Goldman, A. (1970). *A Theory of Human Action*. NY: Prentice-Hall.

Goldstein, K. and Rosenthal, O. (1930). Zum problem der wirkung der farben auf den organismus. *Sweitzer Archiv fur Neurologische Psychiatie* 26, 3–26.

Graham, G. and Stephens, G. L. (1994). Mind and mine. In G. Graham and G. L. Stephens (eds) *Philosophical Psychopathology* (91–109). Cambridge, MA: MIT Press.

Gopnik, A. and Meltzoff, A. N. (1997). *Words, Thoughts, and Theories*. Cambridge, MA: MIT Press.

Gurwitsch, A. (2009). The Collected Works of Aron Gurwitsch (1901–1973), vol. I Constitutive Phenomenology in Historical Perspective. Trans. and (ed.) J. García-Gómez. Dordrecht: Springer.

Gurwitsch, A. (1979). *Human Encounters in the Social World*. Trans. F. Kersten. Pittsburgh: Duquesne University Press.

Gurwitsch, A. (1966). *Studies in Phenomenology and Psychology*. Evanston: Northwestern University Press.

Gurwitsch, A. (1964). *The Field of Consciousness*. Pittsburgh: Duquesne University Press.

Habermas, J. (1987). The Theory of Communicative Action, Vol. 2: Lifeworld and System: A Critique of Functionalist Reason. Trans. T. McCarthy. Boston: Beacon Press.

Haggard, P., Aschersleben, G., Gehrke, J. and Prinz, W. (2002). Action, binding and awareness. In W. Prinz and B. Hommel (eds) *Common Mechanisms in Perception and Action: Attention and Performance*, Vol. XIX (266–285). Oxford: Oxford University Press.

Haith, M. M. (1993). Future-oriented processes in infancy: the case of visual expectations. In C. Granrud (ed.), *Carnegie-Mellon Symposium on Visual Perception and Cognition in Infancy* (235–264). Hillsdale, NJ: Lawrence Erlbaum Associates.

Harvey, I., Di Paolo, E. A., Wood, R., Quinn, M. and Tuci, E. A. (2005). Evolutionary robotics: a new scientific tool for studying cognition. *Artificial Life* 11(1–2), 79–98.

Haugeland, J. (1990). Intentionality all-stars. *Philosophical Perspectives* 4, 383–427.

Head, H. (1920). *Studies in Neurology*. Vol 2. London: Oxford University Press.

Heidegger, M. (1993). The question concerning technology. In D. Krell (ed.), *Basic Writings*. NY: Harper Collins Publishers.

Heidegger, M. (1988). *The Basic Problems of Phenomenology*. Trans. A. Hofstadter. Bloomington: Indiana University Press.

Heidegger, M. (1962). *Being and Time*. Trans. J. Macquarrie and E. Robinson. NY: Harper & Row. Cited with English/German pagination.

Heider, F. and Simmel, M. (1944). An experimental study of apparent behavior. *The American Journal of Psychology* 57(2), 243–259.

Henry, M. (1973). *The Essence of Manifestation* Trans. G. Etzkorn. The Hague: Martinus Nijhoff.

Hobson, P. (2002). *The Cradle of Thought*. London: Macmillan.

Hobson, P. (1993). The emotional origins of social understanding. *Philosophical Psychology* 6, 227–249.

Hobson, P. and Lee, A. (1999). Imitation and identification in autism. *Journal of Child Psychology and Psychiatry* 40, 649–659.

Hohwy, J. (2004). Top-down and bottom-up in delusion formation. *Philosophy, Psychiatry and Psychology* 11, 65–70.

Howe, M. L. (2000). The Fate of Early Memories: Developmental Science and the Retention of Childhood Experiences. Cambridge, MA: MIT Press.

Hume, D., (1739). *A Treatise of Human Nature*. (ed.) L. A. Selby Bigge. Oxford: Clarendon Press, 1975.

Husserl, E. (2006). The Basic Problems of Phenomenology: From the Lectures, Winter Semester, 1910–1911. Dordrecht: Springer.

Husserl, E. (2005). *Phantasy, Image Consciousness, and Memory (1898–1925)*. Trans. J. B. Brough. Collected Works, Vol. XI. Dordrecht: Springer.

Husserl, E. (2001a). *Logical Investigations*. 2 Vols. Trans. J. N. Findlay with corrections D. Moran. London and NY: Routledge.

Husserl, E. (2001b). *Die Bernauer Manuskripte über das Zeitbewusstsein (1917–18)*, Husserliana, Vol. 33. Dordrecht: Kluwer Academic Publishers.

Husserl, E. (1997). *Thing and Space: Lectures of 1907*. Trans. R. Rojcewicz. Dordrecht: Kluwer Academic Publishers.

Husserl, E. (1991). *On the Phenomenology of the Consciousness of Internal Time (1893–1917)*. Trans. J. B. Brough. Dordrecht: Kluwer Academic Publishers.

Husserl, E. (1989). *Ideas Pertaining to a Pure Phenomenology and to a Phenomenological Philosophy – Second Book*. Trans. R. Rojcewicz and A. Schuwer. Dordrecht: Kluwer Academic Publishers.

Husserl, E. (1982). Ideas Pertaining to a Pure Phenomenology and to a Phenomenological Philosophy. First Book. General Introduction to a Pure Phenomenology. Trans. F. Kersten. The Hague: Martinus Nijhoff.

Husserl, E. (1977). *Phenomenological Psychology: Lectures, Summer Semester, 1925*. Trans. J. Scanlon. The Hague: Martinus Nijhoff. German pagination in margins.

Husserl, E. (1973). *Zur Phänomenologie der Intersubjektivität III*, Husserliana XV. Den Haag: Martinus Nijhoff.

Husserl, E. (1970). The Crisis of European Sciences and Transcendental Phenomenology: An Introduction to Phenomenological Philosophy. Trans. D. Carr. Evanston: Northwestern University Press.

Husserl, E. (1965). Phenomenology and the Crisis of Philosophy: Philosophy as a Science and Philosophy and the Crisis of European Man. Trans. Q. Lauer. NY: Harper & Row.

Husserl, E. (1960). *Cartesian Meditations: An Introduction to Phenomenology*. Trans. D. Cairns. Den Haag: Martinus Nijhoff.

Hutto D. D. (2008). Folk Psychological Narratives: The Socio-Cultural Basis of Understanding Reasons. Cambridge, MA: MIT Press.

Hutto, D. D. and Myin, E. (2013). *Radicalizing Enactivism: Basic Minds without Content*. Cambridge, MA: MIT Press.

Iizuka, H. and Di Paolo, E. A. (2007). Minimal agency detection of embodied agents. In F. Almeida e Costa, L. M. Rocha, E. Costa, I. Harvey and A. Coutinho (eds), *Advances in Artificial Life: Proc. of the 9th Euro. Conf. on Artificial Life* (485–494). Berlin, Germany: Springer.

Issartel, J., Marin, L., and Cadopi, M. (2007). Unintended interpersonal coordination: 'can we march to the beat of our own drum'? *Neuroscience Letters* 411, 174–179.

Izquierdo, E. and Buhrmann, T. (2008). Analysis of a dynamical recurrent neural network evolved for two qualitatively different tasks: walking and chemotaxis. In S. Bullock, J. Noble, R. Watson, and M. A. Bedau (eds), *Artificial Life XI: Proceedings of the Eleventh International Conference on the Simulation and Synthesis of Living Systems* (257–264). Cambridge, MA: MIT Press.

Izquierdo-Torres, E. and Di Paolo, E. A. (2005). Is an embodied system ever purely reactive? In M. Capcarrere A. A. Freitas, P. J. Bentley, C. G. Johnson and J. Timmis. (eds), *Advances in Artificial Life: Proc. of the 8th Euro. Conf. on Artificial Life* (252–261). Berlin: Springer-Verlag.

James, W. (1890). *Principles of Psychology*. NY: Dover, 1950.

Jeannerod, M. (2001). Neural simulation of action: a unifying mechanism for motor cognition. *Neuroimage* 14, S103–S109.

Jeannerod, M. and Pacherie, E. (2004). Agency, simulation, and self-identification. *Mind and Language* 19(2), 113–146.

Karmarkar, U. R. and Buonomano, D. V. (2007). Timing in the absence of clocks: encoding time in neural network states. *Neuron* 53, 427–438.

Kelso, J. A. S. (1995). Dynamic Patterns: The Self-Organization of Brain and Behaviour. Cambridge, MA: MIT Press.

Kendon, A. (1990). Conducting Interaction: Patterns of Behavior in Focused Encounters. Cambridge: Cambridge University Press.

Kennedy, J. (2011). Kurt Gödel. *The Stanford Encyclopedia of Philosophy (Fall 2011 Edition)*, Edward N. Zalta (ed.) (http://plato.stanford.edu/archives/fall2011/entries/goedel/ (Accessed 24 July 2012)).

Kern, I. (1977). The three ways to the transcendental phenomenological reduction in the philosophy of Edmund Husserl. In F. Elliston and P. McCromick (eds) *Husserl: Expositions and Appraisals* (126–149). Notre Dame: Notre Dame University Press.

Kortooms, T. (2002). Phenomenology of Time. Edmund Husserl's Analysis of Time-Consciousness. Dordrecht: Kluwer Academic Publishers.

Kosslyn, S. M. (1978). Imagery and internal representation. In E. Rosch and B. B. Lloyd (eds), *Cognition and Categorization* (217–257). Hillsdale: Lawrence Erlbaum.

Kosslyn, S. M. (1980). *Image and Mind*. Cambridge, MA: Harvard University Press.

Lackner, J. R. (1988). Some proprioceptive influences on the perceptual representation of body shape and orientation. *Brain* 3, 281–297.

Lafargue, G., Paillard, J., Lamarre, Y. and Sirigu, Y. (2003). Production and perception of grip force without proprioception: is there a sense of effort in deafferented subjects? *European Journal of Neuroscience* 17(12), 2741–2749.

Lane, T. (2012). Toward an explanatory framework for mental ownership. *Phenomenology and the Cognitive Sciences* 11(2), 251–286.

Langton, C. G. (1989). Artificial life. In C. G. Langton (ed.), *Artificial Life: Proceedings of an Interdisciplinary Workshop on the Synthesis and Simulation of Living Systems*, Santa Fe Institute Studies in the Sciences of Complexity, vol. 4 (1–47). Redwood City, CA: Addison-Wesley.

Lawlor, L. (2009). Becoming and auto-affection (Part II): who are we? Invited Lecture, ICNAP, 2009. Published at http://www.icnap.org/meetings.htm (accessed 15 January 2011).

Leder, D. (1990). *The Absent Body*. Chicago: Chicago University Press.

Legrand, D. and Ruby, P. (2009). What is self specific? A theoretical investigation and a critical review of neuroimaging results. *Psychological Review* 116(1), 252–282.

Lenggenhager, B., Tadi, T., Metzinger, T. and Blanke, O. (2007). Video ergo sum: manipulating bodily self-consciousness. *Science* 317, 1096–1099.

Le Van Quyen, M. and Petitmengin, C. (2002). Neuronal dynamics and conscious experience: an example of reciprocal causation before epileptic seizures. *Phenomenology and the Cognitive Sciences* 1, 169–180.

Levinas, E. (1969). *Totality and Infinity: An Essay on Exteriority*. Trans. A. Lingis, Pittsburgh, PA: Duquesne University Press.

Lew, A. and Butterworth, G. E. (1995). Hand-mouth contact in newborn babies before and after feeding. *Developmental Psychology* 31, 456–463.

Lindblom, J. (2007). Minding the body: interacting socially through embodied action. *Linköping Studies in Science and Technology*. Dissertation No. 1112 Linköpings Universitet.

Lindblom, J. and Ziemke, T. (2007). Embodiment and social interaction: implications for cognitive science. In T. Ziemke, J. Zlatev and R. Frank (eds), *Body, Language, and Mind: Embodiment* (129–162). Berlin: Mouton de Gruyter.

Locke, J. (1690). *An Essay Concerning Human Understanding*. (2nd edition) (1694), Ed. A. C. Fraser. NY: Dover, 1959.

Longo, M. R., Kammers, M., Gomi, H., Tsakiris, M. and Haggard, P. (2009). Contraction of body representation induced by proprioceptive conflict. *Current Biology* 19(17), R27–28.

Lou, H. C., Luber, B., Crupain, M., Keenan, J. P., Nowak, M., Kjaer, T. W., H. A. Sackeim and S. H. Lisanby (2004). Parietal cortex and representation of the mental self. *Proceedings of the National Academy of Sciences (USA)*, 101, 6827–6832.

Löwith, K. (1928). *Das Individuum in der Rolle des Mitmenschen*. In K. Stichweh (ed.) *Sämtliche Schriften*, Vol. 1. (9–197). Stuttgart: J. B. Metzler, 1981.

Lyotard, J-F. (1991). *Phenomenology*. Albany: State University of New York Press.

MacIntyre, A. (1984). *After Virtue*. (2nd edition) Notre Dame: University of Notre Dame Press.

MacKay, D. (1966). Cerebral organizatioin and the conscious control of action. In J. C. Eccles (ed.), *Brain and Conscious Experience* (422–445). NY: Springer.

Malenka, R. C., Angel, R. W., Hampton, B. and Berger, P. A. (1982). Impaired central error correcting behaviour in schizophrenia. *Archives of General Psychiatry* 39, 101–107.

Marbach, E. (2010). Towards a formalism for expressing structures of consciousness. In S. Gallagher and D. Schmicking (eds), *Handbook of Phenomenology and Cognitive Science*. Dordrecht: Springer.

Marbach, E. (1993). Mental Representation and Consciousness: Towards a Phenomenological Theory of Representation and Reference. Dordrecht: Kluwer Academic Publishers.

Marcel, A. (2003). The sense of agency: awareness and ownership of action. In J. Roessler and N. Eilan (eds), *Agency and Self-Awareness* (48–93). Oxford: Oxford University Press.

Marcel, A. (1993). Slippage in the unity of consciousness. *Ciba Foundation Symposium* 174 – *Experimental and Theoretical Studies of Consciousness*. doi: 10.1002/9780470514412.ch9

Marcel, A. J. (1983). Conscious and unconscious perception: an approach to the relations between phenomenal experience and perceptual processes. *Cognitive Psychology* 15, 238–300.

Martin, M. G. F. (1995). Bodily awareness: a sense of ownership. In J. L. Bermudez, A. Marcel and N. Eilan (eds), *The Body and the Self* (267–289). Cambridge, MA: MIT Press.

Maurer, D. and Barrera, M. E. (1981). Infants' perception of natural and distorted arrangements of a schematic face. *Child Development* 52(1), 196–202.

McKenna, W. (1982). *Husserl's Introductions to Phenomenology.* Phaenomenologica, Vol. 89. Dordrecht: Springer.

McTaggart, J. M. E. (1908). The unreality of time. *Mind* 17 (New Series, no. 68), 457–474.

Meltzoff, A. N. (1995). Understanding the intentions of others: re-enactment of intended acts by 18-month-old children. *Developmental Psychology* 31, 838–850.

Meltzoff, A. and Moore, M. K. (1977). Imitation of facial and manual gestures by human neonates. *Science* 198, 75–78.

Meltzoff, A. and Moore, M. K. (1994). Imitation, memory, and the representation of persons. *Infant Behavior and Development* 17, 83–99.

Merleau-Ponty, M. (2010). *Child Psychology and Pedagogy: The Sorbonne Lectures 1949–1952.* Trans. T. Welsh. Evanston: Northewestern University Press.

Merleau-Ponty, M. (1987). *Signs.* Trans. R. C. McCleary. Evanston: Northwestern University Press.

Merleau-Ponty, M. (1968). *The Visible and the Invisible.* Trans. A. Lingis. Evanston: Northwestern University Press.

Merleau-Ponty, M. (1967). *The Structure of Behaviour.* Boston: Beacon Press.

Merleau-Ponty, M. (1964). The Primacy of Perception And Other Essays on Phenomenological Psychology, the Philosophy of Art, History and Politics. Evanston, IL: Northwestern University Press.

Merleau-Ponty, M. (1964). The child's relations with others. Trans. W. Cobb, in M. Merleau-Ponty, *The Primacy of Perception.* Evanston: Northwestern University Press.

Merleau-Ponty, M. (1963). *The Structure of Behavior.* Trans. A. L. Fisher. Pittsburgh: Duquesne University Press.

Merleau-Ponty, M. (1962). *Phenomenology of Perception.* Trans. C. Smith. London: Routledge and Kegan Paul.

Miller, I. (1984). *Husserl, Perception, and Temporal Awareness.* Cambridge, MA: MIT Press.

Miyahara, K. (2011). Neo-pragmatic intentionality and enactive perception: a compromise between extended and enactive minds. *Phenomenology and the Cognitive Sciences* 10(4), 499–519.

Mohanty, J. N. (1989). *Transcendental Phenomenology: An Analytic Account.* Oxford: Basil Blackwell.

Mohanty, J. N. (1971). Husserl's concept of intentionality. *Analecta Husserliana* 1, 100–132.

Moll, H. and Tomasello, M. (2004). 12- and 18-month-old infants follow gaze to spaces behind barriers. *Developmental Science* 7, F1–F9.

Moran, D. (2002). Editor's introduction. In T. Moody and D. Moran (eds) *The Phenomenology Reader* (1–26). London: Routledge.

Moran, D. (2000). *Introduction to Phenomenology*. London: Routledge.

Moreno, A. (2002). Artificial life and philosophy. *Leonardo* 35(4), 401–405.

Mundale, J. and Gallagher, S. (2009). Delusional experience. In J. Bickle (ed). *Oxford Handbook of Philosophy and Neuroscience* (513–521). Oxford: Oxford University Press.

Murray, L. and Trevarthen, C. (1985). Emotional regulations of interactions between two-month-olds and their mothers. In T. M. Field and N. A. Fox (eds), *Social Perception in Infants* (177–197). Norwood, NJ: Ablex Publishing.

Nagel, T. (1974). What is it like to be a bat? *The Philosophical Review* 83, 435–450.

Neisser, U. (1988). Five kinds of self-knowledge. *Philosophical Psychology* 1, 35–59.

Nelson, K. (2003). Narrative and the emergence of a consciousness of self. In G. D. Fireman, T. E. McVay, Jr. O. J. Flanagan (eds) *Narrative and Consciousness*. NY: Oxford University Press.

Noë, A. (2004). *Action in Perception*. Cambridge, MA: MIT Press.

Pacherie, E. (2007). The sense of control and the sense of agency. *Psyche* 13(1). http://jeannicod.ccsd.cnrs.fr/docs/00/35/25/65/PDF/ (Accessed 24 July 2012).

Patocka, J. (1996). *An Introduction to Husserl's Phenomenology*. Trans. E. Kohák. Peru, IL: Carus Publishing Company.

Petitot, J. (2008). Neurogéométrie de la Vision: Modèles Mathématiques et Physiques des Architectures Fonctionnelles. Paris: Editions Ecole Polytechnique.

Petitot, J. (1999). Morphological eidetics for a phenomenology of perception. In J. Petitot, F. J. Varela, B. Pachoud and J.-M. Roy (eds), *Naturalizing Phenomenology: Issues in Contemporary Phenomenology and Cognitive Science* (330–371). Stanford, CA: Stanford University Press.

Petitot, J. Varela, F. J., Pachoud, B. and Roy, J-M. (eds) (1999). *Naturalizing Phenomenology: Issues in Contemporary Phenomenology and Cognitive Science*. Stanford, CA: Stanford University Press.

Petkova, V. I. and Ehrsson, H. H. (2008). If I were you: perceptual illusion of body swapping. PLoS ONE 3(12): e3832. Doi:10.1371/journal.pone.0003832

Pöggeler, O. (1989). *Martin Heidegger's Path of Being.* Trans. D. Magurshak and S. Barber. Atlantic Highlands, NJ: Humanities Press.

Pöppel, E. (1988). *Mindworks: Time and Conscious Experience.* Boston: Harcourt Brace Jovanovich.

Pöppel, E. (1994). Temporal mechanisms in perception. *International Review of Neurobiology* 37, 185–202.

Price, D., Barrell, J. and Rainville, P. (2002). Integrating experiential-phenomenological methods and neuroscience to study neural mechanisms of pain and consciousness. *Consciousness and Cognition* 11, 593–608.

Prinz, J. (2009). Is consciousness embodied? In P. Robbins and M. Aydede (eds), *Cambridge Handbook of Situated Cognition* (419–436). Cambridge: Cambridge University Press.

Proffitt, D. R., Creem, S. H. and Zosh, W. (2001). Seeing mountains in molehills: geographical slant perception. *Psychological Science* 12, 418–423.

Proffitt, D. R., Bhalla, M., Gossweiler, R. and Midgett, J. (1995). Perceiving geographical slant. *Psychonomic Bulletin & Review* 2, 409–428.

Pylyshyn, Z. W. (1973). What the mind's eye tells the mind's brain: a critique of mental imagery. *Psychological Bulletin* 80, 1–24.

Rakoczy, H., Brosche, N., Warneken, F. and Tomasello, M. (2009). Young children's understanding of the context-relativity of normative rules in conventional games. *British Journal of Developmental Psychology* 27, 445–456.

Ratcliffe, M. (2007). Rethinking Commonsense Psychology: A Critique of Folk Psychology, Theory of Mind and Simulation. Basingstoke: Palgrave Macmillan.

Reddy, V. (2008). *How Infants Know Minds.* Cambridge, MA: Harvard University Press.

Ricoeur, P. (1992). *Oneself as Another.* Trans. K. Blamey. Chicago. Chicago University Press.

Ricoeur, P. (1966). *Freedom and Nature: The Voluntary and the Involuntary.* Trans. E. V. Kohák. Evanston: Northwestern University Press.

Rodemeyer, L. M. (2006). *Intersubjective Temporality: It's About Time.* Dordrecht: Springer.

Rowlands, M. (2006). *Body Language.* Cambridge, MA: MIT Press.

Roy, J.-M., Petitot, J., Pachoud, B. and Varela, F. J. (1999). Beyond the gap: an introduction to naturalizing phenomenology. In J. Petitot, F. J. Varlea, B. Pachoud, and J.-M. Roy (eds), *Naturalizing Phenomenology* (1–83). Stanford, CA: Stanford University Press.

Sartre, J-P. (2004). The Imaginary: A Phenomenological Psychology of the Imagination. Trans. J. Webber. London: Routledge.

Sartre, J-P. (1960). *Critique of Dialectical Reason.* NY: Verso.

Sartre, J.-P. (1957). *The Transcendence of the Ego.* Trans. F. Williams and R. Kirkpatrick. NY: The Noonday Press.

Sartre, J.-P. (1956). *Being and Nothingness.* Trans. H. E. Barnes. NY: Philosophical Library.

Sass, L. and Parnas, J. (2003). Schizophrenia, consciousness, and the self. *Schizophrenia Bulletin* 29(3), 427–444.

Saxe, R., Jamal, N. and Powell, L. (2006). My body or yours? The effect of visual perspective on cortical body representations. *Cerebral Cortex* 16, 178–182.

Schechtman, M. (2011). The narrative self. In S. Gallagher (ed.), *The Oxford Handbook of the Self* (394–416). Oxford: Oxford University Press.

Scheler, M. (1954). *The Nature of Sympathy.* Trans. P. Heath. London: Routledge and Kegan Paul.

Schenk, T. and Zihl, J. (1997). Visual motion perception after brain damage: I. Deficits in global motion perception. *Neuropsychologia* 35 (9), 1289–1297.

Schutz, A. (1967). *The Phenomenology of the Social World.* Trans. G. Walsh and F. Lehnert. Evanston: Northwestern University Press.

Schutz, A. and Luckmann, T. (1973 and 1983). *The Structures of the Life-World* (Vols 1 and 2). Trans. R. M. Zaner, T. Engelhardt and D. J. Parent. Evanston: Northwestern University Press.

Searle, J. (1983). *Intentionality: An Essay in the Philosophy of Mind.* Cambridge: Cambridge University Press.

Senju, A., Johnson, M. H. and Csibra, G. (2006). The development and neural basis of referential gaze perception. *Social Neuroscience* 1(3–4), 220–234.

Shoemaker, S. (1984). *Identity, Cause, and Mind.* Cambridge: Cambridge University Press.

Singh, J. R., Knight, T., Rosenlicht, N., Kotun, J. M., Beckley, D. J. and Woods, D. L. (1992). Abnormal premovement brain potentials in schizophrenia. *Schizophrenia Research* 8, 31–41.

Smith, D. W. (2008). Phenomenology. *The Stanford Encyclopedia of Philosophy (Fall 2011 Edition).* Edward N. Zalta (ed.), URL = <http://plato.stanford.edu/archives/fall2011/entries/phenomenology/>. Accessed 24 July 2012.

Smith, D. W. and McIntyre, R. (1982). Husserl and Intentionality: A Study of Mind, Meaning, and Language. Dordrecht: D.Reidel.

Smith, Q. (1977). A phenomenological examination of Husserl's theory of hyletic data. *Philosophy Today* 21, 356–367.

Sokolowski, R. (2000). *Introduction to Phenomenology.* NY: Cambridge University Press.

Sokolowski, R. (1987). Husserl and Frege. *The Journal of Philosophy* 84, 521–528.

Spiegelberg, H. (1960). *The Phenomenological Movement: A Historical Introduction.* 2 Vols. The Hague: Nijhoff. 1960. (2nd edition, 1965; 3rd edition, in collaboration with Karl Schuhmann, 1982).

Steels, L. (1994). The artificial life roots of artificial intelligence. *Artificial Life* 1(1–2), 75–110.

Stein, E. (1964). *On the Problem of Empathy.* Trans. W. Stein. The Hague: Martinus Nijhoff.

Steinbock, A. (1995). *Home and Beyond: Generative Phenomenology after Husserl.* Evanston: Northwestern University Press.

Stephens, G. L. and Graham, G. (2000). *When Self-Consciousness Breaks: Alien Voices and Inserted Thoughts.* Cambridge, MA: MIT Press.

Steuber, K. A. (2006). Rediscovering Empathy: Agency, Folk-Psychology and the Human Sciences. Cambridge, MA: MIT Press.

Strawson, G. (2011). The minimal subject. In S. Gallagher (ed.), *The Oxford Handbook of the Self.* 253–278. Oxford: Oxford University Press.

Strawson, G. (2004). Against narrativity. *Ratio* 17(4), 428–452.

Strawson, G. (1997). The self. *Journal of Consciousness Studies* 4(5–6), 405–428.

Strawson, G. (1999). The self and the SESMET. In S. Gallagher and J. Shear (eds), *Models of the Self* (483–518). Thorverton: Imprint Academic.

Strawson, P. F. (1994). The first person – and others. In Q. Cassam (ed.) *Self-Knowledge* (210–215). Oxford: Oxford University Press.

Taylor, C. (1989). *Sources of the Self.* Cambridge, MA: Harvard University Press.

Thelen, E. and Smith, L. (1994). A Dynamic Systems Approach to the Development of Cognition and Action. Cambridge, MA: MIT Press

Thompson, E. (2007). *Mind in Life: Biology, Phenomenology, and the Sciences of Mind.* Cambridge, MA: Harvard University Press.

Thompson, E., Lutz, A. and Cosmelli, D. (2005). Neurophenomenology: an introduction for neurophilosophers. In A. Brook and K. Akins (eds), *Cognition and the Brain: The Philosophy and Neuroscience Movement.* NY and Cambridge: Cambridge University Press.

Thompson, E. and Varela, F. J. (2001). Radical embodiment: neural dynamics and consciousness. *Trends in Cognitive Sciences* 5, 418–425.

Trevarthen, C. B. (1979). Communication and cooperation in early infancy: a description of primary intersubjectivity. In M. Bullowa (ed.), *Before Speech* (321–348). Cambridge: Cambridge University Press.

Trevarthen, C. and Hubley, P. (1978). Secondary intersubjectivity: confidence, confiding and acts of meaning in the first year. In A. Lock (ed.), *Action, Gesture and Symbol: The Emergence of Language* (183–229). London: Academic Press.

Tsakiris, M., Bosbach S. and Gallagher, S. (2007). On agency and body-ownership: phenomenological and neuroscientific reflections. *Consciousness and Cognition* 16(3), 645–660.

Tsakiris, M. and Haggard, P. (2005). The rubber hand illusion revisited: visuotactile integration and self-attribution. *Journal of Experimental Psychology: Human Perception and Performance* 31(1), 80–91.

Tsakiris, M. and Haggard, P. (2003). Awareness of somatic events associated with a voluntary action. *Experimental Brain Research* 149, 439–446.

Tye, M. (2000). *Consciousness, Color and Content.* Cambridge MA: MIT Press.

Vallar, G. and Ronchi, R. (2009). Somatoparaphrenia: a body delusion. A review of the neuropsychological literature. *Experimental Brain Research* 192, 533–551.

Van Gelder, T. (1996). 'Wooden iron'? Husserlian phenomenology meets cognitive science. *Electronic Journal of Analytic Philosophy* 4; reprinted in J. Petitot, F. J. Varela, B. Pachoud and J-M. Roy (eds), *Naturalizing Phenomenology: Issues in Contemporary Phenomenology and Cognitive Science* (245–265). Stanford, CA: Stanford University Press, 1999.

Velleman, J. D. (2006). *Self to Self: Selected Essays,* Cambridge: Cambridge University Press.

Varela, F. J. (1999). The specious present: a neurophenomenology of time consciousness. In J. Petitot, F. J. Varela, B. Pachoud and J.-M. Roy, (eds) *Naturalizing Phenomenology: Issues in Contemporary Phenomenology and Cognitive Science* (266–314). Stanford, CA: Stanford University Press.

Varela, F. J. (1996). Neurophenomenology: a methodological remedy for the hard problem. *Journal of Consciousness Studies,* 3(4), 330–349.

Varela, F. J. (1995). Resonant cell assemblies: a new approach to cognitive functioning and neuronal synchrony. *Biological Research* 28, 81–95.

Varela, F. J., Lachaux, J. P., Rodriguez, E. and Martinerie, J. (2001). The brainweb: phase-synchronization and long-range integration. *Nature Rev. Neuroscience* 2, 229–239.

Varela, F. J. and Thompson, E. (2003). Neural synchrony and the unity of mind: a neurophenomenological perspective. In A. Cleeremans, (ed.) *The Unity of Consciousness: Binding, Integration and Dissociation* (266–287). NY: Oxford University Press.

Varela, F., Thompson, E. and Rosch, E. (1991). *The Embodied Mind: Cognitive Science and Human Experience.* Cambridge, MA: MIT Press.

Walker, A. S. (1982). Intermodal perception of expressive behaviors by human infants. *Journal of Experimental Child Psychology* 33, 514–535.

Ward, J. (2008). The Frog who Croaked Blue: Synesthesia and the Mixing of the Senses. Hove, UK: Routledge.

Wenke, D. and Haggard, P. (2009). How voluntary actions modulate time perception. *Experimental Brain Research* 196(3), 311–318.

Wheeler, M. (2005). Reconstructing the Cognitive World: The Next Step. Cambridge, MA: MIT Press.

Wheeler, M. (2008). Cognition in context: phenomenology, situated robotics and the frame problem. *International Journal of Philosophical Studies*, 16(3), 323–349.

Wider, K. V. (1997). The Bodily Nature of Consciousness: Sartre and Contemporary Philosophy of Mind. Ithaca: Cornell University Press.

Wilson, M. and Knoblich, G. (2005). The case for motor involvement in perceiving conspecifics. *Psychological Bulletin* 131(3), 460–473.

Wittgenstein, L. (1958). *Philosophical Investigations.* (3rd edition). Trans. G. E. M. Anscombe. Englewood Cliffs, NJ: Prentice Hall.

Wolpert, D. M., Ghahramani, Z. and Jordan, M. I. (1995). An internal model for sensorimotor integration. *Science* 269(5232), 1880–1882.

Woodward, A. L. and Sommerville, J. A. (2000). Twelve-month-old infants interpret action in context. *Psychological Science* 11, 73–77.

Yoshimi, J. (2007). Mathematizing phenomenology. *Phenomenology and the Cognitive Sciences* 6(3), 271–291.

Zahavi, D. (ed.) (2012a). *Oxford Handbook of Contemporary Phenomenology.* Oxford: Oxford University Press.

Zahavi, D. (2012b). Empathy and mirroring: Husserl and Gallese. In R. Breeur and U. Melle (eds), *Life, Subjectivity & Art: Essays in Honor of Rudolf Bernet* (217–254). Dordrecht: Springer.

Zahavi. D. (2010). Phenomenology and the problem of naturalization. In S. Gallagher and D. Schmicking (eds), *Handbook of Phenomenology and Cognitive Science.* Dordrecht: Springer.

Zahavi, D. (2005). Subjectivity and Selfhood: Investigating the First-Person Perspective. Cambridge, MA: MIT Press.

Zahavi, D. (2004). Phenomenology and the project of naturalization. *Phenomenology and the Cognitive Sciences* 3(4), 331–347.

Zahavi, D. (2003). *Husserl's Phenomenology.* Stanford, CA: Stanford University Press.

Zahavi, D. (1999). *Self-Awareness and Alterity: A Phenomenological Investigation*. Evanston: Northwestern University Press.

Zahavi, D. (1994). Husserl's phenomenology of the body. *Études Phénoménologiques* 19, 63–84.

Zahn, R., Talazko, J. and Ebert, D. (2008). Loss of the sense of self-ownership for perceptions of objects in a case of right inferior temporal, parieto-occipital and precentral hypometabolism. *Psychopathology* 41, 397–402.

Zaner, R. (1971). The Problem of Embodiment: Some Contributions to a Phenomenology of the Body. Dordrecht: Springer.

Zihl, J., von Cramon, D. and Mai, N. (1983). Selective disturbance of movement vision after bilateral brain damage. *Brain* 106, 313–340.

Index

CPSIA information can be obtained
at www.ICGtesting.com
Printed in the USA
LVHW010630021220
673143LV00014B/604

9 780230 272491